Advance Praise for

SUBJECTIVITY & TRUTH

"An analytical rendezvous between Foucault's writing on modern forms of power, as they are articulated in the microphysics of subjectivity and technologies of truth, and the contemporary challenges of educational theory and pedagogical practice is long overdue. In *Subjectivity & Truth*, Tina (A.C.) Besley and Michael A. Peters have inaugurated a vigorous discussion on the relevance of Foucault's philosophical writings on subjectivity and truth to the pedagogical and ethical challenges confronting the contemporary educator. In this sophisticated and elegant book, Besley and Peters have dug deep at the wellspring of the interdisciplines of history, philosophy, literature, aesthetics, ethics, and cultural policy, offering an abundance of rich, thoughtful, and illuminating insights on Foucault's extraordinary work. This book takes us beyond the banality of much of critical scholarship now being conducted in the educational field. It should be required reading for all those interested in the relevance of Foucault's thinking to the quotidian work that we do as educational theorists and practitioners."

Cameron McCarthy, University of Illinois at Urbana-Champaign

"It is always surprising how Foucault's philosophical project continues to inspire. Here we have a series of penetrating and brilliant chapters on aspects of Foucault's thought, richly embellished and utilized to inform education and the social sciences. This book represents a new and powerful contribution to the field. It will be important reading for experts and students alike."

Mark Olssen, University of Surrey, United Kingdom;
Author of Michel Foucault: Materialism and Education

"This book represents the polished culmination of years of work by the authors on Foucault. Tina (A.C.) Besley and Michael A. Peters provide an insightful and readable analysis of Foucault's later writings on the self, bodies, truth telling, and governmentality, at the same time skillfully linking this work to a range of other thinkers both ancient and modern. They also, very importantly, provide new applications of Foucault's later period of thought to the field of education, opening up new and exciting ideas and directions for other researchers. This book is thoroughly recommended both for those who wish to know more in general about Foucault's writings on the self and for those who wish to extend those ideas specifically within the area of education."

Clare O'Farrell, Editor of Foucault Studies

"Tina (A.C.) Besley and Michael A. Peters' *Subjectivity & Truth* is a superb contribution to Foucauldian scholarship and the study of education that helps to consider the limits of this commonsense of schooling. Rarely does one find such a wide command over the diverse writings of Foucault and the development of profound insights about contemporary social and educational issues as in this book. The volume provocatively challenges the conventions of policy studies, philosophy, and research. Not discarding the notion of change and agency, it provides strategies to diagnose the limitations of the distinctions between discourse and experience that constitute and consecrate modern school pedagogy and its theories of the child. The argument of the book is neither one of the subjectivity of the individual nor a structuralism that drives contemporary reforms. It is about the 'thought' and systems of reason as historical practices through which the self is produced."

Thomas S. Popkewitz, University of Wisconsin-Madison

"Anyone engaging Foucault today cannot help but be caught up in a whirlwind of theoretical activity fast approaching a neo-Foucauldian or even post-Foucauldian age. It is surely not clear what it means to read and write 'Foucault' today, or perhaps this debate no longer matters. What does matter still are interpretations substantively based in his own writings augmented by authoritative commentary. This book offers both set within and connected to significant contexts, theorizations, and practices of education."

Lynda Stone, University of North Carolina, Chapel Hill

SUBJECTIVITY & TRUTH

Studies in the
Postmodern Theory of Education

Joe L. Kincheloe and Shirley R. Steinberg
General Editors

Vol. 303

PETER LANG
New York • Washington, D.C./Baltimore • Bern
Frankfurt am Main • Berlin • Brussels • Vienna • Oxford

Tina (A.C) Besley & Michael A. Peters

Subjectivity & Truth

Foucault, Education, and the Culture of Self

PETER LANG
New York • Washington, D.C./Baltimore • Bern
Frankfurt am Main • Berlin • Brussels • Vienna • Oxford

Library of Congress Cataloging-in-Publication Data
Besley, Tina (A.C.).
Subjectivity and truth: Foucault, education, and the culture of self /
Tina (A.C) Besley, Michael A. Peters.
p. cm. — (Counterpoints: studies in the postmodern theory of education; v. 303)
Includes bibliographical references and index.
1. Foucault, Michel, 1926–1984. 2. Education—Philosophy. 3. Postmodernism and education.
4. Subjectivity. 5. Self. I. Peters, Michael A. II. Besley, Tina.
LB880.F682S83   370.1—dc22   2007001375
ISBN 978-0-8204-8195-1
ISSN 1058-1634

Bibliographic information published by **Die Deutsche Bibliothek**.
Die Deutsche Bibliothek lists this publication in the "Deutsche
Nationalbibliografie"; detailed bibliographic data is available
on the Internet at http://dnb.ddb.de/.

Cover design by Clear Point Designs

The paper in this book meets the guidelines for permanence and durability
of the Committee on Production Guidelines for Book Longevity
of the Council of Library Resources.

© 2007 Peter Lang Publishing, Inc., New York
29 Broadway, 18th floor, New York, NY 10006
www.peterlang.com

Printed in the United States of America

FOR SIMON AND CHRISTO

Contents

PART THREE. TRUTH-TELLING, RISK AND SUBJECTIVITY

PART FOUR. GOVERNMENTALITY—GOVERNING THE SELF

Acknowledgments

Most of the chapters in this book have been presented as papers at conferences in universities around the world—Mexico (Mexico City, Chiapas, Vera Cruz), Oxford (United Kingdom), Auckland (New Zealand), Champaign (Illinois)—and also over the years as material for various courses taught at the Universities of Glasgow (Scotland), Auckland (New Zealand), Illinois at Urbana-Champaign, and California State at San Bernardino. We would like to thank all those colleagues, discussants and students in different parts of the world who have helped us both individually and as co-authors to refine the ideas that comprise this book. We first came to Foucault's work at the University of Auckland largely through the commentary of Professor James Marshall beginning in the early 1980s before the death of Foucault, although we did not begin to publish on his work until the 1990s. We would like to acknowledge and thank Jim Marshall, a dear friend and colleague, for his inspiration, his support and his careful analysis of Foucault's thinking from which we have greatly benefited. Michael Peters had the pleasure of working and teaching with Jim Marshall over a twenty-year period coauthoring and coediting some seven books, thirty academic papers and twenty chapters. Many of these works grew out of a common interest in Foucault's oeuvre. Jim Marshall was advisor to both Michael Peters and Tina Besley at the University of Auckland. Michael Peters published *Poststructuralism, Politics and Education* in 1996 that contained a chapter on Foucault and wrote several essays in the late 1980s and early 1990s on Foucault's work and its application to educational and social theory. Tina Besley completed her PhD on

Foucault and published *Counseling Youth: Foucault, Power, and the Ethics of Subjectivity* in 2002 (reprinted in 2006 by Sense Publishers). Our combined interest in Foucault goes back many years and our shared ideas and perspectives come into contact with one another particularly over the notion of subjectivity and the philosophy of the subject. Tina Besley and Michael Peters jointly taught a Masters course at the University of Glasgow on 'Modern Education' entitled 'Educating the Self' for over five years (2000–05) that had a strong component on Foucault and before that at the University of Auckland Michael Peters ran a Masters class for five years with Jim Marshall that also made central reference to Foucault. We would like to acknowledge students particularly at the universities of Auckland and Glasgow for their helpful and constructive comments and feedback on our Foucault material presented and discussed in these courses. Many of these students have gone on to complete their PhDs and to work as academics in their own right.

More recently, during our time in Mexico in 2006, we were invited to present seminars on Foucault at a number of Mexican universities. Tina (A.C.) Besley presented seminars based on chapter 3 and added further ideas and perspectives that developed the chapter as a result of useful discussions following the seminar. In this respect we wish to thank Professor Alicia de Alba and the participants at Universidad Nacional Autonoma de Mexico (UNAM), including translator, Sra Lourdes. We would also like to thank Leticia Pons-Bonal and translators who provided an excellent Spanish PowerPoint presentation Alexandra and Susie Mendez at Universidad Nacional Autonoma de Chiapas (UNACH), Tuxla-Guitterez, and Marcella Maria at Universidad Normal Vera Cruz, Xalapa.

Much of the material in this book has been reworked and reedited from earlier conference presentations and publications. Chapter 2 is based on 'Self denial or self mastery: Foucault's genealogy of the confessional self' by Tina Besley previously published in Tina Besley and Richard Edwards (Eds.) *Poststructuralism and the impact of the work of Michel Foucault in Counselling and Guidance,* Special Issue Symposium, *British Journal of Guidance & Counselling,* 33, 3, 2005. Parts of chapter 3 are based on the opening section of an invited keynote address by Michael Peters, 'Why Foucault? New Directions in Anglo-American Educational Research' at the conference 'After Foucault: Perspectives of the Analysis of Discourse and Power in Education,' 29–31 October 2003, The University of Dortmund, and later published in L.A. Pongratz, M. Wimmer, W. Nieke and J. Masschelein (Eds.) *Nach Foucault:dikurs- und machtanaltische Perspektiven der Pädagogik,* Heidelberg, Wiesbaden: VS Verlag. Chapter 4 is based on 'Heidegger and Foucault on Space and Bodies: Geographies of Resistance in Critical Pedagogic Practices' by Michael A. Peters published in Richard Edwards and Robin Usher (Eds.) *Geographies of Resistance in Critical Pedagogic Practices, Space, Curriculum, and Learning,* Information Age Publishing, 2004. Chapter 5 by Michael Peters is an edited version of 'Truth-

Telling as an Educational Practice of the Self: Foucault, Parrhesia and the Ethics of Subjectivity,' published in the *Oxford Review of Education,* 29 (2), 2003, 207–23. Parts of chapter 6, including the first example are from Tina Besley (2004) 'Technologies of the self and *parrhesia:* education, globalization and the politicization of youth in response to the Iraq War 2003' published in Michael A. Peters (Ed.) *Education, Globalization and Citizenship in an age of Terrorism,* Boulder, CO: Paradigm Publishers. Earlier variations were presented at the Foucault Pre-session, AERA, Chicago, April 2003; The Big Day Conference, Centre for Global Citizenship, University of Glasgow, June 2003 and the GENIE conference, Cyprus, July 2003. The second example used in this chapter is based on a paper presented at the Philosophy of Education Society of Australasia conference, held in Auckland, New Zealand, 28–29 November 2003 and a paper published in the *New Zealand Journal of Counselling* (Besley, 2003c, 2003d). The third example is based on a paper presented at the British Educational Research Association conference, Heriot-Watt University, Edinburgh, 12 September 2003 (Besley, 2003b). Chapter 7 draws on 'Neoliberalism, the Enterprise Curriculum, and the Constitution of the Self in Aotearoa/New Zealand' by Michael A. Peters (chapter 1) in Alicia de Alba et al. (2000) *Curriculum in the Postmodern Condition* and 'Neoliberalism and the Governance of Welfare,' Special Issue on Neoliberalism, Christine Cheyne (Ed.), *Sites: A Journal for South Pacific Cultural Studies,* 38: 8–30. Chapter 8 is based on an article by Michael A. Peters 'The New Prudentialism in Education: Actuarial Rationality and the Entrepreneurial Self,' *Educational Theory,* 55 (2) 2005: 123–37; a version was first presented at a Round Table on 'Education and Risk' at the World Congress of Philosophy, Istanbul, 11 August 2003.

Finally, we wish to thank Trevor Thwaites at the University of Auckland, New Zealand for his generous hospitality and for making available the use of his beach house on Rakino Island, a delightfully small and still undeveloped island in the Hauraki Gulf, Auckland, New Zealand, where the sea, wind and birds happily co-exist. Native birds Tuis and Pukekos, together with Chaffinches, Gannets and Gulls of all kinds, and Terns provided the birdsong and musical background against which to focus on the task of completing this manuscript for publication.

Michael A. Peters and Tina (A.C.) Besley
Rakino Island, New Zealand
23 December 2006

Introduction

Together and individually we have been working on Foucault's later oeuvre for many years using him to help theorize on issues of self, ethical self-constitution, governmentality and truth-telling practices. We have also taught together and consistently used and presented Foucault's ideas on the self in courses in educational philosophy and theory, counseling, and social science methodology. As partners we have often run ideas past one another and also, increasingly, written together. Recently we coauthored *Building Knowledge Cultures: Education in the Age of Knowledge Capitalism* (Peters & Besley, 2006) and coedited *Why Foucault? New Directions in Educational Research* (Peters & Besley, 2006). We very much enjoyed the writing process and subsequently we decided that the time was ripe to write and edit work on Foucault we had carried out independently of each other to form the basis of this book. We set out our themes and examined our individual interests blending our thoughts ideas and styles, rewriting and editing of earlier papers to create a cohesive book with four major sections.

In this book we focus our study on an analysis of a selection of Foucault's later works, books, lectures and seminars where he examines questions of the self, subjectivity, sexuality, and truth-telling practices. We apply his understandings to educational discourse to investigate a Foucauldian approach to the self, the body, and subjectivity. In doing so, we divide the book into four sections, each with two chapters.

In the first section entitled 'Technologies of the Self' we begin with Foucault notion of 'the culture of the self,' a phrase that he used in the late 1970s in a course he delivered at the Collège de France under the heading of *The Hermeneutics of the Subject* (Foucault, 2004). The focus on the concept of *culture* that emphasizes the collective dimension of subjectivity (against the Kantian and more highly individualistic liberal forms) is motivated at least in part by the American social critic Christopher Lasch whose work Foucault acknowledges. Chapter 1 entitled 'The Culture of Self' begins with the way in which Foucault considered the hermeneutics of the subject significant for understanding ancient discourses and practices of pedagogy; indeed, how pedagogy itself was conceived and developed as a form of subjectivity based upon a pedagogical relationship that endowed subjects not only with truth-seeking attitudes, values and abilities but also as an historical ontology of ourselves, as shaping the forms of subjectivity that we take for granted today. The chapter investigates Foucault's precise use of the concept of culture in relation to the self as well as investigating the influence of Lasch's work on Foucault, especially the ground-breaking *The Culture of Narcissism* (1979). In the second part of the chapter we also chart and investigate Foucault's notion of 'the care of the self' and the obvious significance of 'reading and writing the self' for conceptions of educational subjectivity.

In chapter 2 we pick up explicitly on the 'confessional self' tracing Foucault's genealogy first by understanding how Foucault's own theorizations of the self changed and second by explaining the influence of both Nietzsche and Heidegger on Foucault's idea of 'technologies of the self' (Foucault, 1988b). The chapter discusses Foucault's understanding of Classical Greek technologies of the self, Christian religious confessional practices, and the secularization of confession in contemporary medico-therapeutic confessional practices. For Foucault confession is a form of truth telling that actively constitutes the self and following Foucault, we contrast ancient Greek and early Christian technologies of self, one based on an ethic of self-denial, the other on a concept of self-mastery. We argue that the latter provides a secular model consonant with the demands of a postmodern world that recognizes the inescapability of desire and the necessity of pleasure in a new body politics.

Section two, entitled 'Space, Body and the Aesthetics of Existence,' extends and develops these themes in a contemporary way. Chapter 3 explores Foucault's notion of the aesthetics of existence by focusing on processes of ethical self-constitution and the ways in which we come to shape our subjectivities through choice-making. We begin by emphasizing an approach from what Foucault called an 'aesthetics of existence' applying it to Foucault's own life and his investigations of questions of the self in the history of madness. We then examine Foucault's thinking on the body, including the notion of embodiment that has become a major theme and trope in educational philosophy and theory. In this chapter we also investigate feminist appropriations of Foucault's work on the body, the female body, and recent theories and conceptions of the masculine body. Body theory, gender studies, and feminism are no longer marginal themes and approaches in educational theory and practice—they are at the very heart of a major rejuvenation of educational theory that takes questions of subjectivity and identity as core issues defining the very nature of education problems.

In the next chapter in this section—'Space and the Body Politic'—we explore the Heideggerian-Foucauldian notion of space as a necessary background to questions of being and subjectivity and as a basis for re-conceptualising the relation between power, knowledge and the body. This line of thinking is developed in the direction of Hubert Dreyfus' phenomenology of learning and his discussion of the body in relation to the Internet.

Section three subtitled 'Truth-telling, Risk and Subjectivity' comprises two chapters concerned with the relation between truth and subjectivity, a theme strongly developed by Foucault. The first chapter of the section 'Truth-Telling as an Educational Practice of the Self' (chapter 5) is based on an examination of Foucault's investigation of *parrhesia*, rendered in English as 'truth-telling.' The chapter discusses six lectures entitled 'Discourse and Truth: The Problematization of Parrhesia' that Foucault gave at the University of California, Berkeley, during late 1983 that were subsequently published as *Fearless Speech* (Foucault, 2001a). In these lectures Foucault problematizes the practices of *parrhesia* concerning the truth teller or *parrhesiastes* and initiated a set of deep-seated cultural practices for the West that evolved to take various political, philosophical and personal forms (Foucault, 2001a, p.11). Foucault outlines the meanings and the evolution of the classical Greek word *'parrhesia'* and its cognates as they enter into and exemplify the changing practices of *truth-telling* in Greek society including 'the use of *parrhesia* in specific types of human relationships' and 'the procedures and techniques employed in such relationships' (Foucault, 2001a, p. 107). Central to Foucault's analysis is the significance of education, how pedagogy was central to 'care of the self,' public life and the crisis of democratic institutions. The Berkeley lectures are seen, in part, as a continuation and elaboration of some of the themes concerning 'technologies of the self' that Foucault (1988a, 1988b) gave as lectures at the University of Vermont a year earlier in 1982 and discussed in chapter 2. Yet there are significant differences in the themes Foucault pursues in these two sets of lectures, the way he pursues them and his characterization of the Platonic model as chapter 5 makes clear.

The second chapter of this section (chapter 6) provides three exemplars of *parrhesia* in action. The first examines new kinds of youth who are constituted in response to globalization, the mass media, information technology and consumer society, who rather than being seen as focussed predominantly on style and lifestyle, became politically radicalised in response to the 2003 war against Iraq, risking a range of punishment from school authorities who seemed unable to reconcile theory of citizenship education curricula with students putting such teachings into action. The second exemplar focuses on a disclosure about sexual abuse made to a school counselor, which examines the risks and courage involved for a girl in making such a disclosure. The final exemplar is one that educational researchers may encounter and the risky issue of 'whistle blowing' they may feel duty bound to undertake.

In section four, 'Governmentality—Governing the Self,' Foucault's notion of governmentality comes to occupy a central place in tying questions of the political formation of the individual to the liberal problematic where government of the self and government of the State coincide. Foucault also includes a pedagogy of the self considered as a form of governmentality as part of the explosion of questions around the State that accompanies its birth in the modern context. Foucault in his governmentality studies investigates both the classical ethical liberalism of Kant, on the one hand, and various forms of neoliberalism, on the other—French, German, and American centered around such figures as Hayek, Böhm, Müller-Almack, Friedman, and Becker. This is certainly a history of the present because it has such strong links to present day forms of neoliberalism and also nuances and gestures that define an approach applicable to 'third way' politics and the development of the social market. Critical in this respect is Foucault's consideration of the political formation of individuals, their relation to the state, new individualizing technologies of the self that revolve around concepts of enterprise culture and the entrepreneurial self. Here Foucault develops a line of thinking that emphasizes ethical self-constitution and the way that we are very much the choices we make, even if those choices are constrained or manipulated. The individual is considered in relation to both the State and the market, especially in his *Naissance de la Biopolitique* (Foucault, 2004b). *Naissance de la Biopolitique* is a course of lectures Foucault (2004b) gave at the Collège de France in 1978–79 on the rise of what he called 'biopolitics,' a notion he first introduces in *Discipline and Punish* (Foucault, 1977) and develops further in his lectures on governmentality.

In summary, then, the book analyzes and problematizes the notion of the self beginning with 'technologies of the self' centered on 'the culture of the self' and describing Foucault's genealogy of the confessional self focusing on the question of self-denial or self-mastery that contrasts the Christian and Greek ethic of subjectivity. In the second section that we have called 'Space, Body and the Aesthetics of Existence' we turn our attention to the body and the aesthetics of existence and also examine space and the body politic. In the third section entitled 'Truth-telling, Risk and Subjectivity' we use Foucault's notion of *parrhesia*, usually translated as 'free speech' (Foucault, 2001) to discuss truth-telling practices of the self and provide an account of truth-telling as an educational practice of the self. We follow this by theorizing the relation between risk and the ethics of subjectivity in what we call '*parrhesia* in action' where we provide three exemplars from education-based contexts. In the fourth and final section, 'Governmentality—Governing the Self,' we first provide an account of the understanding of the neoliberal paradigm of education policy before charting the rise of enterprise culture and the rise of the entrepreneurial self in the final chapter.

PART ONE

Technologies OF THE Self

CHAPTER ONE

The Culture OF Self

PEDAGOGY AND THE HERMENEUTICS OF THE SUBJECT

Ever since the first moment of institutional philosophy the notion of the self has presented itself as an object of inquiry, as a problem, and as a locus for posing questions concerning knowledge, action and ethics. Socrates, Plato and Aristotle in different ways inquired of the self in terms that we might understand today as personhood, or personal identity, although they saw the self as an animated soul. This idea of self as a substance or form seemed dependent upon a *unity* that can act as a source of consciousness, memory and as a basis for self-knowledge. The ancient philosopher Thales asked the question 'what is most difficult?,' replied 'To know yourself.' The invocation 'to know oneself' is also attributed to Socrates and other Greek philosophers as the source of wisdom and the good life. According to the great ancient historian Plutarch 'Know thyself' (*Gnothi se auton*) was inscribed on the lintel above Apollo's temple at Delphi on the slopes of Mount Parnassus in the 6th century B.C. In one sense Western philosophy has been a continuous engagement with the 'problem of subjectivity' and with the self as a locus of both consciousness and experience—a question that is deemed to be open to understanding, analysis and philosophical reflection.

In the modern era beginning with Descartes and Kant the emphasis shifted to a thinking 'I' not only as a source of consciousness and representation but also ultimately as a source of all knowledge, action and ethics. Sometimes this tradition that has been taken up differently by different philosophers is referred to as the 'philosophy of the subject,' where 'subject,' at least in the premodern sense, refers to the political (or civic) domain of a reigning monarch and anchored in a network of 'rights,' 'duties,' 'responsibilities,' and 'privileges' that characterized the feudal relationship. The notion of the subject also prefigured the modern 'citizen,' which as a concept finds its institutional origin in the Greek *polis* or city state and is intimately connected to exercise of freedom and the pursuit of 'well being.'

In the latter part of his life Foucault stepped back from his study of the regimen of sexual behavior and pleasures in antiquity based on *aphrodsia* to extract from it and study the more general problem of 'the subject and truth.' Foucault was interested in the historical form of the relations between the 'subject' and 'truth' and how it took shape in the West. This concern was laid out most clearly in *The Hermeneutics of the Subject: Lectures at the Collège de France 1981–1982* (Foucault, 2005) a course of lectures that Foucault gave in the early 1980s and has only recently been published in English. Foucault gives twenty-four one-hour lectures that explore the general problematic of subjectivity and truth based on a historical examination of the privileging of the Delphic precept 'know yourself' (*gnothi seauton*) over 'care of the self' (*epimeleia heaton*). In these lectures Foucault examines care of the self as a new theoretical point of departure interpreting Socrates himself as a master of care of the self. He also examines reasons for the elimination of care for the self in modern philosophy beginning with Descartes's insistence on self-knowledge and the structure of the *cogito*.

In these ancient discourses pedagogy plays a strong and central role and also in Foucault's deliberations as he takes us on a tour of Plato's *Alcibiades* and the contextualization of the first appearance of 'care of the self,' with its political expectations and pedagogical deficiencies. Pedagogy and the problem of education play a central role in Foucault's discussions. For example, he writes in a lecture of 10 March 1982:

> Let's us call 'pedagogical,' if you like, the transmission of a truth whose function it is to endow any subject whatsoever with aptitudes, capabilities, knowledges and so on, that he did not possess before and that he should possess at the end of the pedagogical relationship. If, then, we call 'pedagogical' this relationship consisting in endowing any subject whomsoever with a series of abilities defined in advance, we can, I think, call 'psychagogical' the transmission of a truth whose function is not to endow any subject with abilities, etcetera, but whose function is to modify the mode of being of the subject to whom we address ourselves (Foucault, 2005, p. 407).

It is helpful to see this course in the series of thirteen courses he gave from 1970 to 1984. The first five courses reflected his early work on knowledge in the human sciences, concerning punishment, penal and psychiatric institutions: 'La Volonté de savoir' (1970–71), 'Théories et Institutions pénales' (1971–72), 'La Société punitive' (1972–73), 'Le Pouvoir psychiatrique' (1973–74), 'Les Anormaux' (1974–75). The remaining eight courses focused squarely on 'governmentality' studies, with a clear emphasis also on the problematic (and hermeneutics) of the subject and the relation between subjectivity and truth: 'It faut défender la société' (1975–76), 'Securité, Territoire, Population' (1977–78), 'Naissance de la biopolitique' (1978–79), 'Du gouvernement des vivants' (1979–80), 'Subjectivité et Vérité' (1980–81), 'L'Herméneutique du subjet' (1981–82), 'Le Gouvernement de soi et des autres' (1982–83), 'Le Gouvernement de soi et des autres: le courage de la verite' (1983–84). *The Hermeneutics of the Subject* and the historical form of the relation between subjectivity and truth is a cornerstone in his governmentality studies and appears in recently published form as *Fearless Speech* (Foucault, 2001a).

This coauthored book constitutes the first systematic exploration of the relevance of Foucault's explorations of subjectivity and truth, and its significance for educational theory of what Foucault referred to on a number of occasions as 'the culture of self,' especially in a course of lecture he gave in Berkeley in the early 1980s.[1] The term itself is a curious one because it indicates that we cannot approach the question of the self without locating it within the network of values and social *practices* that come to characterize a culture at a particular time. The notion of the self belongs to a culture and can really only be understood in relation to a culture comprised of values, social relations and practices. These practices and relations change and are constituted very differently in different historical eras. For Foucault there is no such thing as universal necessities when it comes to human nature; indeed, there is no such thing as human nature; nothing that is that we can advance a theory about which is valid for all ages and across all cultures. Even within the Western tradition there have been marked shifts that center around a quite different set of practices.

This book provides the first systematic analysis and development in educational theory of the later Foucault's concern for the historical form that relations between subjectivity and truth in the history of Western philosophy has taken since antiquity. Our joint intention is to use Foucault's insights on subjectivity and truth as a basis for the investigation of contemporary forms of truth-telling in the constitution of the educational subject. Combined with Foucault's studies of governmentality this constitutes a general problematic for the investigation of new forms of subjectivity including, 'the entrepreneurial self' that has come to characterize neoliberalism as a form of governmentality and the neoliberal paradigm of educational policy.

Michel Foucault in his late work, a year before he died, used the phrase 'culture of self' as the title of his lecture in Berkeley on April 12, 1983, and in the discussion that followed.[2] He used the phrase to explore the theme of the culture of the self as a philosophical and historical question, and philosophy as an activity that taught about the care of the self. Early in that lecture he drew attention once again to Kant's minor essay 'What is Enlightenment?' to emphasize the question 'What are we now?' and more broadly, 'What is truth?' as well as the related question 'How is it possible to know the truth?' Here Foucault employs the term 'historical ontology of ourselves' and views his own later work precisely as an investigation utilizing this mode of historical analysis. Foucault is entranced by Kant's question of the present—'the question of what is happening now' because it bears on what this present actually is and how it might be recognized, distinguished, and deciphered.

In his historical investigations of the formation of ourselves through the history of thought he focuses on three sets of relations: those concerning truth, obligation, and relations to ourselves and to others. In particular, Foucault had turned from his earlier studies of systematic and structural forces that produced the self to examine the relation to oneself and examples of techniques of the self. In these investigations he saw that care of the self (concern for the self) was the main form of ethics in Roman and Greek thought for over a thousand years. For Foucault the concept of 'culture' is central. In *The Hermeneutics of the Subject* Foucault (2005) writes:

> I think we can say that from the Hellenistic and Roman period we see a real development of the 'culture' of the self. I don't want to use the word culture in a sense that is too loose and I will say that we can speak of culture on a number of conditions. First, when there is a set of values with a minimum degree of coordination, subordination, and hierarchy. We can speak of culture when a second condition is satisfied, which is that these values are given both as universal but also as only accessible to a few. A third condition for being able to speak of culture is that a number of precise and regular forms of conduct are necessary for individuals to be able to reach these values. Even more than this, effort and sacrifice is required. In short, to have access to these values you must be able to devote your life to them. Finally, the fourth condition for being able to talk about culture is that access to these values is conditional upon more or less regular techniques and procedures that have been developed, validated, transmitted, and taught, and that are also associated with a whole set of notions, concepts, and theories etcetera: with a field of knowledge (*savoir*) (Foucault, 2005, p. 238).

Around the same time in *Technologies of the Self,* Foucault (1988b) departs from Heidegger's essentialism to focus on *historical ontologies* established through a Nietzschean-styled genealogical investigation. For Foucault, as previously mentioned there are no universal necessities in human nature, but only different technologies through which the subject is created or by which (s)he creates him or herself. Following the work of Nietzsche and the later Heidegger, Foucault reacts against the phenomenological and humanist subject to emphasize modes of subjectivation and the way that human beings become subjects. In so doing he transforms Heidegger's essentialism into a historical inquiry, and he distances himself from Heidegger's universalism and preoccupation with essences. From Heidegger he accepts the relationship between subjectivity and technology, although he gives it a historical cast. In particular, he became interested in techniques of self-formation and how the roots of the modern concept of the self could be located in first and second century Greco-Roman philosophy and in fourth and fifth century Christian spirituality. As he says in 'Truth, Power, Self':

> All my analyses are directed against the idea of universal necessities in human existence. They show the arbitrariness of institutions and show which space of freedom we still can enjoy and how changes can still be made (Foucault, 1988a, p.11).

He was to remark 'I do believe that there is no sovereign, founding subject, a universal form of subject.' He explains further, 'I believe, on the contrary, that the subject is constituted through practices' of subjection to or liberation from 'a number of rules, styles, and inventions to be found in the cultural environment' (Foucault, 1988b, pp. 50–51).

Foucault draws our attention to the ways in which technologies have always been part of culture and society and instrumental in questions of self-formation. He aims 'to sketch a history of the different ways in our culture that humans develop knowledge about themselves . . . [and] to analyze these so-called sciences as very specific 'truth games' related to specific techniques that human beings use to understand themselves.' (Foucault, 1988b, p.17). He outlines four major types of technologies, 'each a matrix of practical reason':

> (1) technologies of production, which permit us to produce, transform, or manipulate things; (2) technologies of signs systems, which permit us to use signs, meanings, symbols, or signification; (3) technologies of power, which determine the conduct of individuals and submit them to certain ends or domination, an objectivizing of the subject; (4) technologies of the self, which permit individuals to effect by their own means or with the help of others a certain number of operations on their own bodies and souls, thoughts, conduct and way of being, so as to transform themselves in order to attain a certain state of happiness, purity, wisdom, perfection, or immortality' (Foucault, 1988b, p. 18).

Foucault explains that, in antiquity, there were two major ethical principles—'know yourself' and 'take care of yourself.' The former came to displace and obscure the latter because the tradition of Christian morality made self-renunciation the condition for salvation. By contrast, taking care of oneself became presented as an immorality. Also, knowledge of the self, as Foucault (1988b, p.22) explains, 'takes on an ever-increasing importance as the first step in the theory of knowledge.'

Foucault then proceeds to investigate the theme of 'taking care of oneself' in antiquity, focusing first on Plato's Alcibiades I and, second, on the Hellenistic period and the Stoics, including Seneca and Plutarch. He investigates techniques employed by the Stoics—the disclosure of the self through letters to friends and the examination of self and conscience—and the truth games of early Christianity that led finally to the whole apparatus of confession.

Foucault investigated 'care of self' versus 'know your self' (latter as a means for taking care of oneself) in the Greco-Roman culture of the self which seemed to create a culture based on autonomous selves, though not separate from its political relations, but geared towards care of themselves and principles of self-cultivation. In this culture a set of obligations to the self grew up not as necessarily rule based or authoritarian but rather as the result of a personal choice aimed at a better life and the possibility of a new type of existence. Curiously, this culture was not religious in any institutional or organized sense even though we might still call it spiritual.

Throughout his work Foucault had been concerned with technologies of power and domination, whereby the self had been objectified through scientific inquiry. By 1981, he became interested in how a human being turns him- or herself into a subject. He became interested in those practices whereby individuals, by their own means or with the help of others, acted on their own bodies, souls, thoughts, conduct, and way of being in order to transform themselves and attain a certain state of perfection or happiness. At this late period of his life he became interested in the Kantian question 'what are we today,' and he indicates that his project on the self was suggested by the late American critic Christopher Lasch and his influential work *The Culture of Narcissism* (1979).

LASCH AND THE CULTURE OF NARCISSISM

It is worth dwelling on Lasch's work momentarily, if anything, because it firmly anchors the self in a notion of culture and understands the self by reference to a culture, in this case, as he suggests in the subtitle, 'American Life in an Age of Diminishing Expectations.' Lasch sums up his provocative thesis in the following statement 'To live for the moment is the prevailing passion—to live for yourself, not for your predecessors or posterity' (Lasch, 1979, p. 5). For Lasch, writing at the end of the 1970s, an 'intense preoccupying self-absorption defines the moral climate of contemporary American society' (p. 25) where 'Self-preservation has replaced self-improvement as the goal of earthly existence' (Lasch, 1979, p. 53). Lasch is arguing that techniques of the self in a capitalist society based on a consumerist ethic has taken leave of its spiritual base and become replaced by self-preservation or one might say, even against Lasch, a kind of 'self-improvement' but of a narrow, instrumental kind. This notion of self-improvement is revealed in an ethic of pleasure and a kind of hedonistic pasttime where 'even the most intimate encounters become a form of mutual exploitation' (Lasch, 1979, p. 65). The main thesis of Lasch's book is that Americans have created a self-absorbed, greedy and frivolous society the intimate heart of which has been transformed by relentless consumerism. The irony is that this self-absorption is not accompanied by increased self-awareness but rather quite the opposite, a thinness in self-understanding and an exploitative relation to others.

Lasch uses the myth and the figure of Narcissus to describe this American culture of the self at the end of the 1970s. The story of Narcissus comes to us in various forms—in the archaic version of the *Oxyrhynchus papyri* (after the archeological site in Egypt and once a prosperous regional city) and in the version related by Ovid's *Metamorphoses* that tells the story of Narcissus, a beautiful youth who spurned the affections of Echo, the wood nymph, only to fall in love with his own reflection. As Ovid writes:

> While he is drinking he beholds himself reflected in the mirrored pool—and loves; loves an imagined body which contains no substance, for he deems the mirrored shade a thing of life to love. . . . All that is lovely in himself he loves, and in his witless way he wants himself:— he who approves is equally approved; he seeks, is sought, he burns and he is burnt (Book 3, edited by Brookes More).

While the myth has been referred to and used many times throughout literary history it was given a distinctive stamp in the work of Sigmund Freud who distinguishes between primary and secondary narcissism where the first form is developmental and adaptive occurring during the normal course of growing up and the second form is pathological and a form of neurosis of an adolescent or adult who has not been properly socialized. As infants we are the center of the universe and parents, while 'mythical and awesome,' exist solely to cater for our every need. Secondary narcissism exists where the child does not complete the normal processes of separation from his parents and individuation because of conflict and injuries sustained within a dysfunctional family (although there is some evidence to suggest genetic influence). In the process the child's sense of self-worth and self-esteem is damaged resulting in an obsessive self-infatuation and leading to the exclusion and insensitivity towards others. Narcissism in this sense is the core of the narcissistic personality disorder as defined by *The Diagnostic and Statistical Manual of Mental Disorders IV* that defines the disorder of the self as a group of five of the following characteristics:

(1) has a grandiose sense of self-importance (e.g., exaggerates achievements and talents, expects to be recognized as superior without commensurate achievements); (2) is preoccupied with fantasies of unlimited success, power, brilliance, beauty, or ideal love; (3) believes that he or she is 'special' and unique and can only be understood by, or should associate with, other special or high-status people (or institutions); (4) requires excessive admiration; (5) has a sense of entitlement, i.e., unreasonable expectations of especially favorable treatment or automatic compliance with his or her expectations; (6) is interpersonally exploitative, i.e., takes advantage of others to achieve his or her own ends; (7) lacks empathy: is unwilling to recognize or identify with the feelings and needs of others; (8) is often envious of others or believes that others are envious of him or her; (9) shows arrogant, haughty behaviors or attitudes.

Lasch's (1979) innovation is to follow Freud's idea mentioned in *Civilization and Its Discontents* that we might talk not only of sick individuals but also of sick or unhealthy cultures. Lasch also broadens his analysis away from individual disorders of the self to locate narcissism as the core of a new American consumerist culture at the end of the 1970s. As he writes:

> The new narcissist is haunted not by guilt but by anxiety. He seeks not to inflict his own certainties on others but to find a meaning in life. Liberated from the superstitions of the past, he doubts even the reality of his own existence. Superficially relaxed and tolerant, he finds little use for dogmas of racial and ethnic purity but at the same time forfeits the security of group loyalties and regards everyone as a rival for the favors conferred by a paternalistic state. His sexual attitudes are permissive rather than puritanical, even though his emancipation from ancient taboos brings him no sexual peace. Fiercely competitive in his demand for approval and acclaim, he distrusts competition because he associates it unconsciously with an unbridled urge to destroy. Hence he repudiates the competitive ideologies that flourished at an earlier stage of capitalist development and distrusts even their limited expression in sports and games. He extols cooperation and teamwork while harboring deeply antisocial impulses. He praises respect for rules and regulations in the secret belief that they do not apply to himself. Acquisitive in the sense that his cravings have no limits, he does not accumulate goods and provisions against the future, in the manner of the acquisitive individualist of nineteenth-century political economy, but demands immediate gratification and lives in a state of restless, perpetually unsatisfied desire (Lasch, 1979, p. 23).

Lasch diagnoses a culture of narcissism in 1970s America—a consumerist culture that promotes the development of a narcissistic self-disorder. It is this cultural analysis of American self-disorders that allegedly interested Michel Foucault, but the influence was mutual and flowed both ways. Lasch reviewed many of Foucault's books in *The New York Times* and *The New York Review of Books* during the 1970s and 1980s extolling Foucault's work as relevant to cultural historians and describing his work as 'brilliant,' 'a tour de force,' 'innovative and controversial,' suggesting 'What is special to him . . . is his demonstration of how institutions create the concept of illness, crime, insanity or sex.' Later and prophetically in *The Minimal*

Self (1984) Lasch, no doubt strongly influenced by Foucault, makes explicit that the insights of traditional religion have retained their vitality. Psychic 'survival' is no longer a meaningful goal, rather, as Lasch argues: 'Self-affirmation remains a possibility precisely to the degree that an older conception of personality, rooted in Judeo-Christian traditions, has persisted alongside a behavioral or therapeutic conception.' (Lasch, 1984, p. 17). In *The Minimal Self* Lasch assigns a new significance to religion, suggesting:

> In the history of civilization . . . vindictive gods give way to gods who show mercy as well and uphold the morality of loving your enemy. Such a morality has never achieved anything like general popularity, but it lives on, even in our own enlightened age, as a reminder both of our fallen state and of our surprising capacity for gratitude, remorse, and forgiveness, by means of which we now and then transcend it (Lasch, 1984, p. 6).

Given the renewed religiosity, the rise of fundamentalisms in an age of uncertainty, the return to scripture and its literal truth, and also the growth of faith schools, both Lasch's and Foucault's work provide useful grids of understanding and analytical tools for investigating the return to the 'fundamentalist self' in terms of new religious practices and precepts and also the continued significance of truth-telling practices in processes of self-formation both inside faith schools and in the wider community. The educational self and 'educating the self' become motifs for a differentiated plural society that with the withering of grand ideologies have led to communities of faith exerting their own educational principles, beliefs and practices.

Lasch's work certainly takes Foucault seriously although he deviates from Foucault's analysis especially in the use of Freud. Where they agree on the fundamentals of the importance of *culture* in understanding the self and they both focus on practices of the self, Foucault situates his study in the world of antiquity and Lasch in contemporary American consumer society. Foucault reacts against Freud and the model of repression that suggests the possibility of liberation from oneself through a 'talking cure.' More than Lasch, Foucault wants to revise or reform if not reject the elements that comprise the Freudian model of analysis.

It does not take much imagination to see the relevance of education as forming 'cultures of the self' not only in the senses explicit in Foucault's work (and Lasch's) but also in profiling the great interrelated problems of subjectivity (knowing one's mind) and intersubjectivity (knowing other minds), which stand at the heart of learning, self-formation, identity, culture and ethics. Central to Foucault's account is a philosophical analysis that anchors the ethical self in the practice of freedom. This emphasis is most obvious in Foucault's analysis of what he calls 'care of the self' that pictures freedom as the ontological condition of ethics and ethics as a social practice linked to games of truth.

ANALYZING CARE OF THE SELF

Paul Rabinow (1997) provides a useful summary of the steps in Foucault's argument about 'care of the self' that are presented here as a series of related premises in summary form:

> *Premise 1:* 'what is ethics, if not the practice of liberty, the considered practice of liberty' (Foucault, 1997a, p. xxv). 'Freedom is the ontological condition of ethics. But ethics is the considered form that freedom takes' (ibid.).

> *Premise 2:* In the Western tradition, 'taking care of oneself requires knowing oneself.' 'To take care of the self is to equip oneself with these truths (p. 281); thus, as Rabinow (1997: xxv) points out quoting Foucault (1997a, p. xxv), 'ethics is linked to the game of truth.'

> *Premise 3:* Ethics is a practice or style of life and the problem for Foucault is to give 'liberty the form of an ethos' (Foucault, 1997a, p. xxv).

> *Premise 4:* The subject 'is not a substance. It is a form, and this form is not primarily or always identical to itself' (Foucault, 1997a, p. xxv).

As Rabinow (1997: xxvi) explains "'Self' is a reflexive pronoun, and has two meanings. *Auto* means 'the same,' but it also conveys the notion of identity. The latter meaning shifts the question from 'What is the self?' to 'What is the foundation on which I shall find my identity?'"

> *Premise 5:* So the emphasis shifts to the historical constitution of these forms and their relation to 'games of truth.' 'A game of truth is a set of procedures that lead to a certain result, which, on the basis of its principles and rules of procedures, may be considered valid or invalid.' 'Why truth? . . . And why must the care of the self occur only through the concern for truth? [This is] *the* question for the West. How did it come about that all of Western culture began to revolve around this obligation of truth . . . ?' (Foucault, 1997a, p. xxv).

Rabinow (1997: xxvi) comments: that given these premises, 'one must conclude equally that "one escaped from a domination of truth" only by playing the game differently.'

> *Premise 6:* 'the relationship between philosophy and politics is permanent and fundamental' (Foucault, 1997a).

And finally *Premise 7*, where Rabinow (1997: xxvi) remarks 'Philosophy, understood as a practice and a problem, is a vocation. The manner in which liberty is taken up by the philosopher is distinctive, differing in intensity and zeal from other free citizens.'

In Rabinow's formulation of Foucault's argument, it is clear that the overriding emphasis is on 'care for the self,' and there is no explicit discussion about 'care for others' or the possibility of inferring the latter from the former (see Foucault, 1984). Perhaps this emphasis on the centrality of truth in relation to the self is to be developed only through the notion of 'others' as an audience—intimate or public—that allows for the politics of confession and (auto)biography.

Arnold Davidson (1997) makes it clear that Foucault, especially in his later work *The Care of the Self* (Foucault, 1990) drew on the work of Pierre Hadot's work on 'spiritual exercises' especially with regard to what Foucault called 'ethics' or the self's relationship to itself or 'ethical self-constitution.' (Pierre Hadot has held the chair of the History of Hellenistic Studies and Roman Thought at the Collège de France since 1982). Davidson suggests that Foucault's four main aspects of the self's relationship to itself are an appropriation of Hadot's four-fold framework for interpreting ancient thought:

> the ethical substance, that part of oneself that is taken to be the relevant domain for ethical judgement; the mode of subjection, the way in which the individual established his relation to moral obligations and rules; the self-forming activity or ethical work that one performs on oneself in order to transform oneself into an ethical subject; and, finally, the telos, the mode of being at which one aims in behaving ethically (Davidson, 1997, pp. 200–201).

Hadot emphasized that in ancient schools of thought philosophy was considered to be a way of life, a quest for wisdom, a way of being and, ultimately a way of transforming the self. Spiritual exercises were a form of pedagogy designed to teach its practitioners the philosophical life that had both a moral and existential value. These exercises were aimed at nothing less than a transformation of one's worldview and one's personality involving all aspects of one's being, including intellect, imagination, sensibility and will. Hadot claimed that in the figure of Socrates we find a set of dialogical spiritual exercises that epitomized the Socratic injunction 'Know thyself!' and provided a model for a relationship of the self to itself that constituted the basis of all spiritual exercise. In this model, Hadot draws our attention to the primacy of the process one adopts to a problem rather than the solution. Hadot's (1987) major work *Exercises spirituels et philosophie antique* shows how this set of dialogical relations of the self (with itself) is at the very center of a total transformation of one's being (see Davidson, 1997). It is a model that could both complement and correct certain emphases in Foucault's later thinking about truth and subjectivity.

Foucault's (1997b) essay, 'Writing the Self,' clearly draws on Hadot's work.[3] Foucault's essay analyses a passage from Athanasius's *Vita Antoni* about writing the self that involve 'the actions and movements of our souls as though to make them mutually known to one another, and let us be sure that out of shame at being known, we will cease sinning and have nothing perverse in our hearts' (cited in Foucault, 1997b, p. 234). 'Self-writing' . . . 'offsets the dangers of solitude' and exposes our deeds to a possible gaze; at the same time the practice works on thoughts as well as actions, which brings it into line with the role of confession (in the early Christian literature). It permits, at the same time, a retrospective analysis of 'the role of writing in the philosophical culture of the self just prior to Christianity: its close tie with apprenticeship; its applicability to movements of thought; its role as a test of truth' (Foucault, 1997b, p. 235). Reading and writing are part of 'arts of the self' which contribute to what Foucault calls the 'aesthetics of existence' and also a basis for the government of self and others.

READING AND WRITING THE SELF

In his investigations of 'spiritual exercises' in Latin antiquity Hadot (1995, p. 81) describes in the philosophy of the Stoics the way in which 'thought, as it were, takes itself as its own subject-matter' as the basis for an art of living where the individual is transformed into an authentic state of heightened self-consciousness providing both inner peace and freedom. No systematic treatise of these exercises has come down to us and Hadot reconstructs them from a close reading of ancient texts in order to emphasize the consequences of such thought for philosophy itself. By reference to Philo of Alexandria Hadot enumerates the following list: research (*zetesis*), thorough investigation (*skepsis*), reading (*anagnosis*), listening (*akroasis*), attention (*prosoche*), self-mastery (*enkrateia*), indifference to indifferent things, meditations (*meletai*), therapies of the passions, remembrance of good things, and the accomplishment of duties.[2] The specifically intellectual exercises of reading, listening, research, and investigation provide the substance for meditation, which can be distinguished from attention (the fundamental spiritual attitude of the Stoics), and from the practical exercises designed to create habits. In this context, Hadot analyses the Hellenistic and Roman spiritual exercises in terms of learning to live, learning to dialogue (first brought to Western consciousness in the figure of Socrates), learning to die, and learning how to read. It is especially this last notion that is worth pondering in relation to pedagogy. The quest for self-realization and improvement is the final goal of the spiritual exercises and this goal, Hadot (1995, p. 102) informs us is shared by all philosophical schools of antiquity. Through 'spiritual exercises'— including 'reading' and 'writing'—the self is liberated from its egoism, its passions and its anxieties. This thought must sound so familiar to us late moderns, especially in a post-Foucauldian age, at a time when the self as subject (and object of its own gaze) has been the basis of so much debate in terms of both the Cartesian picture (the self as a unified, transparent, essence) that held us captive and *technologies of self*.

Foucault (1986) drew on Hadot's work on 'spiritual exercises' when he was completing *The Care of the Self*, and Hadot, in a piece entitled "Reflections on the Idea of the 'Cultivation of the self'" (Hadot, 1995, pp. 206–13), takes Foucault to task for the inaccuracies of his interpretation of Greco-Roman ethics as 'an ethics of the pleasure one takes in oneself' (Hadot, 1995, p. 207). Foucault (1997b) writes a stunning essay entitled 'Writing the Self' that also, it seems, draws on Hadot's groundbreaking work. Foucault's essay is part of what he calls his studies of 'arts of the self,' which are designed to explore the 'aesthetics of existence' and to inquire into the government of self and others that characterizes his later work.

Foucault's essay analyzes a passage from Athanasius's *Vita Antoni*. The opening sentence of the text to which Foucault refers weighs so precisely on the preceding discussion:

> Here is one thing to observe to ensure that one does not sin. Let us each take note of and write down the actions and movements of our souls as though to make them mutually known to one another, and let us be sure that out of shame at being known, we will cease sinning and have nothing perverse in our hearts (cited in Foucault, 1997b, p. 234).

Foucault notes that this 'self-writing' 'offsets the dangers of solitude' and exposes our deeds to a possible gaze; at the same time the practice works on *thoughts* as well as actions, which brings it into line with the role of confession (in the early Christian literature). It permits, at the same time, a retrospective analysis of

> the role of writing in the philosophical culture of the self just prior to Christianity: its close tie with apprenticeship; its applicability to movements of thought; its role as a test of truth (Foucault, 1997b, p. 235).

These elements are to be found in Seneca and Plutarch but take a different form and are based upon different values. As he says,

> No technique, no professional skill can be acquired without exercise; nor can one learn the art of living, the *techne tou biou*, without an *askesis* that must be understood as a training of the self by the self (Foucault, 1997b, p. 235).

In relation to the ancients Hadot suggests we must *learn how to read* them. Whether it be the dialogues of Plato, the class notes of Aristotle, or the treatises of Plotinus we must learn to take into account the concrete situation in which they were produced. As he writes:

> They are the products of a philosophical school, in the most concrete sense of the term, in which a master forms his disciples, trying to guide them to self-transformation and -realization. Thus, the written work is a reflection of *pedagogical*, psychagogic, and methodological preoccupations (Hadot, 1995, pp. 104–5, our emphasis).

Foucault's work, we would argue, is instructive when investigating modern forms of pedagogy, and the historical transition from church- to state-based forms of formal schooling. In *The Use of Pleasure,* Foucault talks of technologies of the self as 'models proposed for setting up and developing relationships with the self, for self-reflection, self-knowledge, self-examination, for deciphering the self by oneself, for the transformation one seeks to accomplish with oneself as object.' (Foucault, 1986, p. 29)

Nikolas Rose comments:

> Western man, Michel Foucault argued, has become a confessing animal. The truthful rendering into speech of who one is, to one's parents, one's teachers, one's doctor, one's lover, and oneself, is installed at the heart of contemporary procedures of individualization. In confessing, one is subjectified by another, for one confesses in the actual or imagined presence of a figure who prescribes the form of the confession, the words and rituals through which it should be made, who appreciates, judges, consoles, or understands. But in confessing, one also constitutes oneself. In the act of speaking, through the obligation to produce words that are true to an inner reality, through the self-examination that precedes and accompanies speech, one becomes a subject for oneself. Confession, then, is the diagram of a certain form of subjectification that binds us to others at the very moment we affirm our identity (Rose, 1989, p. 240).

Foucault reminds us that confession originated with Catholicism. He views it as the principal technology that emerged for Catholicism to manage the sexual lives of believers. With the counterreformation confession underwent a profound change so that it came to apply to not just acts but also to one's *thoughts.* In the 18th century confession developed as a complex technology of secular discourses proliferating in pedagogy, medicine, psychiatry, and literature, and reaching its secular highpoint in Freud's 'talking cure.' Since Freud one might say that the secularization of confession has been 'scientized' through clinical codifications, personal examinations, histological techniques, the general documentation and date collection of personal data, the proliferation of interpretive schemas and the development of a whole host of therapeutic techniques for 'normalization.'

With these new techniques for normalization and individualization we are 'obliged to be free': self-inspection replaces the confessional as new forms of self-regulation become manifest. As Rose writes:

> Writing was one central technique. Not that writing was a new acquisition for technologies of the self; it extends from Socrates' letters to Augustine's confessions. But for the seventeenth century Puritans, the confessional diary, constituted what William Paden terms 'an account book of one's state of sin,' which effected, through the work of writing, a measurement of the self against biblical standards. The diary was a mirror of one's sinfulness, but a mirror one held oneself. The self-inscription of the diary both calibrated one's lapses, and bore witness to the survival of one's faith; the self was to become both sinner and judge (Rose, 1989, p. 220).

Discipline 'entails training in the minute arts of self-scrutiny, self-evaluation, and self-regulation ranging from the control of the body, speech, and movement in school, through the mental drill inculcated in school and university, to the Puritan practices of self-inspection and obedience to divine reason' (Rose, 1989, p. 222).

Foucault alerts us to the way that modern pedagogies are secular technologies of the self in which self-regulation and self-examination comes to occupy center ground. Philosophy in a *pedagogical sense* is always autobiographical and that, insofar as we belong to a particular form of life, we are compelled to recreate ourselves through narrative. Foucault emphasizes the power/knowledge grid in which we turn the gaze of examination back upon our selves as objects.

In a Foucauldian-inspired investigation we might inquire into the pedagogical cultures within which children learn to tell the truth about themselves, by what means, and how these truth-telling discourses are central to the narrative creation and reconstruction of the self.

Children learn the art of discourse against a background of truth (even in fiction) and also learn the cultural compulsion to tell the truth. Autobiography and truth-telling are central to pedagogical discourses, for every pedagogical interaction also presupposes a background of truth-telling. Autobiography sets up a sense of agency as the child learns to look back and reflect on past actions and decisions. In our Western society children learn to be 'autononomous,' at least insofar as that means responsibility for oneself, one's actions and those under one's care. The role of biography and autobiography is broader than its consideration as a specialist genre within literature, and it is in philosophical forms linked strongly with the becoming of the self, not only through basic social and psychological processes as 'reading' and 'writing' the self but also through other forms of media and representations. Self-representation also takes various forms in the sculptural, plastic and visual arts where we see many different kinds of self-portraiture. In the performing and the visual arts we experience both scripted and unscripted (free expression) kinds of self-representation and self-recognition. These forms find a particular expression during the Florentine Renaissance with what Jacob Burkthardt understood as the birth of modern individualism. Renaissance humanism is best seen as a form of pedagogy rather than a systematic philosophy—'the pedagogy of individualism'—devoted through the liberal arts, through reading and writing, but also through its parts or specific disciplines (rhetoric, grammar, dialectic) (see Peters, 2001). Games of truth and the development of different disciplinary discourses, that through its rules, produced truths were aimed at the development of moral character and the direct shaping of the Renaissance individual both as a city dweller as well as a civic and church subject.

Almost certainly we are witnessing a shift from the shaping of an individual of classical liberalism—the ethical individual of Kantian humanism—to a market individualism of neoliberalism where the self is shaped as a utility maximizer, a free and contractual individual, who is self-constituted through the market choices and investment decisions that he/she makes. Lasch points to the forms of self disorders that accompanies a culture of narcissism, both narcissistic self and minimal self. In face of increasingly technical and functional forms of literacy and of schooling, we might inquire whether school in an age of consumerism promotes a relation to the self based on truth-telling or whether this relation has been replaced by another primary ethos: happiness, security, survival, success, 'self-improvement,' wealth.

CHAPTER TWO

The Genealogy OF THE Confessional Self

Self-Denial or Self-Mastery?

Of ourselves we are not 'knowers.' . . .

NIETZSCHE, *THE GENEALOGY OF MORALS*

INTRODUCTION

This chapter uses the work on the self, and the genealogy of confession as a technology of the self, of Michel Foucault, the iconoclast French philosopher-historian (1926–1984). Foucault provides us with 'creative, controversial, and original thinking on philosophical-historical-social ideas. Yet he did not propose any grand, global, utopian, or systematic solution to societal ills' (Besley, 2002a, p. 2). Foucault was not a counselor or psychotherapist. Nevertheless he obtained his *licence de psychologie* in 1951 and a diploma in psychopathology in 1952, subsequently working in a psychiatric hospital in the 1950s. *Madness and Civilization: A History of Insanity in the Age of Reason* formed the major thesis for his doctorate (Foucault, 1965). In something of a confession, Foucault states:

> In a sense, I have always wanted my books to be fragments from an autobiography. My books have always been my personal problems with madness, with prisons, with sexuality . . . each of my works is a part of my own biography (Foucault, cited in Macey, 1993, p. xii).

In other words, the personal and the philosophical ideas of Foucault are inextricably entwined. Foucault's critique opens up possibilities for us to sort out how we might see, understand and, in turn, negotiate our subjectivity and the power relations in our world.

For Foucault 'technologies of domination' and 'technologies of the self' produce effects that constitute the self, both defining the individual and controlling their conduct. His focus is on questions of subjectivity and the shaping and regulation of identities, on a relational self where intersubjectivity becomes central—a self that acknowledges and is constituted by difference and the Other. Foucauldian philosophical notions of 'technologies' and in particular 'technologies of the self' are derived from Nietzsche's 'genealogy' and Heidegger's understanding of technology. Foucault develops Nietzschean and Heideggerian concepts into 'technologies of the self' in relation to a reconsideration Greco-Roman antiquity and early Christianity.

The chapter begins with an outline of Foucault's changing understandings about the self. The second section, subtitled 'Nietzsche and Heidegger—influences on Foucault,' explores Foucault's Nietzschean-inspired method of genealogy and the influence of Heidegger's work as a basis for Foucault's understanding of 'technology' in relation to the self. The third section, 'technologies of the self,' provides a genealogy of Foucault's notions of confession that are outlined in *Technologies of the Self* (Foucault, 1988b), with subsections on Classical Greek technologies of the self, Christian religious confessional practices, and medico-therapeutic confessional practices: the secularisation of confession. This chapter argues that confession is a form of truth telling that constitutes the self. Following Foucault, it suggests that confession, as a technology of self, should be based less on an ethic of self-denial than on one of self-mastery. Self-mastery provides a secular model consonant with the demands of a postmodern world that recognises the inescapability of desire and the necessity of pleasure in a new body politics.

FOUCAULT'S CHANGING UNDERSTANDINGS OF THE SELF

Late in his life, when discussing his work in the seminar, *Technologies of the Self,* Foucault said that his project had been to historicise and analyse how in Western culture the specific 'truth games' in the social sciences such as economics, biology, psychiatry, medicine, and penology (prisons/criminology) have developed knowledge and techniques for people to understand themselves (Foucault, 1988b).

Foucault never focused specifically on education or pedagogy, although he did make some highly original and suggestive comments in earlier works like *Discipline and Punish* (Foucault, 1977) which emphasized the application of technologies of domination through the political subjugation of 'docile bodies' in the grip of disciplinary powers and the way the self is produced by processes of objectification, classification and normalization in the human sciences. Other commentators have addressed the relevance of his writings to education and some have applied his methods to educational issues (e.g., Ball, 1990; Marshall, 1996; Olssen, 1999; Baker, 2001; Peters & Besley, 2007).

For Foucault, power is not simply something negative used by one person or group to oppress others but can also be productive, positive, and a set of complex strategies where there is also resistance(s) (Besley, 2002a). For Foucault, power is *power-knowledge* since

> power produces knowledge and . . . power and knowledge directly imply one another: that there is no power relation without the correlative constitution of a field of knowledge, nor any knowledge that does not presuppose and constitute at the same time power relations (Foucault, 1977, p. 27).

Although Foucault defended the 'determinist' emphasis in *Discipline and Punish*, admitting that not enough was said about agency, once he redefined power to include agency as self-regulation, through both technologies of the self and ethical self-constitution, he overcame some of the problematic political implications in his earlier work (see Afterword in Rabinow, 1997; Foucault, 1986, 1988a, 1990; McNay, 1992). His later work emphasises self-determination or agency as self-regulation where individuals are continually in the process of constituting themselves as ethical subjects (ethical self-constitution). He emphasized that individuals are continually in the process of constituting themselves as ethical subjects through both technologies of the self and ethical self-constitution, and a notion of power that is not simply based upon repression, coercion, or domination. By this later point Foucault saw individuals 'as self-determining agents capable of challenging and resisting the structures of domination in modern society,' doing this for themselves without necessarily needing a priest or a therapist (McNay, 1992, p. 4).

In his later works, Foucault not only provided quite a shift from earlier discourses on the self, but also brought in notions of disciplinarity, governmentality, freedom and ethics as well as focusing on corporeality, politics and power and understanding the self in its historico-social context.

Foucault took up Heidegger's critiques of subjectivity and Cartesian-Kantian rationality in terms of power, knowledge and discourse—a stance against humanism that is tantamount to a rejection of phenomenology. Heidegger's influence on Foucault's thinking is discussed in a later section.

Foucault harnessed Heideggerian notions of *techne* and technology, innovatively adding these notions to his understanding the self as technologies of the self in his reconsideration of Greco-Roman antiquity and early Christianity (Foucault, 1988b). However, unlike Heidegger (1977) who focused on understanding the 'essence' or presence of being (*dasein*) Foucault historicised questions of ontology and was not concerned about notions of *aletheia* or uncovering any inner, hidden truth or essence of self. Foucault substituted genealogical investigations of the subject for the philosophical attempt to define the essence of human nature, aiming to reveal the contingent and historical conditions of existence. For Foucault, the self or subject 'is not a substance. It is a form, and this form is not primarily or always identical to itself' (Foucault, 1997a). Self means both *auto* or 'the same' and also implies understanding one's identity. There is no universal necessity of human nature. Once we realise this we will feel much freer than we ever experienced ourselves.

Governmentality (Foucault's neologism for government rationality) emerges with the development of liberalism and is directed through the notion of policing, administration and governance of individuals (Foucault, 1979, 1991). For Foucault 'governmentality' means the complex of calculations, programs, policies, strategies, reflections and tactics that shape the conduct of individuals, 'the conduct of conduct' for acting upon the actions of others in order to achieve certain ends. Those ends are 'not just to control, subdue, discipline, normalize, or reform them, but also to make them more intelligent, wise, happy, virtuous, healthy, productive, docile, enterprising, fulfilled, self-esteeming, empowered, or whatever' (Rose, 1998, p. 12). Governmentality is not simply about control in its negative sense but also in its positive sense, in its contribution to the security of society. Foucault poses questions about the *how* of government—'how to govern oneself, how to be governed, how to govern others, by whom the people will accept being governed, how to become the best possible governor' (Foucault, 1991, p. 87). Self-government is connected with morality; governing the family is related to economy and ruling the state to politics.

The History of Sexuality, Vol. I (Foucault, 1980a) presents a change from technologies of domination. A common assumption of Western culture, that the body and its desires—its sexuality—reveal the truth about the self is explored in this book. From this assumption it is then proposed that if one tells the 'truth' about one's sexuality, this deepest truth about the self will become apparent and then one can live an authentic life that is in touch with one's true self. Foucault's work on sexuality is concerned with problematising how pleasure, desire and sexuality—the regimes of power-knowledge-pleasure—as components of the art of living or an 'aesthetics of existence' have become discourses that shape the construction of ourselves as both the 'truth' of our sexuality is revealed as is the 'truth' of ourselves, as 'technologies of the self' (Foucault, 1986, p. 11). Chapter 3 discusses Foucault's use of Nietzsche's notion of the aesthetics of existence. Foucault (1988b) points out that since a common cultural feature is the paradoxical combination of prohibitions against sexuality on the one hand and strong incitations to speak the truth on the other, his project became focused on a history of this link, asking how individuals had been made to understand themselves in terms of what was forbidden—i.e., the relationship between truth and asceticism.

In 'The Ethics of the Concern for Self as a Practice of Freedom' (Foucault, 1997a), an interview in 1984, the year of his death, Foucault explains the change in his thinking about the relations of subjectivity and truth. In his earlier thinking he had conceived of the relationship between the subject and 'games of truth' in terms of either coercive practices (psychiatry or prison) or theoretical-scientific discourses e.g., the analysis of wealth, language and living beings in *The Order of Things* (Foucault, 1973). In his later writings he breaks with this relationship to emphasize games of truth not as a coercive practice, but rather as *an ascetic practice of self-formation*. 'Ascetic' in this context means an 'exercise of self upon the self by which one attempts to develop and transform oneself, and to attain a certain mode of being' (Foucault, 1997a, p. 282).

'Work' completed by the self upon itself is an *ascetic* practice that is to be understood not in terms of more traditional left-wing *models of liberation*, but rather as (Kantian) *practices of freedom*. This is an essential distinction for Foucault because the notion of liberation suggests that there is a hidden self or inner nature or essence that has been 'concealed, alienated, or imprisoned in and by mechanisms of repression' (Foucault, 1997a, p. 282). The process of liberation, on this model, liberates the 'true' self from its bondage or repression. By contrast, Foucault historicizes questions of ontology: there are no essences only 'becomings,' only a phenomenology or hermeneutics of the self—the forging of an identity through processes of self-formation.

Foucault (1997a) contrasts two different models of self-interpretation: liberation and freedom, suggesting that the latter is broader than the former and historically necessary once a country or people have attained a degree of independence and set up political society. For Foucault, liberation is not enough and the practices of freedom do not preclude liberation, but they enable individuals and society to define 'admissible and acceptable forms of existence or political society' (Foucault, 1997a, p. 283). For example, a person in chains is not free and although they may have some choices, these are severely limited by their lack of freedom. They have to be liberated or freed from their total domination so they have the freedom to practice their own ethics. Ethics is a practice or style of life. Freedom that equates to liberation is therefore a pre-condition of ethics, since ethics are the practices of the 'free' person. Foucault suggests that the ethical problem of freedom in relation to sexuality is politically and philosophically more important than a simple insistence on liberating sexual desire. In other words, he wishes to understand freedom as the ontological condition for ethics especially when freedom takes the form of a kind of informed reflection. This general understanding he begins to outline in terms of the ancient Greek imperative of 'care for the self,' which he discusses in 'technologies of the self—a seminar presented at the University of Vermont in the fall of 1982 (Foucault, 1988b).

NIETZSCHE AND HEIDEGGER—INFLUENCES ON FOUCAULT

Michel Foucault was strongly influenced by his readings of both Friedrich Nietzsche and Martin Heidegger and indebted to them for ideas that led him to emphasize the close conceptual relations between the notions of truth, power and subjectivity in his genealogical investigations. He started reading these two philosophers in the early 1950s. Foucault makes clear his intellectual debt to Heidegger, who he says 'has always been the essential philosopher . . . My entire philosophical development was determined by my reading of Heidegger' (Foucault, 1985, p. 8). This is not to say that Foucault was first and foremost a Heideggerian, for he was influenced by many other writers (see Besley, 2002a; Marshall, 1996; Olssen, 1999), but he acknowledges that Heidegger was crucial for his understanding of Nietzsche. Without Heidegger he may not have read Nietzsche whose work he had tried to read, but found that reading it alone did not appeal, 'whereas Nietzsche and Heidegger, that was a philosophical shock!' (Foucault, 1985, p. 9). In a late interview Foucault even described himself as Nietzschean:

> I am simply Nietzschean, and I try to see, on a number of points, and to the extent that it is possible, with the aid of Nietzsche's texts . . . what can be done in this domain (Foucault, 1988, p. 251).

While he wrote only one substantial paper on Nietzsche (Foucault, 1977) and nothing directly on Heidegger, it is clear that Foucault's works bear the unmistakable imprints of these two great thinkers. On Nietzsche's influence on Foucault see Shrift (1995). On Heidegger's influence on Foucault see Dreyfus (1998; 1999). Foucault's books are, of course, scattered with references to both thinkers. In regard to Heidegger, it is an interesting question, given his intellectual debts, why Foucault provided little direct acknowledgment of his work or influence upon him.

Nietzsche inspired Foucault to analyse the modes by which human beings *became* subjects without according either power or desire conceptual priority over the other, as had been the case in the discourses of Marxism (with its accent on *power*) and of Freudianism (with its accent on *desire*). This enabled Foucault to develop novel ways to retheorize and conceive anew the operation of *power* and *desire* in the constitution and self-overcoming of human subjects.

From Nietzsche, Foucault also intellectually inherited the concept and method of genealogy, a conception clearly influenced by Friedrich Nietzsche's *The Genealogy of Morals* (Foucault, 1980c, 1984b, 1984c; Nietzsche [1887] 1956). Genealogy is a form of historical analysis that inquires into the formation and structure of value accorded Man, Reason, and Truth through a variety of techniques, including both etymological and *linguistic* inquiry alongside the investigation of the *history* of concepts. See Nietzsche's famous and, apparently, only footnote in the entire corpus of his work, which appears after the first essay of the *Genealogy of Morals* (orig. 1887; 1956, p. 188).

Foucauldian genealogy is radically different from traditional historical analysis. It is a history of the present, which begins by posing a question or problematizing the present and how a problem is currently expressed by historicizing or re-evaluating the past in the light of current concerns. Genealogy is conducted by moving backward in a process of descent and emergence rather than through evolution or a process of development. It forms a critical ontology of our selves. For Foucault, living in one's own time involved the ethical constitution of self through a critical reflexiveness about the culture and forces that operated to constitute it (see Besley, 2002a).

Genealogy challenges the humanist idea that the self is unified and fully transparent to itself and that consciousness is linear, storing memories in the same way as a novel progresses a plot. It also challenges the progressivist agendas of the Enlightenment by emphasizing dispersion, disparity, and difference, taken-for-granted universal 'truths' about life. In *Discipline and Punish*, the body becomes both an object of knowledge and a site where power is exercised (Foucault, 1977). Foucault points out two forms of 'subjugated knowledges' (such as disciplinary networks of power or the arts of existence or the practices of sexuality in the ancient world) that are lowly ranked and considered inadequate for the accepted standards of knowledge and science:

> One constitutes previously established, erudite knowledges that have been buried, hidden, disguised, masked, removed, or written out by revisionist histories; another involves local, popular, or indigenous knowledges that are marginalized or denied space to perform (Besley, 2002a, p. 17).

In recovering these knowledges, we can rediscover the history of struggle and conflict and challenge the power-knowledge institutions and scientific discourses

(Foucault, 1980c). It is these subjugated knowledges that the Foucauldian-influenced narrative therapy seeks to harness in developing alternative narratives that challenge the dominant stories in people's lives (Besley, 2002a, 2002b).

For Foucault, as for Nietzsche, genealogy *replaces* ontology. Foucault's investigations into the modes by which human beings are made into subjects are, above all, historical investigations. For Foucault, as for Nietzsche, there are no *essences* of human beings and, therefore, also no possibility for universalist theories concerning the *nature* of human beings. Given that there is no human nature, fixed once and for all—no essential or universalisable nature—there is no question of a *science* of human nature (à la Hobbes or Hume) or the possibility of building other theories (of politics, of education, or of rights) on the basis of this alleged nature. All questions of ontology, in the hands of Nietzsche and Foucault, become radically historized. Thus, there is no sovereign individual or transcendental subject, but only human beings who have been historically constituted as subjects in different ways at different times.

Any one who has read *Discipline and Punish* cannot help but be struck by the extent to which Nietzsche's discussion of punishment in the second essay of the *Genealogy*—its analysis of debt and its inscription on the body—permeates Foucault's method and investigations of discipline, power and knowledge in the institutions regulated by the emergent human sciences. It is also clear that Foucault broadly accepted Nietzsche's perspectival notion of truth, yet the degree to which we can properly ascribe him Nietzsche's view is fraught with difficulty, given the complexity and changing character of Nietzsche's own views, and the continuing development of Foucault's thought. It is clear that Foucault, at least toward the end of his life, denied neither the classical ideal of truth as correspondence to an independently existing world nor the 'analytics of truth,' even although the early Nietzsche (1979) cast doubt precisely on this ideal. For Nietzsche, as an opening quotation demonstrates, truth is a convenient fiction, merely a belief about the possession of truth. Foucault's innovation was to historicize 'truth,' first, materially in discourse as 'regimes of truth' and, second, in practices as 'games of truth.'

Foucault makes clear his intellectual debt to Heidegger. He took up Heidegger's critiques of subjectivity and Cartesian-Kantian rationality in terms of power, knowledge and discourse. A shift from ontology to the history of Being is reflected in Heidegger's philosophy. Hence Foucault's stance against humanism is a rejection of phenomenology for he sees the subject as being within a particular historic-cultural context or genealogical narrative. Similar to Heidegger, Foucault explored ancient Greek philosophy and took some of his ideas on archaeological method from him—ideas about uncovering that Heidegger derived from Husserl. For Husserl some objects were clearly disclosed in consciousness while others were obscure or on the fringe.

In this respect, one notion that Heidegger focused on was *aletheia* (ancient Greek for 'truth' that included notions of revealing, unveiling or disclosing). Such 'truths' about oneself can involve various forms of confession about the self with thoughts feelings actions being disclosed or brought out of concealment. This stands in contrast to correspondence theories about truth that considers something to be truthful when statements and objects are matched and which are so prevalent in science and in law. In his later work, Foucault harnessed another Heideggerian notion, that of *techne* and technology. Both *aletheia* and *techne* as discussed in Heidegger's, essay 'Questions Concerning Technology' (1977) are explored here (Heidegger's essay was written in 1949 and revised in 1955).

In *The Question Concerning Technology*, Heidegger questions our relationship to the essence of modern technology, which, he argues, treats everything, including people, 'as a resource that aims at efficiency—toward driving on to the maximum yield at the minimum expense' (Heidegger, 1977, p. 15). Heidegger argued that *aletheia* is the fundamental, first truth because beings or subjects can only be known, encountered or experienced as beings if they are unconcealed and that since statements and their objects are beings, they must come before any correspondence or adequation truth that matches them up. Unlike Heidegger though who focuses on understanding the 'essence' or coming into presence of being or *dasein*, Foucault historicises questions of ontology and in the process is therefore not concerned about notions of *aletheia* or uncovering any inner, hidden truth or essence of self. He too looks to the Ancient Greeks for understandings about self, but not to the pre-Socratics that Heidegger particularly focused on (Heraclitus, Parmenides and Anaximander). Foucault's work, especially the seminar, *Technologies of the Self* (1989) looks to the Stoics and Alcibiades.

In introducing his theme of *questioning* technology, or finding ways of thinking about it, Heidegger warns we are never free whether or not we accept or deny this, but worse still, 'we are delivered over to it in the worst possible way when we regard it as something neutral; for this conception of it, to which we particularly like to do homage, makes us utterly blind to the essence of technology' (Heidegger, 1977, p. 4).

First, Heidegger points out the current instrumental and anthropological definition of technology as both a means to an end and a human activity that manufactures and uses tools of various kinds. However, Heidegger is concerned about our mastering it so that it doesn't slip from human control, about our relationship to its essence, but this is not revealed by an instrumental definition. Second, Heidegger points out that 'wherever ends are pursued and means are employed, wherever instrumentality reigns, there reigns causality' and proceeds to explore the four causes that philosophy teaches: *causa materialis, causa formalis, causa finalis and causa efficiens* (Heidegger, 1977, p. 6).

He points to the importance to us today of Plato's understanding in *Symposium* 205b, 'Every occasion for whatever passes over and goes forward into presencing from that which is not presencing is *poiesis*, a bringing-forth [*Her-vor-bringen*]' (Heidegger, 1977, p. 10). *Poiesis* can be both unaided *(physis)* and aided *(techne)*. *Physis* (Greek for nature) is unaided bringing-forth, like a bud blossoming, something within nature and *techne*, aided bringing-forth, involves nature's being assisted by craft persons or technicians. For the ancient Greeks, *techne*—the relationship between nature and human activity—comprised three dimensions, 'the arts of the mind' (thinking), fine arts and 'the activities and skills of the craftsman' (which were not separate for the Greeks) (Heidegger, 1997, p. 13). Heidegger alerts us that until Plato's time *techne* was linked with *episteme*, both words meaning 'knowing in the widest sense ... to be at home in something, to understand and be expert in it. Such knowing provides an opening up. As an opening up it is a revealing' (Heidegger, 1977, 13). Furthermore, 'it is as a revealing, and not as manufacturing, that *techne* is a bringing-forth' (Heidegger, 1977, p. 13). Therefore, 'technology is a mode of revealing. Technology comes to presence in the realm where revealing and unconcealment take place, where *aletheia*, truth, happens' (Heidegger, 1977, p. 13). For Heidegger, Greek technology was 'the gentleness of 'bringing-forth' rather than the violence of making this happen'—an important difference between earlier and modern epochs (Young, 2002, p. 40).

Heidegger points out that modern machine-power technology began in the latter eighteenth century, growing out of the modern physical sciences that developed over a century prior, establishing 'the deceptive illusion that modern technology is applied physical science' (Heidegger, 1977, p. 23). But this illusion is caused because there is no questioning of our relationship to the essence of modern technology, which Heidegger points out is shown in 'Enframing'[das Gestell].[1] Rather than something intrinsically technological or machinelike, Enframing is 'the way in which the real reveals itself as standing-reserve' (Heidegger, 1977, p. 23). Standing-reserve is not simply stock that is waiting to be used rather it is the revealing of modern technology that challenges nature to supply or expose energy that is unlocked, transformed, stored, distributed—a resource. In explanation, Heidegger is highly critical of the relationship of modern technology to nature pointing out that the difference between peasant farming and the mechanized food industry means that the earth is not there simply to be tilled but to yield to machines in ways that '*sets* upon [*stellt*] nature' (Heidegger, 1977, p. 15). Heidegger holds a somewhat romanticised view of nature and man's relationship to it in earlier times, suggesting that the earlier relationship was more harmonious, respectful and gentle. Heidegger (1977, p. 16) points out that 'setting-upon, in the sense of challenging-forth' happens as 'the energy concealed in nature is unlocked' (Heidegger, 1977, p. 16). This implies a violence or violation that 'is more than mere damage or harm' in modern technology (Young, 2002, p. 52). As Julian Young (2002) argues, earlier technological practices were no less violent in their treatment of nature, but because of the nature of their technology the scale is reduced—it takes longer to effect change with handtools although fire can of course rapidly and violently destroy habitats.

Furthermore the earth is not just to be cultivated but to yield coal to be mines, stockpiled and used as steam power for factories and water is now seen as a means of providing hydroelectric power. In this manner modern technology is always an 'expediting that is always directed from the beginning toward furthering something else' (Heidegger, 1977, p. 15). It treats everything, including people, as a resource that aims at the efficiency to produce the maximum yield or productivity.

Heidegger quotes Hölderlin, to point out that while modern technology holds high danger for humans (e.g., ecological destruction, nuclear war) at the same time, within it there is a saving power that takes root and eventually grows. He suggests that through reflection people will come to see that 'all saving power must be of a higher essence than what is endangered, though at the same time kindred to it' (Heidegger, 1977, p. 34). Since *techne* once 'a single manifold revealing' encompassed the fine arts as part of *poiesis*, 'the poetical pervades every art, every revealing of coming into presence of the beautiful' therefore maybe it is the arts that foster the saving power (Heigegger, 1977, 34). What is salient about technology is that:

> the human being is, then, essentially, uniquely, and almost always a worker, a technological being engaged in a technological activity. But (the first thinker clearly to articulate this point was Arthur Schopenhauer) work requires that things are represented, that they show up, in work-suitable, 'ready-to-hand' instrumental, technological ways (Young, 2002, p. 48).

And in this regard what is new is about modern technology is that in being different from earlier forms it invokes a new understanding of being where humans are not simply subjects who objectify and dominate the world through technology. Rather, as a consequence of modern technology, humans are constituted by this technology. Hubert Dreyfus points out that for both Foucault and Heidegger, it is the practices of the modern world that produce a different kind of subject 'constituted as the source of a deep inner truth about itself' (Dreyfus, 2002, p. 18).

TECHNOLOGIES OF THE SELF—CONFESSING OURSELVES: A GENEALOGY

In *Technologies of the Self*, Foucault uses his method of genealogy to first examine the place of knowing the self and care of the self in the first two centuries AD of Greco-Roman philosophy. Then he moves to the fourth and fifth centuries of the

Roman Empire when Christian spirituality and monastic principles were prevalent. This chapter now traces some of these practices or technologies of the self and associated forms of confession. This section outlines three nonlinear phases, namely, classical Greek technologies of the self, Christian religious confessional practices, and medico-therapeutic confessional practices that show historico-philosophic shifts from self-mastery to self-denial and back to self-mastery that Foucault discuses in 'Technologies of the Self' (Foucault, 1988b).

Foucault sets out a typology of four interrelated 'technologies'—namely, technologies of production, technologies of sign systems, technologies of power (or domination) and technologies of the self. Each is a set of practical reason that is permeated by a form of domination that implies some type of training and changing or shaping of individuals. Instead of an instrumental understanding of 'technology,' Foucault uses technology in the Heideggerian sense as a way of revealing truth and focuses on technologies of power and technologies of the self. In an interview he notes that he may have concentrated 'too much on the technology of domination and power' (Foucault, 1988a, p. 19).

Technologies of power 'determine the conduct of individuals and submit them to certain ends or domination, an objectivizing of the subject' (Foucault, 1988b, p. 18). His earlier work emphasized the application of such technologies of domination through the political subjugation of 'docile bodies' in the grip of disciplinary powers and the way the self is produced by processes of objectification, classification and normalization in the human sciences (Foucault, 1977). Nevertheless, for him **both** technologies of domination and technologies of the self produce effects that constitute the self (or subjectivity). Taken together, technologies of domination and of the self define the individual and control their conduct as they make the individual a significant element for the state through the exercise of a form of power, which Foucault coined as 'governmentality' in becoming useful, docile, practical citizens (Foucault, 1988c). In turn, Foucault's two notions of technologies of domination and technologies of the self (1988b) can be used as a means for investigation of the constitution of postmodern youth under the impact of globalisation.

Technologies of the self, are ways the various 'operations on their own bodies and souls, thoughts, conduct, and way of being,' that people make either by themselves or with the help of others, in order to transform themselves to reach a 'state of happiness, purity, wisdom, perfection, or immortality' (Foucault, 1988b, p. 18). Confession is one such technology and care of the self.

> Why truth? . . . and why must the care of the self occur only through the concern for truth? [This is] *the* question for the West. How did it come about that all of Western culture began to revolve around this obligation of truth . . . ? (Foucault, 1997a, p. 281).

The compulsion to tell the truth is highly valued in Western society. In our contemporary society, which is arguably a 'confessional age,' where telling all and telling the truth about oneself rather than keeping secrets is *de rigueur*. For example, on TV talk shows (such as Oprah, Riki Lake, Jerry Springer, Kilroy, Trisha, etc.) people publicly confess their stories of physical, sexual, and emotional abuse; alcoholism and drug use; sexual practices, affairs, harassment, and even incest. On websites and through media-based public confessions of some wrong-doing by prominent politicians (e.g., Bill Clinton) we nowadays witness confessional practices affecting mass audiences. This provides us with an interface between the public and personal domains. With the addition of an emphasis on writing confessional diaries, journals, memoirs, autobiographies, as well as confessional fiction, the picture expands. Moreover, many people now opt to see a therapist or counselor for their personal problems. Hence we have confessional practices occurring in both public and private arenas. This poses many questions, such as why are audiences—readers, television audiences, Internet users—so interested in public self-revelation? Why do so many people feel a compulsion to confess? Why do some chose to do so publicly and others privately? How do we know if the confessor is lying by omission or commission, embroidering the truth, or shading it? What is the effect on us of confessing our selves either publicly or privately?

Confession is a deep-seated cultural practice in the West that involves a declaration and disclosure, acknowledgment or admission of a fault, weakness or crime and is expected to be the 'truth' that discloses one's actions and private feelings or opinions. In confessing our selves, an other (real or virtual) is required as an audience that will hear, understand, possibly judge and punish and maybe accept and forgive as they reflect back to us who we are. In confessing, we reveal part of our identity. The role of the other is dialogical and highly ambiguous since it involves plural roles—such as witness, accomplice, recipient, mediator, judge and enabler. Understandably there seems to be a tension between the impulse to confess and, in turn, to reveal the self to others and the desire to keep something hidden.

There are various forms of confession. In its religious form, confession involves the verbal acknowledgment of one's sins to another. One is duty bound to perform this confession as repentance in the hope of absolution. In the literary sense, 'confession' also contains elements of identifying the self in a deliberate, self-conscious attempt to explain and express oneself to an audience. Unlike the public confession, other confessional situations are private ones. For example, the professional counseling or psychotherapy relationship offers the chance of confessing with the assurance that the counselor is bound by ethical conventions of confidentiality. Confession then is both a communicative and an expressive act, a narrative in which we (re)create ourselves by creating our own narrative, reworking the past, in public, or at least in dialogue with another. Contemporary notions of confession are derived not simply from the influence of the Roman Catholic Church and its strategies for confessing one's 'sins' but also from ancient, pre-Christian philosophical notions (Foucault, 1980a, 1988b).

Classical Greek Technologies of the Self—Self Mastery

Foucault examined the first two centuries AD of Greco-Roman philosophy and the fourth and fifth centuries of the Roman Empire when Christian spirituality and monastic principles were prevalent. Foucault argued that the Delphic moral principle, 'know thyself' (*gnothi sauton*) became dominant, taking precedence over another ancient principle and set of practices, 'to take care of yourself,' or to be concerned with oneself (*epimelesthai sautou*) (Foucault, 1988b). According to Foucault, 'care of the self' formed one of the main rules for personal and social conduct and for the art of life in ancient Greek cities. The two principles were interconnected, and it was actually from the principle of care of the self that the Delphic principle was brought into operation as a form of technical advice or rules to be followed when the oracle was consulted. Foucault accepted that the ancient Greek notion of care of the self was an inclusive one that involved *care for others* and precluded the possibility of tyranny because a tyrant did not, by definition, take care of the self since he[2] did not take care of others. Foucault stated that *care for others* became an explicit ethic later on and should not be put before care of the self (see Foucault, 1984; 1997a).

Foucault argues that over time there was an inversion of the traditional hierarchy of the two ancient principles so that Delphic 'know yourself' became dominant and took precedence over 'care of the self,' to be concerned with oneself and to work to improve oneself. From being a matter of self-mastery in the classical Greek, it changed to an emphasis on learning to shape one's own inner character (Foucault, 1988b).

Such an inversion has continued into modern Western culture partly as a result of 'know yourself' being the principle that Plato privileged and which subsequently became hugely influential in philosophy following Descartes and the Enlightenment emphasis on the thinking subject (*cogito ergo sum*—I think therefore I am) as the first step in epistemology. Foucault argues that 'know yourself' is the fundamental austere principle that influences morality nowadays, because we tend to view 'care of the self' in rather negative terms as something immoral, narcissistic, or selfish and an escape from rules.

Foucault (1988b, p. 27) elaborated on both the Greek (Platonic and Stoic) techniques of self, which 'was not abstract advice but a widespread activity, a network of obligations and services to the soul' that recommended setting aside time for the self each day for meditation, preparing and writing:

> to study, to read, to prepare for misfortune or death ... Writing was also important in the culture of taking care of oneself ... taking notes on oneself to be reread, writing treatises and letters to friends to help them, and keeping notebooks in order to reactivate for oneself the truths as needed (Foucault, 1988b, p. 27).

Using as examples, the letters of Socrates, Cicero and Marcus Aurelius, Foucault discusses how writing about the self is an ancient Western tradition connected with care of the self that developed in the 1st and 2nd centuries, well before Augustine wrote his *Confessions*. Writing enabled increased examination and vigilance of one's moods and so intensified and widened how people thought of themselves and promoted self-understanding and self-mastery.

Foucault traces another change in techniques in care of the self that had prevailed in Pythagorean culture and re-emerged under Stoicism in the imperial period. Rather than Platonic style dialogue, a new pedagogical relationship that emphasized silence and listening developed, 'where the master/teacher speaks and doesn't ask questions and the disciple doesn't answer but must listen and keep silent ... This is the positive condition for acquiring truth' (Foucault, 1988b, p. 32). Perhaps Foucault's emphasis on the centrality of truth in relation to the self is to be developed only through the notion of the 'other' as an audience—intimate or public—that allows for the politics of confession and (auto)biography.

The Stoic techniques of care of the self include first, 'letters to friends and disclosure of self'; second, the 'examination of self and conscience, including a review of what was to be done, of what should have been done and a comparison of the two'; third, '*askesis*, not a disclosure of the secret self but a remembering'; and fourth, 'the interpretation of dreams' (Foucault, 1988b, pp. 34–38). Foucault remarks that, despite being a popular practice, the Stoics were mostly critical and sceptical about the interpretation of dreams. He points out that rather than renunciation, this is 'the progressive consideration of self, or mastery over oneself, obtained not through the renunciation of reality but through the acquisition and assimilation of truth ... that is characterised by *paraskeuazo* ("to get prepared")' (Foucault, 1988b, p. 35). Two forms of preparation exercises emerged. One, the *melete*, was a philosophical meditation that trained one's *thoughts* about how one would respond to hypothetical situations. The second, the *gymnasia*, was a *physical* training experience that could involve physical privation, hardship, purification rituals and sexual abstinence. The latter could perhaps be considered a form of self-denial, but was in fact together with the former, a means of overall self-mastery.

It is interesting to note the re-emergence of many of these practices of the self, apart from physical training, in the different helping professions or 'psy' therapies (Rose, 1998) (e.g. psychiatrists, psychologists, psychoanalysts, psychotherapists, counselors, doctors etc) in the 19th and 20th centuries and Foucault does a real service in pointing us to the philosophical and historical roots of some of these.

Christian Religious Confessional Practices—Self Denial

The procedures of confession have altered considerably over time. The impact of Christianity cannot be underestimated in the Western world even though many people may now adopt a more secular view of life. Confession has been profoundly influenced by confessional techniques embodied in protestant and Puritan notions of the self and its relation to God and by Romantic, Rousseauian notions of the self (Gutman, 1988; Paden, 1988). In most religious contexts, the sins that needed to be confessed mostly equated with sexual morality. As a consequence, in time religious confession became the principal technology for managing the sexual lives of believers, for confessing the 'truth' about one's sexual thoughts and behaviours. This aspect is taken up by Freud in his notions of repression and also by Foucault in his three volumes, *The History of Sexuality* (Foucault, 1980a, 1986, 1990). One form of disclosure of the self is confession.

Foucault (1988b) points out that in the first centuries, two main forms of disclosing the self emerged in early Christianity—*exomologesis* and *exagoreusis*. Despite being very different, the former being a dramatic form, the latter a verbalized one, what they have in common is that disclosing the self involves renouncing one's self or will. *Exomologesis* or 'recognition of fact' was a public approach that lasted until the 15th–16th centuries, whereby Christians disclosed themselves through publicly acknowledging both their faith and by recognizing themselves as both 'a sinner and penitent' (Foucault, 1988b, p. 41). If they had committed very serious sins, they would seek penance from a bishop, explaining their faults and why they sought this status. They would remain in a state of penance for several years, observing punishments such as fasting, clothing and sexual restrictions that publicly exhibited or disclosed their shame, humility and modesty until they became reconciled or atoned for their sins. Foucault says that this is not confession as such, 'it was not a way for the sinner to explain his sins but a way to present himself as a sinner' (Foucault, 1988b, p. 42). Foucault, points out the paradox that 'exposé is the heart of *exomologesis* . . . it rubs out the sin and yet reveals the sinner' (Foucault, 1988b, p. 42).

Penance became elaborated around notions of torture, martyrdom and death, of renouncing self, identity and life in preferring to die rather than compromising or abandoning one's faith. Christian penance did not involve establishing an identity but 'a break with one's past identity,' the refusal or renunciation of self, so that 'self-revelation is at the same time self-destruction' (Foucault, 1988, p. 43). Whereas for the classical Greek Stoics the 'examination of self, judgement, and discipline' that lead to self-knowledge by 'memorizing rules' was a private matter, for Christians 'the penitent superimposes truth about self by violent rupture and dissociation' through a form of *exomologesis* that is public, 'symbolic, ritual and theatrical' but not verbal (Foucault, 1988b, p. 43).

Foucault (1988b) asserts that in the 4th century a different and more important set of technologies for disclosing the self—*exagoreusis* that were derived from some Stoic technologies of the self—emerged in Christianity. Self-examination then took the form of verbalizing exercises or prayers that took account of one's daily actions in relation to rules (as in Senecan self-examination). With monastic life, different confessional practices developed based on the principles of obedience and contemplation and confession developed a hermeneutic role in examining the self in relation to one's hidden inner thoughts and purity. Christian hermeneutics of the self imply 'that there is something hidden in ourselves and that we are always in a self-illusion, which hides the secret' (Foucault, 1988b, p. 46). Furthermore, because evil was believed to be hidden and unstated and 'because evil thoughts cannot be expressed without difficulty and shame' (Foucault, 1988b, p. 47), the only way to weigh the quality, reality and purity of our thoughts, is to permanently verbalize thoughts or 'confess' all one's thoughts, intentions and consciousness to a master. Since it was only after a verbal confession that the devil went out of the person, confession became 'a mark of truth.' However, since it is impossible to permanently verbally confess, the result was 'to make everything that couldn't be expressed into a sin' (Foucault, 1988b, p. 48). *Exagoreusis* was 'an analytical and continual verbalization of thoughts carried on in the relation of complete obedience to someone else . . . the renunciation of one's own will and of one's own self' (Foucault, 1988b, p. 48).

The classical Greek practice of *askesis* differs significantly from the Christian counterpart of ascetic practices. Foucault pointed out that for the ancient Greeks the ethical principle of self consisted of *self-mastery*, but by comparison, it shifted to become *self-renunciation* in the Christian era (Foucault, 1988b). In the Greek, the goal is establishing of a specific relationship to oneself—of self possession, self-sovereignty, self-mastery. In the Christian, it is renunciation of the self. Foucault argues that Christian asceticism involves detachment from the world, whereas Greco-Roman practices were concerned with 'endowing the individual with the preparation and the moral equipment that will permit him to fully confront the world in an ethical and rational manner' (Foucault, 2001a, p. 55).

Thus the crucial difference revolved around two quite different ethical notions. Self-mastery implied both a control of the passions and a moderation in all things, but also a worldliness that involved being in and part of the world of the free citizen in a democratic society. Self-renunciation as a form of Christian asceticism involved a set of two interlinked truths obligations: one set surrounded 'the faith, the book, the dogma' and another 'the self, the soul the heart' (Foucault, 1981, cited in Foucault, 2001a, p. 139). The tasks involved in the latter, include first a 'clearing up all the illusions, temptations, and seductions which can occur in the mind, and discovering the reality of what is going on within ourselves' and second getting free from attachment to the self, 'not because the self is an illusion, but because the self is much too real' (Foucault, 1981, cited in Foucault, 2001a, p.139). These tasks implied self-negation and a withdrawal from the world, in what forms a 'spiral of truth formulation and reality renouncement, which is at the heart of Christian techniques of the self' (Foucault, 1981, cited in Foucault, 2001a, p. 139). Confessional practices form a technology of the self—speaking, reading and writing the self—that shifted from the religious world to medical then to therapeutic and pedagogical models in secular contemporary societies (Foucault, 1988b; Peters, 2000).

Medico-Therapeutic Confessional Practices— Confession without Self-Renunciation

Until the mid-16th century confession in the Church was an annual event, so the confession of and surveillance of sexuality was quite limited (Foucault, 1980b). After the Reformation, confession changed profoundly to involve not just one's acts but also one's thoughts. Foucault suggests that the 18th century saw 'brutal medical techniques emerging, which consist in simply demanding that the subject tells his or her story, or narrate it in writing' (Foucault, 1980b, p. 215).

Foucault's work on sexuality is concerned with problematizing how pleasure, desire and sexuality—the regimes of power-knowledge-pleasure—as components of the art of living or 'an aesthetics of existence' have become discourses that shape the construction of ourselves as both the 'truth' of our sexuality and ourselves (Foucault, 1986, p.10).

Foucault argues that Western society, unlike other societies that have an *ars erotica* (erotic art) whereby truth is drawn from pleasure itself, has *scientia sexualis* (scientized sexuality) procedures for telling the truth of sexuality. Sexual confession became constituted in scientific terms through a codification of speaking, speculation about causality, ideas about latent sexuality, the use of interpretation, and the medicalization of the effects of confession (see Foucault, 1980a, pp. 59–70). Power-knowledge resides in confession, not in the person who speaks but in the one who questions and listens. Foucault (1980a) points to the techniques of both the examination and the confessional or therapeutic situation, where a person is required to speak about their psyche or emotions to a doctor, priest or therapist. This expert in both observation and interpretation would determine whether or not the truth, or an underlying truth that the person was unaware of, had been spoken. To access this inner self or 'truth,' professionals may administer certain 'technologies' for speaking, listening, recording, transcribing and redistributing what is said. This is a means for examining the conscious, the unconscious, and for confessing one's innermost thoughts, feelings, attitudes, desires and motives about the self and one's relationships with others. The professional's expert knowledge might be used to reinterpret and reconstruct what a person says. However, in the therapeutic process, as one gains this form of self-knowledge, one also becomes known to others involved in the process, which can, in turn, constitute the self.

From the medical model of healing, where a patient 'confesses' the problem and inadvertently reveals the 'truth' as part of the diagnostic clinical examination, there was a shift to a therapeutic model where both the confession and examination are deliberately used for uncovering the truth about one's sexuality and one's self (Foucault, 1980a). In the process, the therapy can create a new kind of pleasure: pleasure in telling the truth of pleasure. But speaking the truth is not only descriptive. In confession, one is expected to tell the truth about oneself—a basic assumption that most therapists and counselors continue to make about their clients. In a focus on the techniques of the self, which are designed to explore the aesthetics of existence and to inquire into the government of self and others, Foucault discusses writing the self as a means of counteracting the dangers of solitude and of exposing our deeds to the gaze (Foucault, 1988b, 1997b). At the same time, because it works on thoughts as well as actions, writing the self becomes a form of confession.

Foucault points to the shift of confessional practices from the religious world to medical then to therapeutic and pedagogical models in secular contemporary societies. Over time the movement towards the care of the self *by* the self removes the necessity for dialogue:

> A medical model was substituted for Plato's pedagogical model. The care of the self isn't another kind of pedagogy; it has to become permanent medical care. Permanent medical care is one of the central features of the care of the self. One must become the doctor of oneself (Foucault, 1988b, p. 31).

Foucault concluded his seminar on technologies of the self with the highly significant point that the verbalization techniques of disclosing the self through confession have been important in the development of the human sciences where they have been transposed and inserted into this different context 'in order to use them without renunciation of the self but to constitute, positively, a new self. To use these techniques without renouncing oneself constitutes a decisive break' (Foucault, 1988b,

p. 49). He implies that instead of knowing the self and in fact denying the self, as occurs in the religious form of confession, the newer therapeutic techniques of the self can use confessional practices without such denial of the self. Instead they use practices that build on the strengths of the self to even develop self-mastery as a form of care of the self. Because language has a performative function, speaking the truth about oneself makes, constitutes, or constructs or forms one's self. By these discursive means and through these technologies, a human being turns him or herself into a subject.

As confession became secularized, a range of techniques emerged in the human sciences—in pedagogy, medicine, psychiatry and literature—with a highpoint being psychoanalysis or Freud's 'talking cure.' Since Freud, the secular form of confession could be argued as having been 'scientized' through new techniques of normalization and individualization that include clinical codifications, personal examinations, case-study techniques, the general documentation and collection of personal data, the proliferation of interpretive schemas and the development of a whole host of therapeutic techniques for 'normalization' (Foucault, 1977). In turn, these 'oblige' us to be free, as self-inspection and new forms of self-regulation replace the confessional. This new form of confession is an affirmation of our self and our identity that involves 'contemporary procedures of individualization' that 'binds us to others at the very moment we affirm our identity' (Rose, 1989, p. 240). In truthfully confessing who one is to others (e.g., to parents, teachers, friends, lovers and oneself, etc.) ' . . . one is subjectified by another . . . who prescribes the form of the confession, the words and rituals through which it should be made, who appreciates, judges, consoles, or understands' (Rose, 1989, p. 240). Through speech acts of confession, a person constitutes his/her self.

Foucault writes of technologies of the self as 'models proposed for setting up and developing relationships with the self, for self-reflection, self-knowledge, self-examination, for deciphering the self by oneself, for the transformation one seeks to accomplish with oneself as object' (Foucault, 1986, p. 29). When the subject is confessing and creating its 'self,' it seems to feel compelled to tell the truth about itself. Therefore, confession involves a type of 'discipline' that 'entails training in the minute arts of self-scrutiny, self-evaluation, and self-regulation, ranging from the control of the body, speech, and movement in school, through the mental drill inculcated in school and university, to the Puritan practices of self-inspection and obedience to divine reason' (Rose, 1989, p. 222). Whilst confession is autobiographical, compelling us to narratively recreate ourselves, it is also about assigning truth-seeking meaning to our lives. People can be assisted in this through a whole variety of therapeutic endeavours such as counseling. In secular society, therapeutic forms of confession, where the psychotherapist or counselor could be considered akin to the priest, have replaced the theological form. Although the use of listening techniques and the uncovering of 'self' are similar, the elements of advice, admonition and punishment that are involved in the religious forms of confession are certainly no part of contemporary counseling—a practice predicated on the assumption that the client is telling the truth about him-herself.

CONCLUSION: SELF-DENIAL OR SELF-MASTERY?

The foregoing has argued that confession is a form of truth telling that constitutes the self. Following Foucault, we suggest that confession as a technology of self should be based less on an ethic of self-denial than one of self-mastery. For self-mastery provides a secular model consonant with the demands of a postmodern world that recognises the inescapability of desire and the necessity of pleasure in a new body politics.

Self-denial involves renouncing one's own interests in favour of the interests of others. It also means denying aspects of one's self, self-abnegation, self-renunciation; self-discipline or self-control in not gratifying, abstaining or indulging one's desires or impulses, abstinence, asceticism, austerity and also connotations of selflessness and self-sacrifice. In extreme religious forms it may involve mortification of the flesh.

Notions of self-denial remain prominent in many religious contexts, especially those of a more fundamentalist orientation. For a protestant religious example see John Wesley's sermon 48, Self Denial, at http://gbgm-umc.org/umhistory/wesley/sermons/serm-048.stm, which is based upon Luke 9: 23, 'And He said to them all, If any man will come after me, let him deny himself, and take up his cross daily, and follow me.' In this sermon Wesley points out that 'men who take nature, not grace, for their guide, abhor the very sound of it [denial].' Professor Finney's lectures of 1841 elaborate further on the notion (e.g., http://www.gospeltruth.net/18410E/410317_self_denial.htm). Other websites similarly detail what self-denial is and what it is not (e.g., http://www.gracegems.org/ Books2/traits13.htm). Such religiously oriented notions of self-denial continue the Christian ascetic tradition that emphasizes the denial of the body and especially its sexuality and desires. A question that arises, which is beyond the scope of this chapter, is if there is a form of counseling that can encompass such a position yet be consistent with the aims of counseling.

Religious and associated philosophical thought is also invoked in many contemporary formulations of self-mastery, but rather than being derived from Christianity, or for that matter the other Abrahamaic religions (i.e., Judaism or Islam), the turn is to Eastern religions or philosophies such as Taoism and Zen Bhuddism. Furthermore, the emphasis tends to be on the whole person, body, mind, emotions and spirit, rather than one's relationship with God. For example, see 'The Self Mastery Foundation' at http://www.selfmastery.com/article.asp?pageid=9 which:

> incorporates Taoist and Zen spiritual philosophy, with 21st century science, to create a practical program for the modern mind. Our purpose is to develop strong individuals physically, mentally, and emotionally. We teach people to understand and surpass their limitations, and find ways around them to attain their peak performance. A good balance of physical and mental exercises helps create strong individuals. Gradual training programs bring students in touch with themselves and the world around them. Classes and seminars include Martial Arts, Meditation, and Energy Awareness exercises.

The 'Self Mastery International' website declares their purpose to 'promote the resurgence of personal values as a tool for self empowerment and increased personal and professional performance' (http://www.selfmasteryintl.com/). Another website, http://anunda.com/self-mastery.htm, suggests that through 'self mastery, the seeker becomes a traveller, beyond religion, tradition, the teachings, doctrine and dogma. Spiritual practice is then, a communion with Life in the moment of Living.' Another organisation, the 'Self-Mastery' website (http://www.livelyup.com/Self-Mastery.htm), takes a largely Kantian of self-mastery as being a rational autonomous chooser, with mastery meaning

> the full command or control of a subject. Therefore, all self-mastery requires is being your own boss or director, the Chairman of the Board for your life, consciously choosing for yourself the thoughts and actions that will make you who and what you want to be. Just seize the controls, instead of being pushed and pulled around by outside factors, and your life is back in your hands.

In similar vein is 'The Top 200 Secrets of Success and the Pillars of Self-Mastery' at http://www.robinsharma.com/2001ife.html

By incorporating Eastern religious traditions into their formulations of self-mastery, some of these organisations recognise the body without denigrating or denying it unlike ascetic forms of Christianity. However, Eastern notions tend to promote a transcendental self, which by negating the ego, also negates the self.

Foucault's viewpoint on the self was not a transcendental one. His analysis questions historical necessity and, while he maps the ethical contours of a period, he also provides historical models of the self that can be used to articulate contemporary issues. It might be argued that in the age of global consumer culture the ethical self is neither modelled on techniques of self-denial (Nietzsche's analysis of ascetic practices in *The Genealogy of Morals*) or (Stoic) practices of self-mastery alone—though both may have continuing relevance in certain ways—but rather it is based on an ethics of the 'aesthetics of existence,' a continual shaping, fashioning and presentation of the body. In an extreme form this speaks of self-indulgence rather than self-denial or self-mastery—what Christopher Lasch (1979; 1984) called the 'narcissistic self' and later the 'minimal self.' When one is considering the self, self-indulgence and desire tend to be downplayed since they are often viewed as something not quite proper or appropriate, especially by the 'moral majority' and people with strong religious convictions. Understandings of desire acknowledge the body, the emotional and include the sexual and maybe even Bacchanalian appetites. Considering the level of discomfort many people seem to have in broaching such aspects of life, and considering the prevalence of the dualism privileging thinking over the body since Descartes' time, it is perhaps not surprising that in considering self mastery, it is reason that tends to be privileged in what may be viewed as something of an avoidance technique, but one that has serious implications for our culture:

> The Cartesian dualism repeats and extends a separation of the soul/mind from the body first developed in Plato's philosophy, that encouraged an equation between soul, rationality, and the world of eternal forms on the one hand, and the body, the appetites, and the transitory world of appearances, on the other. The dualism is a form of metaphysics and a source of confusion and nihilism (dissolution and fragmentation) with negative results that bifurcate Western culture ... Such prioritising has assigned power over the latter category (e.g. male over female, rationality over emotion, culture/society over nature, white over black, able over disabled and so on) that has been used for social and political ends, not least the subordination of women (Besley, 2003e, p. 60).

In ancient schools of thought, philosophy was considered to be a way of life, a quest for wisdom, a way of being and, ultimately a way of transforming the self. Spiritual exercises were a form of pedagogy designed to teach its practitioners the philosophical life that had both a moral and an existential value. These exercises were aimed at self-mastery, nothing less than a transformation of one's worldview and personality by involving all aspects of one's being, including intellect, imagination, sensibility and will. In the process, the person became a responsible citizen. Socrates provided a set of dialogical spiritual exercises that epitomized the injunction 'know thyself' and provided a model for a relationship of the self to itself and a total transformation of one's being (see Davidson, 1997a). In this model, the process of dealing with a problem takes primacy over the solution (Hadot, 1987). This provides counseling with an ancient philosophical basis or model, at once transformative, ethical, dialogic and pedagogical. It is a model that could both complement and correct certain emphases in Foucault's later thinking about truth and subjectivity and care of the self. For counseling, an emphasis on process is of prime importance since the solution of problems is generally not the counselor's responsibility. The emphasis is on processes that enable the person to find the resources to access their own solutions.

Christianity adopted and modified themes from ancient philosophy but made renouncing the self to the will of God the condition for salvation. Yet paradoxically self-denial required that one know oneself, and this in turn revealed the self. Foucault argues that over time where the ancient principle of care of the self once preceded know thyself (Delphic maxim) these became inverted. Foucault argues for the return of the ancient maxim of 'care of the self' and its components of self-mastery because, since the Enlightenment, the Delphic maxim became overriding and inextricably linked with constituting subjects who are able to be governed.

Foucault's genealogy highlights the politics and ethics in questions of the self, of caring for the self and self-knowledge (or ignorance). Foucault (1988b) argued that a binary of self-denial versus self-mastery had been prevalent at different points of time and thus entailed different technologies of the self and, in turn, different ways of constituting the self. While self-denial and self-mastery are ethical sets, the protocols of which dominate practices of the self, clearly today it may be the case that self-mastery might be achieved through self-denial (and vice versa). Part of the intent behind Foucault's analysis is to alert us to the way things can be otherwise.

Foucault's model of the care of the self in relation to practices of freedom, his account of power-knowledge and his Kantian-like basis for ethics that considers the way in which choices under certain conditions creates who we become, provides a philosophical approach that offers counselors an ethically suitable way of dealing with their clients. This highlights the importance of various technologies of the self, confessing the self through 'writing' and 'reading' the self alongside conversational or dialogical forms and 'talking' or confessing the self. Foucault's understanding of the self's relationship to itself points to various ways that 'psy' science professionals such as counselors can help people to ethically constitute themselves: by ethical work that a person performs on him-hersef with the aim of becoming an ethical subject; the way in which individuals relate to moral obligations and rules; and the type of person one aims to become in behaving ethically.

PART TWO

Space, Body AND THE Aesthetics OF Existence

CHAPTER THREE

The Body AND THE Aesthetics OF Existence

INTRODUCTION

The self is not just the mind, but also involves the body and in the postmodern world, the aesthetics of existence are inexorably linked with the commodification of our world and existence. Our relationship to commodities and the self is no longer based on 'need,' but more on a desire that can never be satisfied so we seek new objects to consume in a system where choices are infinite, and desire and pleasure become integral parts of material and social production that in turn produce or construct more desire/pleasure (Baudrillard, 1998). Commodifying pressures result in an increasing importance being placed upon the appearance and presentation of the body as constitutive of self-identity, on possessing 'desired' goods and the pursuit of particular lifestyles. The idealised corporeal images of youth, beauty, health and fitness support body maintenance and related industries ensuring that the body is attractively packaged, marketed and sold. Health no longer simply involves caring for the body and seeking its optimal functioning, but involves disciplining its appearance, movement and control so that it looks presentable and hence becomes marketable all the while transmitting a whole host of codes/signs about the values and attitudes of the owner of such a body. Today, the firm, well-toned and muscled body indicates a 'correct attitude' implying personal qualities such as determination, willpower, energy. It displays the ability to 'make something' of oneself and an asceticism that is to a certain extent a denial of self—at least a denial of impulses to indulge the self—a self-discipline that controls desires to overindulge in epicurean pleasures. It shows that one 'cares' about oneself and about how one appears to others. Whilst in premodern times, bodily discipline and asceticism was sought to serve spiritual ends through repressing the temptations of the flesh, today the concern has shifted to the aesthetic cultivation of outer appearance and the hedonistic expression of desire.

On one line of body criticism that we might christen 'body aesthetics' the body becomes the site for a range of critical practices in the arts and humanities for the investigation of cultural representations, constructions and inscriptions of power and hierarchies of value. This includes the investigation of the sociopolitical context of procedures for 'body contouring'—liposuction, abdominoplasty, lifts, nips and tucks—as well as the philosophical significance of the search for the perfect body through methodologies and means that historicize the body and provide it with a history. Body aesthetics may also focus on ethnic and cultural specificity of bodies in relation to aesthetic traditions and ideals, and the intimate connection between medical practice, politics and aesthetics on the understanding that 'design is politics.' It may also involve a kind of projection into posthuman forms of prosthesis, exosomatic development, and the virtual body. From this perspective, we can analyze the social pathologies that cause *disorders of bodies* (rather than the *self*) especially those that are amenable to political economy such as eating disorders (at both ends of the spectrum—'obesity' and 'anorexia'), the death-denying emphasis on the exercised body, the 'healthy' body and the plethora of diet routines promoted by fitness clubs, the pharma-industry, body shape and the fast food industry, and the relation between aesthetics and sports, and so on, but that is beyond the scope of this book. It is clear however, that body aesthetics is a complex field embracing normative, historical and scientific elements.

Ontological questions are raised concerning the nature of bodily order and corporeal transgression. Despite the Enlightenment's making rationality almost a cult or a virtue, paradoxically, it has irrationally overestimated rationality's power to control either the emotions or the body. Bodies are clearly subject to discipline and control through discourse—i.e., to (rational) management and control—and through institutions such as prisons, asylums, factories and schools. On the one hand the rational impulse is for discipline, control and order and on the other hand the corporeal impulse is of chaos and transgression, being sensual rather than ascetic, fluid rather than static, volatile rather than fixed. Nietzsche (1956) reminds us that the will or passions are stronger than the mind, threatening to overturn the rationally ordered world. But this is to continue to promote the old dualisms rather than a more integrated sense of embodied subjectivity. Since our transgressive bodies/recalcitrant minds will always find points of resistance and escape, understanding and incorporating a contemporary philosophy of the embodied self provides a more optimistic view of the body and the emotions in contemporary society, opening space for new possibilities.

Michel Foucault was drawn late in life in *The History of Sexuality*, to study the 'arts of the self' in Greco-Roman culture as a basis, following Nietzsche, for what he called an 'aesthetics of existence' (Foucault, 1980a). By this, he meant a set of creative and experimental processes and techniques by which an individual turns him- or herself into a work of art. For Nietzsche, it was above all the figure of the musician that best represented the mode of creative self-transformation, although he also talked of the philosopher-artist. By contrast, Foucault in his famous essay 'Writing the Self' emphasized the writer and writing. Yet, at the same time, he was also to question the notion of the author and the author-function. Foucault, while rejecting the phenomenological account of the subject, held on to the body as a site of power relations occupying a spatial-temporal location in development of Western institutions. The aesthetics of existence was also part of Foucault's genealogical strategy to move us from the concepts and discourses of 'desire,' 'lack' and 'repression' that have controlled sexuality in the modern era.

This chapter explores Foucault's notion of the aesthetics of existence by focusing on processes of ethical self-constitution—an aesthetic 'sculpting' of the self—and, in particular, the ways in which we come to shape our lives through the capacity of choice-making. The chapter begins by emphasising the consistency of an approach from an 'aesthetics of existence' to Foucault's life and his relations to questions of the self in the history of madness. It then in examines Foucault's work on the body, including the notion of embodiment, which becomes the basis for exploring Foucault's thought in relation to feminism, the female body, conceptions of masculinity and the male body as well as raising some questions concerning contemporary body politics.

WHO IS FOUCAULT?

The question 'who is Foucault?' has more often been asked than 'why Foucault?' For instance, James D. Faubion begins his edited collection of Foucault's work in *Aesthetics, Method and Epistemology* with exactly that question, to which he answers:

> The possibilities seem endless: structuralist, idealist, neoconservative, post-structuralist, antihumanist, irrationalist, radical relativist, theorist of power, missionary of transgression, aestheticist, dying man, saint, or, if nothing else post-modern (Foucault, 1998a, p. xiii).

These labels designed to answer the 'who' or 'what' of Foucault, are, of course, not necessarily mutually contradictory, but they are *not* categories or descriptions that Foucault would apply to himself. And Foucault was very testy and vitriolic against those who ascribed him positions he did not hold or those who offered descriptions of him that did not fit. In his Foreword to the English edition of *The Order of Things* (Foucault, 1973, p. xiv), he wrote:

> In France, certain half-witted 'commentators' persist in labelling me a 'structuralist.' I have been unable to get it into their tiny minds that I have used none of the methods, concepts, or key terms that characterise structural analysis.

He acknowledged 'certain similarities' between his own work and that of the 'structuralists.' He went on to suggest, given the problematic of structuralism that emphasized the unconscious and a decentring of the author, that it would be strange for him to claim that his work was independent of conditions and rules of which I am very largely unaware' (Foucault, 1973, p. xiv). Elsewhere, he denied he knew what the term postmodernism meant, or indeed, even the meaning of the term 'modernity' (Foucault, 1998c), yet he granted that structuralism had a determinate meaning, although only in retrospect. In the same interview, he was to remark: 'I have never been a Freudian, I have never been a Marxist, and I have never been a structuralist' (Foucault, 1998c, p. 437). In another autobiographical comment, Foucault proceeds negatively, by noting how others have classified him and by taking considerable enjoyment from casting aspersions on these descriptions:

> I think I have been situated in most squares on the political checkerboard, one after another and sometimes simultaneously: as anarchist, leftist, ostentatious or disguised Marxist, nihilist, explicit or secret anti-marxist, technocrat in the service of Gaullism, new liberal etc. An American professor complained that a crypto-marxist like me was invited to the U.S.A., and I was denounced by the press in Eastern Europe for being an accomplice of the dissidents. None of these descriptions is important by itself; taken together, on the other hand, they mean something. And I must admit that I rather like what they mean (Foucault, 1984d, pp. 383–84).

These denials, labels and self-descriptions raise an issue immediately concerning the construction of 'self and others' in relation to the descriptions we accept or deny, or even those that we have thrust upon us, despite our best efforts to shape the ways in which we are perceived or received. Self-descriptions are complex entities often containing narrative elements, whole roles or parts of which are prescripted in larger scenarios, or even in the distribution of multiple roles and the speaking and acting chances of which we avail ourselves. Yet to treat these self-descriptions or such ascriptions as simply narrative *humanist* constructions, with the actor at the centre, tends to ignore many of the quasistructuralist objections Foucault entertained about the 'author.' Already we can see an incipient ethos for a form of counseling that avoids the pitfalls of humanist narratives—the commitment to essentialist categories and chronological life-histories that mark the passage of the hero or heroine (or antihero) according to the privileged voice of the author or biographer.

Foucault once famously remarked: 'The coming into being of the "author" constitutes the privileged moment of individualisation in the history of ideas, knowledge, literature, philosophy and the sciences' (Foucault, 1998b, p. 205). Such a statement is doubly paradoxical when applied to Foucault himself for the so-called 'disappearance or death of the author' significantly is not something that applies to Foucault, either as a scholar who during his productive life initiated new inquiries and approaches, or as the convenient name for a body or corpus of 'work' that connects with contemporary movements and goes beyond them. Nor is it apt for the consideration of Foucault and his role in contemporary 'theory,' when the processes of reification and canonisation of both the man and his work began even before his death in 1984. (Saint Foucault—the Left have a tendency toward hagiography; another form of canonisation). Yet Foucault also was acutely aware of the Nietzschean trope of an 'aesthetics of existence' and the ways in which we can or should remake ourselves. These are the principles of *self-constitution* and transformation, at once ethical and political, applied as much to the citizen, the consumer, and the student as to the public intellectual, the writer, and the theorist. If it is the case that we can remake ourselves through art, through writing, especially utilising spiritual exercises initiated by the Greeks in the Western tradition, using the arts of self-reflection through artistic techniques of reading and writing, then why not through everyday conversation and interaction?

Clearly, Foucault remodels himself and his thinking changes and evolves throughout his life. Indeed, he was forever reformulating what he saw as his own 'project.' In their study of Foucault's work, Dreyfus and Rabinow (1983) propose four stages: a Heideggerian stage (typified by his study of madness and reason), an archaeological or quasistructuralist stage (characterised by *The Archaeology of Knowledge* and *The Order of Things*), a genealogical stage and, finally an ethical stage. The shift from the archaeological to the genealogical stage in Foucault's writings is well represented in *Discipline and Punish* (Foucault, 1977), a work that has direct relevance to educational theory. Like *The History of Sexuality, Discipline and Punish* exhibits a Nietzschean genealogical turn focused upon studies of the *will to knowledge* understood as reflecting both discursive and nondiscursive (i.e., institutional) practices and, in particular, the complex relations among power, knowledge and the body. In *Discipline and Punish,* Foucault is concerned with the body as an object of certain disciplinary technologies of power. He examines the genealogy of forms of punishment and the development of the modern penal institution, discussing in turn torture (beginning with the gruesome account of Damien the regicide), punishment, discipline, and the prison.

In the early 1980s, Denis Huisman asked François Ewald to reedit the entry on Foucault for a new edition of the *Dictionnaire des Philosophes*. As the translator, Robert Hurley remarks in a footnote to the text 'Foucault,' 'The text submitted to Huisman was written almost entirely by Foucault himself, and signed anonymously "Maurice Florence"' (p. 458). Foucault begins that text with the following words: 'To the extent that Foucault fits into the philosophical tradition, it is the *critical* tradition of Kant, and his project could be called *A Critical History of Thought*' (Foucault, 1998d, p. 459). Later he defines a critical history of thought as,

> an analysis of the conditions under which certain relations of subject to object are formed or modified, insofar as those relations constitute a possible knowledge [*savoir*] . . . In short, it is a matter of determining its mode of 'subjectivation' . . . and objectivation . . . What are the processes of subjectivation and objectivation that make it possible for the subject qua subject to become an object of knowledge [*connaissance*], as a subject? (Foucault, 1998d, pp. 450–60).

He describes himself as undertaking the constitution of the subject both as an object of knowledge within certain scientific discourses or truth games we call the 'human sciences' (both empirical and normative) and as an object for himself. This is the history of subjectivity insofar as it involves 'the way the subject experiences himself in a game of truth where it relates to himself' (Foucault, 1998d, p. 461), such as in the history of sexuality. Already, counseling as a narrative 'art of the self' or a scientific discourse plays the truth game and from Foucault's point of view can be considered as one means of constituting the subject.

It is the kind of self-description that Foucault gives elsewhere. In an interview a year before his death, Foucault (1983) 'confessed' to Paul Rabinow and Hubert Dreyfus that his real quarry was *not* an investigation of power but rather the history of the ways in which human beings are constituted as subjects, a process that involved power relations as an integral aspect of the production of discourses involving truths.

> My objective . . . has been to create a history of the different modes by which, in our culture, human beings are made subjects. My work has dealt with three modes of objectification which transform human beings into subjects . . . The first is the modes of inquiry which try to give themselves the status of the sciences . . . In the second part of my work, I have studied the objectivisating of the subject in what I shall call 'dividing practices' . . . Finally, I have sought to study—it is my current work—the way a human being turns him- or herself into a subject. For example, I have chosen the domain of sexuality . . . Thus it is not power, but the subject, that is the general theme of my research.

It is true that I became quite involved with the question of power. It soon appeared to me that, while the human subject is placed in relations of production and of signification, he is equally placed in power relations that are very complex (Foucault, 2000, orig. 1983: 326–27).

Paul Veyne commented after Foucault's death that in his very first lecture at the Collège de France, Foucault contrasted an 'analytic philosophy of truth in general' with his own preference 'for critical thought that would take the form of an ontology of ourselves, of an ontology of the present'; he went so far, that day, as to relate his own work to 'the form of reflection that extends from Hegel to the Frankfurt School via Nietzsche and Max Weber' (Veyne,1997, p. 226). Veyne warns us not to take that circumstantial analogy too far and he puts us on a course that connects Foucault strongly to Nietzsche and Heidegger.

Foucault undoubtedly was strongly influenced by his readings of both Nietzsche and Heidegger and indebted to them for ideas that led him to emphasize and unpack the conceptual and historical relations between notions of truth, power and subjectivity in his genealogical investigations. We can talk here then of Foucault's Nietzsche or Foucault's Heidegger—how Foucault remakes Nietzsche and Heidegger, how he *uses* them in his work. Conversely, we might talk of Nietzsche's Foucault or Heidegger's Foucault, for their work or some selection of it, transformed the Foucauldian corpus, the *body* of Foucault.

FOUCAULT AND THE HISTORY OF MADNESS

The growing avalanche of Foucault-inspired papers in counseling, health, social work, sociology and psychoanalysis and every branch of psychotherapy, from gay therapy through identity issues of self-formation to family therapy, testifies not only to the power of Foucault's work and its continuing legacy but also an intense fascination with the man himself.[1] This ought not be surprising given Foucault's paradoxical self-referentialism as the basis of his speaking, reading and writing, and also the way in which his life presents and represents itself, calling out for some form of analysis consistent with his philosophy. And this is so, despite his protestations and Barthesian tropes concerning the status of author, his Heideggerian-inspired questioning of humanism and the human sciences, and his declaration that 'Man' is a recent invention.

He was fond of referring to and quoting his colleague and friend Pierre Hadot, who occupied the Chair of Hellenistic Studies at the Collège de France, that philosophy was a *way of life*. Autobiographically speaking, Foucault's life and career presents itself as one, from the earliest stage, tied to limit-experiences and the possibilities for self-overcoming found in transgressive sexual pleasures. This is to free himself, so James Miller claims, from the fascism of the self. There is a nugget here for a systematic counseling philosophy based on the concept of limit-experiences.

Also, from the earliest point in his career, Foucault located his work self-consciously at the interstices of psychology, history, medicine, criminology, literature and political philosophy. He received degrees in both psychology and philosophy; studied with Jean Hyppolite from the age of nineteen; and wrote four works in the early period, each detailing the discursive practices involved with the production of knowledge in psychiatry (*Folie et déraison*, 1961), clinical psychology (*Maladie mentale et psycholgie*, 1962), medicine (*Naissance de la clinique*, 1963) and the human sciences (*Les mots et les choses*, 1966).[2] His very first works, then, concerned the crossovers between phenomenology and existential psychology evident in his introduction to the Heideggerian, Ludwig Binswanger's *Traum und existenz* (*Dream and Existence*), published later as 'Dream, Imagination and Existence,' and *Maladie mentale et personalité* (1954).

Foucault turned to Husserl's phenomenology to critique Freudian dream interpretation for reducing the meaning of symbolic content to semantics and thus missing the full expressive content of dreams. (Might narrative therapy run the danger of paying too much attention to the story and not enough on the image or the expressive contents of word-based images?) Yet while phenomenology is a more adequate account, he maintained, it is still tied to the Cartesian project that reduces knowledge to self-knowledge. It cannot therefore move outside its solipsistic orbit to take account of the understanding of language, represented better in the structuralist linguistics of the time that decentred the speaking and writing subject and thus also called into question the entire *subjective turn* and the humanism it implied that dominated French philosophy from Descartes to Sartre. To reduce the problem of the interpretation of dreams (or of the subject or of the subject's story) to self-knowledge is to ignore the rules written into language that structure our consciousness and help make us human beings of a certain kind. This 'grammar of the self' is largely unconscious, the 'deep grammar' of the culture and language that weighs on us heavily when we are born into a culture.

Foucault's own critical project took shape in reaction to phenomenology, structuralism and hermeneutics, although he participated in the existential phenomenological movement for a brief time. This wedded him to the emerging international and poorly named 'anti-psychiatry' movement led by David Cooper and the Glaswegian-born, R.D. Laing. Against hermeneutics, he argued the world had its own structures. Against structuralism, he argued the materiality of linguistic practices constitute meaning. Against phenomenology, he argued for the non-foundational historical construction of social phenomena. Considered as an application to forms of counseling based on narrative, there is a pressing question: What are the hidden narratological structures that form our narrative conscious and shape not only our self-descriptions, but also our perceptions of the world?

Foucault's reception in the English-speaking world was mistakenly aligned with both existentialism and phenomenology. R.D. Laing edited the first English translation of Foucault's *Madness and Civilization* in a series entitled 'Studies in Existentialism and Phenomenology' for the Tavistock Institute. As Daniel Burston (2002) documents, 'Foucault had divorced himself from phenomenology some five years earlier, but Laing stubbornly insisted on regarding him as a phenomenologist.' And further, as Burston reports, while 'Laing's regard for Foucault never wavered ... Laing's esteem for Foucault was never quite reciprocated' (http://www.janushead. org/4–1/burstonpol.cfm). By all accounts, their meeting finally in 1975 was badly strained.

Existentialism and phenomenology in different ways considered madness and mental illness as a *property of a subject* rather than as a social category historically constructed. This was a major difference between the existentialist understanding and the poststructuralist innovation. Foucault, for instance, in *Folie de déraison* demonstrated the conceptual shifts that the category of 'madness' underwent as it replaced 'leprosy' as the disease of the outcast and shifted its status from divine inspiration in the Renaissance to physical exclusion and confinement in the seventeenth century. In this archaeological history of knowledge 'madness' focused less on the human attributes of the knowing subject as a reasoning, rational and autonomous self than on the *history of social categories* that had material effects. The history of madness, Foucault argued, was closely tied to the history of certain concepts and could not be divorced from the history of reason itself, a history in the modern period at least also part and parcel of the history of the subject. In the Renaissance, for example, Foucault maintains madness was experienced as a lens through which to view the terrifying phantasies of the night represented brilliantly in the paintings of Bruegel and Dürer, *and* also as the ironic counterpart to reason as in Erasmus' *In Praise of Folly*. With the 'great confinement' of the classical age, Foucault draws our attention to practices revealed in manuals and records that pinpoint a different experience *and* moral evaluation. 'Madness' becomes part of the category of 'unreason' and condemned as an 'orginary choice,' involving especially idleness over work, that requires administrative control for fear of contagion.[3] Again, here we might construct a genealogy of counseling that problematises its own originary concepts in the unquestioned humanism of those that predated and later led the human growth potential movement, especially in the U.S.A.

For Foucault, then, madness or mental illness cannot be seen as a *natural* fact to be studied scientifically in order to yield both its status as disease and its treatment. It emerges rather as a cultural and historical construct, the product of certain *knowledge practices* in medicine and psychiatry, supported by a grid of administrative routines and techniques. Thus, the history of madness must be written in terms of the history of reason, rationality and the subject and the metavalues of freedom and control, knowledge and power. If this is the case for Foucault, then we can appreciate that his analysis of the claims of psychoanalysis and medicine to treat the suffering of the afflicted will similarly be both historical and political.

Foucault, for instance, is very suspicious of the claim that psychoanalysis can *liberate* individuals from suffering. He believes that this idea of liberation and the whole ideological baggage of 'individual freedom' has played a pernicious role in the history of human freedom, disguising and veiling the intrusion of *disciplinary* power. Disciplinary power is a kind of power that operates outside the state through the disciplines, techniques and forms of knowledge associated with the rise of the human sciences. This is perhaps most pronounced when it comes to the area of sexual freedom and its control and regulation through modern regimes of sexuality. It might also be argued that forms of counseling as developed in schools participated in sustaining this disciplinary power.

THE AESTHETICS OF EXISTENCE

In his earlier works on institutions, such as his analysis of asylums, the clinic, the hospital, the prison and the school, Foucault emphasized external constraints on the individuals through the disciplinary power of the disciplines. In his later work, Foucault develops a framework to theorise the self, which not only allows for the exercise of individual agency, but also recognises in it the ethics of *self-constitution* and 'arts of the self.'

For instance, in his now-famous argument concerning 'care of the self,' Foucault (1990) recognises freedom as the ontological condition of ethics. Ethics is seen to be the practice of liberty. In the Western tradition, taking care of oneself requires a certain kind of knowledge of oneself, first made clear in the Delphic invocation 'To know oneself' as an ultimate goal. To take care of one's self then requires a knowledge of the self and its truths. In this way, Foucault links ethics to the game of truth through the *discursive production* of truths about the self. Foucault argues that the subject is not a substance but rather *a form*, which is not always identical to itself. There are many locutions in our language that testify to this condition: 'He is not himself today'; 'She is beside herself,' etc. Ethics, then, for Foucault, becomes a *practice* or way of life that gives freedom the form of an ethos. Historically in the West, the subject has given form to his/her life through the pursuit of freedom revolving around the concern for truth, a game with a set of principles and rules of procedures that enabled the subject to escape domination if only (s)he knew how to play the game properly. This is a truth-game in which the stakes could not be higher: self-survival, self-assertion (in the original sense), self-mastery. It was a game that linked the ethical constitution of the self to the practice of freedom through the pursuit of truth. Games of truth in modernity took many different forms that emerged culturally in a broad variety of related practices: not only portraiture and self-portrait, biography and autobiography, but also more specifically forms of taking, reading and writing involving essential spiritual practices in Greco-Roman times that later shifted to confession, where the centrality of truth and truth-telling (*parrhesia*) was paramount.

The same sorts of concerns for truth and truth games in pursuit of an 'aesthetics of existence' drives Foucault's (2001a) discussion of *parrhesia* or truth-telling in early Greece. Truth-telling is a speech activity revolving around four questions— 'who is able to tell the truth, about what, with what consequences, and with what relation to power.' It emerged as distinct philosophical problems with Socrates and was pursued in his confrontations with the Sophists in dialogues concerning politics, rhetorics and ethics.

Chapters 5 and 6 elaborate further on parrhesia. Foucault further states

> My intention was not to deal with the problem of truth, but with the problem of truth-teller or truth-telling as an activity . . . What I wanted to analyse was how the truth-teller's role was variously problematised in Greek philosophy. And what I wanted to show you was that Greek philosophy has raised the question of truth from the point of view of the criteria for true statements and sound reasoning, this same Greek philosophy has also raised the problem of truth from the point of view of truth-telling as an activity (Foucault, 2001a, pp. 65–66).

Foucault's interest in the self sought to understand the Nietzschean project of aesthetic self-transformation as an ethical and political project and above all a matter of understanding the relationship to oneself. By contrast with Nietzsche, Foucault substituted political concepts for aesthetic ones and democratic aspirations for culturally elitist ones. Self-transformation and creation thus is a process within postmodern, liberal democracy that might be taken up by anyone at all and frequently is, as in the relation of forms of freedom tied to thought and expression and these to the notion of democracy: freedom of thought and freedom of expression as the basis for educational self-transformation. Foucault provides us with an approach that enables us to understand both how *liberal subjects* constitutes themselves through choice-making, where freedom is the necessary first premise of an historical ontology of ourselves. He also provides us with an understanding of how modern liberalism makes the connection between government and self-government, between direction from above and self-regulation (or autonomy, where *auto* means 'self' and *nomos* means 'law').

Nikolas Rose, the neo-Foucauldian, argues that in our culture psychotherapies have displaced the older religious techniques of spiritual guidance, because they, along with psychology and related discourses and practices—the 'psy sciences'—have produced knowledges that have transformed human beings into modern selves, which are above all regarded to be free, autonomous and their own agents. He argues:

> This modern form of human being is thought to become a self most fully when he or she is able to chose, is able to make a life for themselves in their everyday existence, to become the actor in their own narrative. This notion of the self that is free to choose is not simply an abstract cultural notion, it is embodied in a whole series of practices throughout our society (http://www.academyanalyticarts.org/rose2.htm).

Rose considers practices of consumption as the most notable that define the kind of self we are through the choices we make and the goods we purchase, so that modern selves are not merely free to choose but *obliged* to do so. The modern self, as Sartre (1948) writes in *Existentialism is a Humanism* is 'condemned to be free' and the self is shaped by the moral choices 'it' makes. The modern self thus enters a network of obligations; it is *forced* to be free, to make choices and to be responsible, even if the burden of choice-making is overwhelming. The history of a life, one's life, is therefore the outcome of a series of accumulated choices made over a period of time for which we are held responsible. The emergence of the modern self, for Rose as much as for Foucault, is defined through relations of freedom and power. While power can involve coercion, repression and even denial, it can also involve relations of tutelage, mastery and subjection. Power is for Foucault essentially productive or creative and, as Rose comments, it is best seen as action on the action of others (Foucault, 1986), as shaping the conduct of others. Yet this action on the action of others presupposes the freedom of the other. In other words, the political rationality of government in liberal societies depends upon individual freedom and power works most effectively when it 'works by shaping the way in which individuals enact their freedom.'

Consider the application to counseling, which presupposes 'consent' of the subject. On this interpretation counseling consists in 'the ways in which the therapist shapes the way in which human beings enact their freedom' (Rose, n.d.). Counselors employ and provide clients with the means to become subjects. They enable the subject to avail themselves of 'technologies of the self' (Foucault, 1988b, p. 18).

In liberal societies, the freedom of the self and its inescapable necessity for making choices defines our modern sensibilities, subjectivities and increasingly the institutions of the social market. We would argue that counselors need to become aware of the extent to which 'choice' is no longer innocent and how it is now at the centre of a struggle to define the ethos of public service. Is there a distinctive left conception of choice that can improve the way the poor and the disadvantaged exercise choice in their personal and daily lives? With the shift to a public service based on the ethos of individual consumer choice-making, more and more choosing blurs the line between the public and the private and highlights the centrality and importance of choice-making in an emerging political economy of public service and society more generally, at least in advanced liberal societies. In this new environment, counselors who are given a Foucauldian education will be able to offer their professional expertise as a group who can help to question choice-making, historicise and understand it, in part, as the aesthetic process by which the individual in the modern world becomes a creative choice-making subject able to transcend him- herself and establish a different relationship to him- herself. They may even be better placed to offer this conception of the subject of freedom responsibilising and constituting themselves through choice-making where the guiding ideal focuses on choice-making as the practice of freedom.

Thus, forms of counseling inspired or informed by Foucault's insights must begin with its own historical reflection on its status as a *practice* and a *discipline* to recognise its disciplinary power and the ways in which it has become institutionalised in the matrix of formal and informal juridical, legal rules and supported through a host of bureaucratic routines and techniques. It must also begin to recognise, with the late Foucault, the significance of *choice-making* as the means through which liberal subjects govern and constitute themselves. Counseling is a specific disciplinary formation and body of knowledge and techniques for encouraging the 'client' to *become* a subject. It employs a regime of choice-making techniques to make the subject responsible and to recognise that his/her own freedom is an aspect of the practice of making choices, which also have the capacity to morally shape, sculpt and transform the self. It is important here to note the difference and overlaps between different kinds of choice-making: the moral choice-making of the Kantian ethical subject versus the economic choice-making of classical liberal political economy evident in the figure of *homo economicus*. Recognising the genealogy of choice-making regimes and their historical significance does not take account of how consumer choice-making is also an 'aesthetics of existence' in the sense that our market choices determine what we eat and therefore our body shape, what we wear and therefore how we present ourselves, what we listen to and watch and therefore our 'style,' both personal style (as in self-stylisation) and 'life style.'

FOUCAULT ON THE BODY

The history of subjectivity and the human subject for Foucault was intimately tied to the body. Foucault examines the long Western tradition of the philosophy of the subject by which he means a *problematique* dominating the modern *episteme* that privileges the subject-as-mind as the foundation of all knowledge, action and signification. As mentioned briefly earlier, Foucault was strongly influenced by arguments concerning the body and the importance of space by the phenomenological tradition of Nietzsche, Heidegger, Husserl, Merleau-Ponty, Sartre and Beauvoir and by structuralist methodologies employed by the Annales School (Bloch, Febvre, Braudel) and Marxist thinkers (Althusser, Lefebvre).[4] Against the mainstream philosophical tradition, Foucault radically decenters both the traditional Cartesian notion of a unified subjectivity and the Hegelian subject that comes into play only through struggle, the dialectic and politics of recognition. From his very early conceptions the subject is already historicized and materialized in relation to discursive and institutional practices that focus on the body. In other words, Foucault historicizes questions of ontology, substituting genealogical investigations of the subject for the philosophical attempt to define the essence of human nature. In this inquiry then Foucault is aware of the importance of *locating* the subject in time and space by focusing on the body. This move is important in historizing the body, in disturbing the naturalization of the body and its cultural givenness—a step prior to recognizing its mode of analysis in aesthetics and arts education by focusing on its representation, performance, movement, and cultural signification.

Foucault concentrates the body in modern society and analyses it as a product of power relations. In *Discipline and Punish,* he begins with a powerful description of the torture of Damiens the regicide—'the body of the condemned'—whose flesh is torn away and whose body is cut, burnt with red-hot pincers and sulphur, and, later drawn and quartered, consumed by fire, and reduced to ashes (Foucault, 1977). Foucault elaborates in detail the gruesome and meticulous approach of the executioner who works on the body to cause maximum pain in the public gaze. He contrasts this very public execution and spectacle with the timetable for young prisoners issued by Léon Faucher eighty years later. The relationship between punishment and the body has changed:

> The body now serves as an instrument or intermediary: if one intervenes upon it to imprison it, or make it work, it is in order to deprive the individual of a liberty that is regarded both as a right and as property ... [Now] the body ... is caught up in a system of constraints and privations, obligations and prohibitions. Physical pain ... is no longer the constituent element of the penalty (Foucault, 1977, p. 11).

While 'The gloomy festival of punishment was dying out' (p. 8), which also meant the 'decline of the spectacle' (p. 10) and the end of the tortured body, the hold on the body did not disappear entirely. Now this modern punishment worked on the body to strike at the soul and Foucault interprets his goal as 'a correlative history of the modern soul' (p. 23) to 'try to study the metamorphosis of punitive methods on the basis of a political technology of the body in which might be read a common history of power relations . . . (p. 24). As he says more directly in a way that distinguishes him as a political theorist and explains his significance to feminists,

> the body is also directly involved in a political field. . . . Power relations have an immediate hold upon it; they invest it, mark it, train it, torture it, force it to carry out tasks, to perform ceremonies, to emit signs. This is directly connected to the economic system, for the body is both useful and productive. But the body as labour power is possible 'only if it is caught up in a system of subjection' (Foucault, 1977, p. 26).

In short, 'the body becomes a useful force only if it is both a productive body and a subjected body' (Foucault, 1977, p. 26).

In the same chapter of *Discipline and Punish*, Foucault describes and analyzes a political system with the King's body at the centre. Yet in the nineteenth century, Foucault suggests that the 'body of society' becomes a new principle. The social body is protected through a series of dividing practices involving the segregation of the sick, the quarantining of 'degenerates,' the schooling of boys and girls, and the exclusion of delinquents. In the early interview *Body/Power* (given in 1975) Foucault says: 'the phenomenon of the social body is the effect not of a consensus but of the materiality of power operating on the very bodies of individuals' (Foucault, 1980, p. 55). These relations of power do not obey the Hegelian form of the dialectic but rather take the path of a strategic development of a political struggle which involves both the mastery of the body, achieved through an institutional investment in the power of the body, and the counterattack in the same body. We must remember that questions of design and aesthetics are very much a part of these political investigations even if they do not privilege questions of art.

Foucault upsets the normal understanding when he claims that we should set aside the thesis that power in our capitalist societies has denied the reality of the body in favour of the mind or consciousness. In fact nothing is more material, physical, corporeal than the exercise of power. He encourages the question of what mode of investment of the body is necessary and adequate for the functioning of a capitalist society like ours. In the period from the eighteenth to the beginning of the twentieth century the investment of the body by power was 'heavy, ponderous, meticulous and constant' as evidenced in the disciplinary regimes of schools, hospitals, barracks, factories and the like. Then in the 1960s, it began to be realised that 'such a cumbersome form of power was no longer indispensable' and 'that industrial societies could content themselves with a much looser form of power over the body.' As he insists: 'One needs to study what kind of body the current society needs' (Foucault, 1977, p. 58). And this speculation cannot be approached today without reflection upon and investigation of the body as the site of desire, the object of narcissism, and the constant relay of commodity fetish that one finds contemporary fashion, in various forms of the consumption of the body, and in the seemingly endless forms of self-fashioning promised through diet, exercise, sport, and medical procedures that all have come to mark neoliberal forms of body subjectivity under late capitalism.

In 'Docile Bodies' that begins part 3 of *Discipline and Punish*, Foucault continues the analysis, arguing 'The Classical age discovered the body as an object and target of power' (Foucault, 1977, p. 136). The anatomico-metaphysical approach to the body was supplemented and overlapped by the technico-political, which, through the disciplines, addressed the docility and usefulness of the body. As Foucault puts it

> The historical moment of the disciplines was the moment when *an art of the human body was born,* which was directed not only at the growth of its skills, nor at the intensification of its subjection, but at the formation of a relation that in the mechanism itself makes it more obedient as it becomes more useful . . . (Foucault, 1977, pp. 137–38, our emphasis).

We can note here already the Nietzschean trope of an 'aesthetics of existence' and a 'physiognomy of values' as the body manipulated and shape is at once both aesthetic and political.

In the seventeenth century 'bio-power' emerged as a coherent political technology based on a new power over life, which takes two main forms: the body as machine and as the regulator of population, which focuses on the reproductive capacity of the human body. The first form of bio-power occurs in the military, in schools and the workplace, and is aimed at a more productive, more disciplined, and useful population; the second occurs in demography, wealth analysis, and ideology, and seeks to control the population on a statistical level. The study of population soon became 'political arithmetic' and as administrators needed detailed knowledge about their own state they developed welfare and state mechanisms designed to create a happy, well-fed, healthy and docile population.

In the *History of Sexuality* Foucault examines the power/knowledge *dispositif* of modern sexuality and how the will to knowledge constituted a science of sexuality ('scientia sexualis') and a 'discursive explosion' producing the truth of sex (Foucault, 1980a). Foucault questions the 'repressive hypothesis' and the account of power on which it rests. For Foucault power is exercised rather than possessed, and it is immanent to economic, scientific, sexual relations. It comes from below rather than from above, and it is both intentional and nonsubjective. Further, power is always accompanied by resistance. Through this perspective, Foucault suggests, we can escape the Sovereign/Law ('juridical') notion of power. Thus, sexuality is not a drive, but a 'dense transfer point' for power relations that work through bodies. Foucault refers to four figures here: Hysterization of women's bodies (hysterical woman); Pedagogization of children's sex (masturbating child); Socialization of procreation (Malthusian couple); Psychiatrization of perversions (perverse adult), that together link the stimulation of bodies and intensification of pleasures with the incitement to discourse and the formation of knowledges (Foucault, 1980a).

His last two books on Greco-Roman sexuality, *The Use of Pleasure* and *The Care of the Self*, turned to ancient conceptions of the ethical self, comparing pagan and Christian ethics through their approaches to sexuality (Foucault, 1986; 1990). Where the Christian code forbids most forms of sexual activity except within sanctioned circumstances, the ancient Greeks emphasized the proper use of pleasures in moderation but also engagement in the full range of sexual activities. Pagan sexual ethics exemplified an 'aesthetics of the self' where the self became responsible for the creation of a beautiful and enjoyable existence. The role of aesethetics and art in the religious life of the body has still to be unpacked.

THE BODY HAS A HISTORY

That the body also has a history is a central insight that emerged during the 1980s on the basis of a radical concordance of insights derived from the intersection of phenomenology, art history, psychoanalysis, historical criticism, feminist and gender studies, and the whole gamut of postmodern studies. These approaches had simultaneously embraced the linguistic, the cultural and the spatial turns, and together prefigured the rise of a new multidisciplinarity that based its objects of study outside traditional disciplinary boundaries (see Peters, 1999c). Body theory and criticism emerged in the 1980s and was given a particular orientation by Michel Foucault's work that helped to make 'the body' a category of social and political analysis and an object of historical analysis. Foucault drew his lessons from the phenomenological tradition of French thought on the body (Sartre, Beauvoir, Merleau-Ponty) that emphasized its materiality and the sociocultural specificity of its embodiedness, inscribed by power relations and at the same time marked by gender, race and class.

Before Foucault, Sartre had written of the empirical ego—the physical-psycho self—as the unifying materiality, differentiating himself from both Kant and

Husserl, who tried to show that the 'I' is the formal structure of consciousness. Beauvoir theorized woman as Other and in a series of philosophical novels had examined the particularities of specific embodied relationships to the Other. *The Second Sex* originally published in 1949 made the sexed body into an object of phenomenological investigation for the first time. Merleau-Ponty, for his part, highlighted the difference between the objective body and the phenomenal body, a difference reflected also in terms of objective and existential space. Drawing on Heidegger, Merleau-Ponty understood the 'lived body' as the site of consciousness and perception, thus avoiding Descartes' mind-body dualism and the reductionism predicated upon it. These were Foucault's immediate inheritances, supplemented by his readings of Nietszche, Freud and Heidegger.

Foucault's form of historical or genealogical analysis recently has led to a range of studies that theorizes the body in relation to its adornment, symbology and representation (art and aesthetics), its age and gender (feminism, gender studies), its extension, pain and repair (medicine), its physical limits (sport), its cultural specificity (anthropology) and its social construction (sociology), its constraints and torture (penology and war studies) and the body as a site and locus for a set of power relations (politics) that runs through all these related fields. These analyses fundamentally disturbed the Romantic essentialism and naturalism that had depicted the body as unity—an unchanging and ahistorical category immune to social and political analysis.

Indeed, it was the combination of aesthetics and feminism that first initiated and propelled body criticism. From the Greek ideal of Venus de Milo to Rubens' *The Three Graces* in the 17th century to the heroin-chic anorexia of the Milano catwalk, female body fashions indicated in a plain manner the changing ideals of 'beauty' and their enmeshment in the politics of desire and consumerism. In a myriad of studies across the range of disciplines and arts the body has emerged as the cornerstone of a new form of criticism, which is at once both historical and materialist: *the body as a site of power, desire, thought, action, constraint, control and freedom.* Foucault also taught us of the power of the Nietzschean trope—the body as a work of art—which also pointed to the notion of self-fashioning and self-stylization of the body.

In part this signals a watershed in cultural theory of the body as a category of analysis, where the body has developed the same ontological status as the notion of *practice.* Both of these are now seen as new sociological and cultural givens that help us to map new constellations of self/body image, concept and assertion, as well as providing means of social, group and collective analysis. The body as a category now customarily feeds theoretical developments in feminism, postcolonial theory, queer theory, gender theory, performance theory, cybertheory, and race theory. At the same time, the history of the body and of body criticism indicates a profound shift in an understanding of 'ourselves,' particularly in the West, from the religious and doc-trinal visions that pictured human beings as enduring souls able to survive the rot-ting of the flesh, emphasizing the shift to a situated material and anatomical body that could be modified, healed, exercized and improved ('medicalized') giving rise to the suspicion, as Roy Porter (2003, p. 472) expressed it in *Flesh in the Age of Reason,* 'the doctrine of mind over matter stood for power over the people.'

EMBODIMENT

Descartes considered that the mind/soul has no physical extension (*res non exten-sa*) yet possesses the capacity to think (*res cogitans*) while the body has physical exten-sion but no capacity to think. In trying to reconcile the emerging sciences with his Catholic beliefs, the separation of the mind and body provided Descartes with a neat solution. In terms of this dichotomy the mind/soul remained within the domain of theology, and science dealt with the body (Strathern, 1996). Yet, as Wittgenstein (1953) and Heidegger (1962 [1927]) both forcefully argue, Descartes' mind/body dualism put modern philosophy and the human sciences on the wrong track, one that not only separates the mind and body, privileging the former over the latter, but also encourages the adoption of a broader set of deep-seated dualisms. Fundamentally, the Cartesian dualism repeats and extends a separation of the soul/mind from the body first developed in Plato's philosophy that encouraged an equation between soul, rationality, and the world of eternal forms on the one hand, and the body, the appetites, and the transitory world of appearances, on the other. The dualism is a form of metaphysics and a source of confusion and nihilism (dis-solution and fragmentation) with negative results that bifurcate Western culture (see Heidegger, 1962 [1927]); Wittgenstein, 1953 and other cultural theorists influenced by them e.g., Crossley, 2001; Lloyd, 1984; Peeples, 1999; Strathern, 1996). Such pri-oritising has assigned power over the latter category (e.g., male over female, ratio-nality over emotion, culture/society over nature, white over black, able over disabled, and so on) that has been used for social and political ends, not least the subordina-tion of women.

In challenging the Cartesian dualism, Merleau-Ponty (1962; 1968) aimed 'to show that all our mental operations in fact are constrained by the characteristics of our bodies,' by 'the influence of spatiotemporal factors on perception, through the concepts of perspective, field, and horizon' (Strathern, 1996, pp. 36–37). Therefore, 'once we recognise that there is a mental component in all bodily states and, con-versely, a physical component in all mental states, the boundary between mental and other illnesses disappears' Strathern (1996, p. 4).

The term 'embodiment,' which tends to be used interchangeably with 'corpo-reality,' is the new paradigm for the philosophy of the body that has developed from four major sources: the phenomenological work of continental philosophy, feminist philosophy, questions of identity and from the distinction between humans and artificial intelligence (Proudfoot, 2003). It emphasises that all knowledge, rationality and desire is embodied. It focuses on the concrete and the here-and-now and does so by recognising the temporality and finitude of the human subject and also the relations—social, economic and political—that embodied selves enter into. It encompasses the question of intersubjectivity—the embodied and relational view of the self that is essential to the question of education and communication between people. 'Embodiment' does not privilege one side of the Cartesian dichotomy (i.e., mind) over the other (i.e., body) but seeks to unsettle the dualism by recognising a new interconnectedness and holism of the mental in the physical and the physical in the mental.

By adopting a materialist social ontology which focuses on the body and cultural practices, where the notion of cultural practice implies a kind of agency of an acting *embodied* self, we begin to reconceptualise the notion of labour as a set of bodily practices with a focus on an *aesthetics of the self*—the presentation of the body and forms of bodily style—in the new knowledge or symbolic economy. The new philosophy of the body, drawing on phenomenology dating from Heidegger (1962) and Merleau-Ponty (1962; 1968) would therefore contain the following elements[5]:

1. the *physicality* of the human body, including its neuro-physiological, hormonal, muscular-skeletal and prosthetic components;
2. *continuous bodily activity* including the manifestation and significance of the various dimensions of individuality that mark embodied subjects in the public world;
3. the *lived body,* that is, the body as it is experienced and the embodied nature of knowledge, rationality and the emotions;
4. the *surface of the body* upon which the marks of culture are inscribed. This surface is the flesh, which is "symbolically and meaningfully punctured, incised, decorated, clothed, done up, disguised and stylised" (Schatzki and Natter, 1996, p. 5).
5. the *libidinal body* as the site of desire;
6. the *bio-body* as the home of well-being, health and sexual reproduction;
7. the *productive or labouring body* as the site of intellect and work (energy expended in the reproduction of life);
8. the *social body* as the network of discursive and institutional practices.

These are the important dimensions, which can serve as a basis in the analysis of the schooling of the student body to reproduce and maintain social order.

Schatzki and Natter (1996) argue that social order requires care of corporeality—emphasizing four aspects of the body (its physicality, activities, experiences and surface presentations) where, taking cognisance of gender, ethnic and class differences, bodies are socially contextualised and are constituted as individual subjects. They point out that the body is socially moulded or shaped through a web of sociocultural practices and conditioning within discourses, practices and institutions. For example, social activities like drinking alcohol can produce health conditions that require therapy and/or medical intervention and may construct a gendered discourse that is more accepting of male alcoholism than of female alcoholism.

FOUCAULT, FEMINISM AND THE FEMALE BODY

There is an implicit gender component in Western philosophical thought regarding the mind and the body with a genealogy that extends at least back to the ancient Greeks, to Plato, and has been endorsed in one form or other by the three major Abrahmaic religions—Judaism, Christianity and Islam—through the story of Adam and Eve. This story has positioned the body as shameful, as something to be covered up and laid blame for the breakdown of the relationship between humans and God on women (Khuri, 2001; Peeples, 1999). Religious notions have created, reinforced and been supported by cultural practices that have provided much of the rationale for the deliberate domination of the female by the male. The male has tended to be equated with reason and culture. The female, by contrast, has tended to be equated with the body, the emotions and nature. Moreover, when it has been represented either anatomically and/or philosophically, the body has almost invariably been white and male, which leaves the status and visibility of women and other ethnicities in question (Meyers, 1999). Furthermore, the influential psychoanalytic theories of both Freud and Lacan tend to favour dualistic notions of the body as both sexed and gendered. The effect has been the systematic devaluation and even degradation of anything related to the female such as 'female' emotions or the female body and the objectification of the female body which leads to subordination of women in many cultural milieu (Khuri, 2001; Lloyd, 1994; Meyers, 1999; Peeples, 1999; Strathern, 1996). The body, especially the female body, has been hidden and constricted by mind/body dualisms, dress and religious imperatives, therefore both recognising and revealing the body opposes this positioning.

This mind/body separation is echoed in the male/female dualism evident, for instance, in Augustine's *Confessions* (1992 [orig. 397–401 A.D.]). Following Plato,

Augustine praises intellectual friendship between males and places it above the plea-sures of heterosexual intercourse (Strathern, 1996). The effect of such idealisation has been to denigrate the female and her relationships and the relationships between the sexes while re-enforcing the mind. Interestingly, Augustine, as did most of Christianity, ignored the homo-erotic component of the Platonic ideal, effectively denying this by his silence.

Feminist critiques of the mind/body dualism and its reappraisal of the body, especially in relation to the questions of subjectivity and identity, provide a way of talking about the body that does not simply attempt to overturn the dualism in favour of the body (e.g., Bordo, 1993; Butler, 1990, 1993; Chodorow, 1978; Gilligan, 1982; Young, 1997). Feminist theories of the body—'our bodies, ourselves'—have drawn on phenomenology of the body and anthropology of the body (e.g., de Beauvoir, 1972 and Merleau-Ponty, 1962; 1968), as theoretical sources for arriving at a new conception where the body is located as a site of personal identity, social relations and political institutions, that focus on the link between the body as a site of perception and knowledge and its representation or the semantic field of the body.

Feminist scholars have been perhaps the most active in providing a gendered critique of Foucault and, at the same time, responsible for appropriating his work and extending it in positive and useful ways. Feminist theorists, for instance, have developed Foucauldian insights about the relations between power, the body and sexuality. These insights have been developed alongside a strong tradition of body theorizing going back at least as far as Simone de Beauvoir in the 1940s, culminat-ing in the publication of *The Second Sex* in 1949. De Beauvoir was influenced by Sartre but also Henri Bergson's philosophy of becoming (*élan vital*) and Richard Wright, the African-American writer, whose work of the lived experience of oppressed black people provided a model for analysing women's oppression.[6] Phenomenology, structuralism and poststructuralism was developed in new ways by a new generation of French feminists including Kristeva, Cixous, and Irigaray. Feminists in the U.S., UK, Australia, diasporic intellectuals, and increasingly those in the Third World used this range of resources in philosophy, politics, art history, and in the creative arts, to explore new directions in body criticism focused around the history of body image, the body and visual culture, bodily inscription, mutila-tion, interpersonal and gender relations, and the control of sexuality. The field is now so advanced and complex that there is no easy characterization of all its strands.[7]

In general, it is probably safe to say that feminists operating with Foucault want to argue that the female body is constituted through its social, medical, symbolic and cultural inscriptions. It can no longer be regarded as a cultural given and can only be understood and interpreted in terms of its cultural meanings, which include the full range of cultural representations—both literal and figurative—and surgical and cosmetic interventions. The body is a site of representation and inscription of power and its materiality is the space of symbolic value.

Aurelia Armstrong (2003) provides the following useful summary of the way in which feminists have appropriated Foucault insights:

> Firstly, Foucault's analyses of the productive dimensions of disciplinary powers which is exercised outside the narrowly defined political domain overlap with the feminist project of exploring the micropolitics of personal life and exposing the mechanics of patriarchal power at the most intimate levels of women's experience. Secondly, Foucault's treatment of power and its relation to the body and sexuality has provided feminist social and political theorists with some useful conceptual tools for the analysis of the social construction of gender and sexuality and contributed to the critique of essentialism within feminism. Finally, Foucault's identification of the body as the principal target of power has been used by feminists to analyze contemporary forms of social control over women's bodies and minds. (See 'Foucault and Feminism' at http://www.iep.utm.edu/f/foucfem.htm (accessed 18/5/05).

Foucault's work, although not his alone, has also stimulated interest in related questions concerning identity, subjectivity and resistance. In broad terms it is probably better to say that Foucault-inspired feminist body criticism has fed into a range of 'theoretical modes of exploration of the body' that have developed as 'complementary elements of feminist aesthetics' (see Korsmeyer's (2004) section on 'The Body in Philosophy and Art' in Feminist Aesthetics at http://plato.stanford.edu/entries-/feminism-aesthetics/#5 (accessed 18/5/05). Korsmeyer (2004) catalogues the 'gendering of sense experience,' for example, through making food a medium of art works, new genre of performance art aimed at a critique of dominant art-cultural representations and traditions such as the nude and focusing on the 'arousal of disgust as an aesthetic response' through picturing taboo aspects of women's bodies including, menstrual blood and excrement. This exploration of viscous interiority functions as a critique of the imposition of past aesthetic standards concerning 'beauty' that have dominated and repressed women.[8]

MASCULINITY AND THE MALE BODY

Masculinity research is now a field over ten years old. One of the standard texts simply called *Masculinities* by R.W. Connell was first published in 1995. In that introduction to the field Connell traces a history of Western masculinity and provides a theory of masculinities, proposing strategies for the politics of gender equality. He notes that in education the literature attempts to deal with pressing problems of the making of masculinity in schools within the problematic of identity formation in youth, together with issues of discipline and learning problems for boys. According to Connell (2005) rethinking masculinities involves an understanding of gender politics and a stance of profeminism, a commitment to enhancing men's lives, as well as recognition of diversities among men. It concerns a recognition of the construction of masculinity in everyday life and, in particular, the importance of economic and institutional structures, together with the significance of differences among masculinities and the dynamic character of gender. As Connell (2005, p. 51) comments:

> a wholly semiotic or cultural account of gender is no more tenable than a biological reductionist one. The surface on which cultural meanings are inscribed is not featureless, and it does not stay still.

Connell's work and that of others on masculinities has been picked up recently by the Women's Commission for Refugee Women and Children (2005) and developed in the publication *Masculinities: Male Roles and Male Involvement in the Promotion of Gender Equality: A Resource Packet* (http://www.womenscommission.org/pdf/masc_res.pdf) with the goal of developing

> a resource packet on masculinities and male inclusion in gender mainstreaming covering definitions, approaches, application in the refugee context and tools. Male inclusion/masculinities have been a gap in gender mainstreaming efforts and are vital in order to move the gender equality agenda forward.

The Commission notes that

> "Masculinity" does not exist except in contrast to "femininity." It is a relatively recent historical product of massive societal change. Certainly, women have always been regarded as different from men—but usually (and no more positively), as in the case of Western Europe pre-1700s, as incomplete or inferior examples of the same character. The stratification and cementing of gender roles along currently understood lines did not take place in large part until later.

The Commission recognizes that 'the role of men and boys in achieving gender equality' is crucial and

> urged all key stakeholders including governments, UN organizations and civil society, to promote action at all levels in fields such as education, health services, training, media and the workplace to increase the contribution of men and boys to furthering gender equality.[1] In order to initiate work on gender equality and male involvement therein, critical examination of men's power and privilege and current constructs of "masculinities" are necessary prerequisites.

This is a clear example of the important effects of social science in promoting social change and social justice. The implications are not hard to find for education. For example, consider the following quotation:

> Men and boys are, in most cultures, socialized to be competitive, aggressive and dominant. Political and economic power are valued and rewarded. Physically and financially powerful men are viewed as desirable by women and enviable by other men. Men are also, at times,

socialized to be sexually promiscuous, even sexually irresponsible. Amongst themselves, men often brag about their sexual prowess—long a means of establishing status between men. The role of "stud" has often been coveted and valued in many societies, by both men and women.

The Commission makes reference to Connell's work several times as a foundation text in the area, but neither source actually mentions Foucault even though Foucault's studies of the history of sexuality helped to establish that even the most obvious and taken-for-granted sexual categories are social constructs open to investigation and change. Foucault was responsible not only for initiating studies of models of sexuality in ancient times but also for demonstrating that the category of 'homosexual' is a social construct scarcely more than a hundred years old.

Foucault argued that pederasty and pedarastic education was problematized in ancient Greek culture especially in terms of an intense moral concern with chastity. It is certainly true of ancient Greek texts that there is a shared concern for whether pederasty is right or wrong and whether it should be chaste or erotic. We are less than historically conscious of the way in which pedarastic education was an essential part of ancient Greek philosophy partly because the historical record in the modern period has been purged of sources and references and reconstructed in homophobic terms. Homosexuality as a seemingly fundamental religio-sexual category has been carefully constructed and subject to all kinds of 'medical,' psychiatric, juridical and legislative interpretations.

This is how *glbtq,* an online encyclopedia of gay, lesbian, bisexual, transgender and queer culture (http://www.glbtq.com/) expresses the point in relation to Foucault's work:

> One of the leading philosophers of the twentieth century, Michel Foucault has had an enormous influence on our understanding of the lesbian and gay literary heritage and the cultural forces surrounding it.
>
> In his explorations of power and his examinations of the history of sexuality, Foucault traces the ways in which discourse shapes perception, focusing often on those individuals and practices considered marginal or abnormal, but finding in them keys to understanding the fragile and imperfect ways that power is deployed by the upper classes, the medical establishment, the scientific community, and the literary and political elite.
>
> In doing so, Foucault successfully challenges our notion of the "normal" and calls our attention to the historical contexts determining the narrow designations that restrict human freedom (http://www.glbtq.com/literature/foucault_m.html).

Certainly, a politics of the body is encouraged as part of the legacy of Foucault's work. It is an aspect of his work that the educational establishment has yet to come to terms with and only recently a topic for educational theorists. It is also a politics that applied to Foucault himself and his own body, as Tom Epps in 'The Body of Foucault' (http://www.ccru.net/swarm3/3_foucault.htm) points out so brilliantly:

> The human body is a site of extraordinary specialization. Whilst certain cells contribute to the provision of sophisticated transportation, communication or security systems, others, relieved of the necessity to search out nutrition or defend themselves, are able to perform specific localized functions within, for example, the skin, the heart or the brain. . . .

> Towards the end of his life, Foucault's body became an increasingly intricate ecology with the relationships between cellular guests, hosts and viral intermediaries delicately balanced. With an immune system diverted into the production of Human Immunodeficiency Virus, the functional advantages of maintaining the acutely specialized cellular structures associated with humanity became increasingly tenuous.

CHAPTER FOUR

Space AND THE Body Politic

INTRODUCTION

How can we have been misled into thinking 'the social' and 'the educational' without the consideration of space? The notion of space and the politics of space implicitly enter into conceptions of 'the public' and 'the body' (the body politic). The public is inherently spatial, referring to the structure and the morphology of a shared place, reflecting a materiality. Public spaces exist in many different forms; boulevards, parks and gardens but also cafes, malls, markets and city centres. These spaces can be also enclosed spaces of public institutions such as universities, schools and libraries. In education, the question of public space cannot be separated from the question of literature, considered as a public institution. Jürgen Habermas has written of the development of the 'public sphere'—a developing public space that is intimately connected to the logic of democracy and citizenship, and hence, public debate and participation. As Michael Davie has argued 'Public space is the sphere of the *polis,* as opposed to the *oikos,* which is proper to each individual. At a different scale, it can also be the space of the State, that of political power, that of the relationship between the State and the population.'[1]

It is also important to distinguish between the exploration of space as a sociological issue—the spatial dimensions of social processes—and the theoretical use of spatial master metaphors. Silber (1995) comments on the increasing currency of spatial metaphors—'fields,' 'space,' 'boundaries'—in contemporary sociological thinking, from Marx's infrastructure/superstructure distinction, Simmel's 'social distance and proximity,' Sorokin's forgotten idea of sociocultural space, to Giddens (1984) 'structuration theory,' as the 'first systematic incorporation of space, both physical and social, into a theory of general sociological character' (Silber, 1995). She focuses, first, upon Pierre Bourdieu's (1985a,b; 1989) influential conceptions of social space and field(s) as the strongest theoretical use of spatial metaphors in sociological theory. Secondly, she discusses Harrison White's (1992) *Identity and Control* as the first systematic statement of 'network theory,' before examining what she calls 'weaker' usages of spatial metaphors and the theoretical logic of spatial metaphors. Silber (1995) concludes that spatial metaphors have begun to displace constructs and metaphors emblematic of positivism while also reflecting the prevalent distrust of any kind of encompassing and totalising paradigm.

The point at which temporality slid into spatial, so to speak, marked a radical break with the Enlightenment and the belief in continuous progress. This was accompanied by a radical decentering of the subject and the Cartesian/Kantian conception of knowledge which had set up the aspatial problem set of modern philosophy but which had echoes of the Western tradition initiated by Plato. Modern philosophy inherited a series of distinctions—reality/appearance, mind/body, morality/prudence, scheme/content—that denied temporality but also, in a different way, spatiality. The philosophy of the body that developed out of phenomenology and became strongly evident in the work of Maurice Merleau-Ponty, Simone de Beauvoir and Jean-Paul Sartre, emphasized the fact that bodies inhabit space but that they do not do so as objects. Martin Heidegger dealt explicitly with the notion of space as a secondary aspect of his ontology, ultimately dependent on temporality, and Michel Foucault acknowledged the inherent political nature of space.

The shift from an anthropocentric view and the Enlightenment ideology of continuous progress can be found in the seeds of revolutionary thinking at the end of the nineteenth century in 'new scientific thought, pictorial perspective, and writing, all of which favored discontinuity and deconstruction.' Dosse (1997, p. 356) explains further what he calls 'temporality slides into spatiality' by reference to 'the sounding of the postmodern hour' in the history of structuralism:

> From the arbitrariness of the Sausserean sign to the new mathematical and physical models to quantum theory to the Impressionist's dislocation of the classical perspective, followed by that of the Cubists, a new vision of the world imposed discontinuity: the referent was held at bay . . .

> Historical consciousness was repressed by a planetary, topographical consciousness [Lacan's dictum that the unconscious is structured like a language]. Temporality shifted into spatial. Being removed from the natural order gave way to a search for unvarying logics born of the nature/culture conjoining (Dosse, 1997, pp. 356–57)

The 'cooled' relationship to temporality characterised structuralist commitments to synchrony over diachrony, atemporal or a new kind of spatiality that entered contemporary theory in terms of the structures of mind, society, culture, knowledge and history itself. Yet the Nietzschean-Heideggerian roots of poststructuralism in the early 1960s began to question these commitments. Poststructuralism, as a specifically *philosophical* response to the alleged scientific status of structuralism—to its status as a megaparadigm for the social sciences—and as a movement which, under the inspiration of Friedrich Nietzsche, Martin Heidegger, and others, sought to decenter the 'structures,' systematicity and scientific status of structuralism, to critique its underlying metaphysics and to extend it a number of different directions, while at the same time preserving central elements of structuralism's critique of the humanist subject (see Peters, 1999b).

This chapter builds upon earlier work in this area (Peters, 1996b) which outlined an 'architecture of resistance' in educational theory, examining in turn, geographical space and what Peters called 'the postmodernisation of education,' architectural space, especially in relation to Foucault's work on institutional enclosure and the hope of a 'critical regionalism,' and, finally, what Peters, following Deleuze, called 'networked spaces of societies of control.' In particular, Peters was interested in following Deleuze and Foucault, in mapping the new open spaces of education, based on processes of free-floating control that characterised the shifts from disciplinary to control societies, from closed to open systems. He ended with a plea to take the politics of space seriously and, in particular, to investigate the way that the new spatiality was, above all, a questioning of historicism and historicist assumptions in educational thinking. He also emphasized that the politics of space is based upon the way in which space is fundamental to the exercise of power. We can appreciate Foucault's insight by postulating the relationships between space and power at the macrolevel (witness the new global political economy of education based on the open system); at the mesolevel (in terms of the rearrangement of institutional spaces); and at the microlevel (in relation to 'the classroom' or the 'lecture theatre').

However, this chapter takes a different tack by reviewing work that explores a Heideggerian-Foucauldian line of thinking (see Elden, 2001) seeking to develop this perspective for a reconsideration of space as an essential part of critical pedagogic practices. The chapter begins from an examination of Heidegger's work to consider the importance of space in relation to the understanding of time, history and Being. Heidegger's *ontology of space* in relation to *Dasein* is a prominent theme in his later philosophy, one that is crucial to understanding his critique of modern technology and of modernity in general. It provides an important set of considerations not only for understanding pedagogy in modernity but also for understanding pedagogical practice in relation to the contemporary technologization of education and, in particular, various technological forms of education, including distance education. The chapter explores the question of spatial ontology in relation to Hubert Dreyfus' (2002) *On the Internet,* as an exemplification of the critical issues it raises for pedagogy.

In the next section, the chapter investigates the Heidegger-Foucault connection and Foucault's (1986b) 'Of Other Spaces' as a basis for reconceptualising the relation between power, knowledge and the body. Foucault demonstrates the relations between power, knowledge and the body in spatial terms and by reference to disciplinary societies based upon forms of enclosure. The body occupies space; as opposed to the nonmaterialisation of the mind, the body has a temporal-spatial location. It is an analysis of the body that must become the basis for pedagogical practices that are critical. The body has recently become a desideratum for a range of disparate studies in the arts, humanities and the sciences for a philosophical rescue operation that aims—against the dualisms bedevilling modern philosophy elevating the mind at the expense of the body, and temporality over space—to rehabilitate the body as a site for reason, perception, knowledge and learning. This re-evaluation has been driven by a range of factors: the attempt to overcome the dualism of mind/body metaphysics (Wittgenstein, Dewey, Heidegger); the resurfacing of a phenomenology of the body (Sartre, de Beauvoir, Merleau-Ponty) in the continuing rapprochement of so-called analytic and continental philosophy; the movement within continental philosophy that emphasises the finitude, temporality, and corporeality of the self (Heidegger) and, also, the historizing of questions of ontology (Nietzsche, Foucault); and, the development of feminist philosophies where embodiedness, especially in relation to sex and gender, have played a central role (see Peters, 2002b).

Finally, the chapter explores the implications of this line of argument for geographies of resistance in critical pedagogic practices. The argument, then, is at one and the same time an explication of the importance of space and an analysis of space in terms of Heidegger's ontology, Dreyfus' phenomenology of learning, and Foucault's analysis of disciplinary societies.

HEIDEGGER AND THE SPATIAL ONTOLOGY OF BEING

The notion of 'dwelling,' which represents Heidegger's reappraisal of the concept of space in relation to Dasein, appears in two late essays 'Building Dwelling Thinking' and ' . . . Poetically Man Dwells . . . ' (Heidegger, 1971). Julian Young (2002, p. 63) identifies three phenomena, what he calls after Heidegger, 'the loss of the gods, the violence of technology, and homelessness, the loss of dwelling' as the destitution or sickness of modernity. Modern technology conquers space, abolishing 'remoteness.' At the same time, paradoxically, in its 'abolition of remoteness,' technology brings about a profound 'distancing' from things and the world. As Malpas (2000, pp. 205–6) explains:

> Although technology is, as Heidegger acknowledges, a *mode* of disclosedness or revealing, its particular 'en-framing' of things also entails a covering-over of things as they extend beyond the technological frame: within the domain of the technological, things are disclosed, not as *things*, but as *resources, material,* or *'stock'* (*'Bestand'*—often translated as 'standing-reserve')—as commodities to be transformed, stored, and consumed in a way that obliterates difference and renders everything in a one-dimensional sameness.

Thus through modern technology the world is reduced to a uniform system of consumable resources and while disclosedness or revealing still occurs, it is hidden from us. Disclosedness is only possible through a certain form of being-in-the-world or 'dwelling' in which things are revealed to us in their complex embeddedness in the world. The problem is that technology threatens this possibility of 'dwelling' and the disclosedness of the world. Not surprisingly, Young maintains 'dwelling can plausibly be said to constitute the central topic of the thinking of the late Heidegger' (Young, 2000, pp. 187–88).

Malpas (2000) claims spatiality plays a central role both in Heidegger's critique of modern technology (and modernity) and also in his account of being-in-the-world (dwelling). Yet in Heidegger's early work *Being and Time* (1961 [orig. 1927]) spatiality is both derived from and considered as secondary to temporality. Malpas (2000) following Dreyfus' (1991) influential account claims that Heidegger is confused. Heidegger, Dreyfus argues, confuses two senses of 'Being-in' when he coins the term 'Being-in-the-world': a spatial sense (as 'in a box'—'inclusion' or 'containment') and an existential sense ('in the army,' 'in love,' 'involvement'). The spatial sense Heidegger understands in a characteristically modern sense due to Descartes, as bodily extension. Dreyfus' criticism is that Heidegger fails to distinguish '*public* space from the centered spatiality of each *individual* human being': the former operates as a field of presence—the condition for things being near or far—which is to be distinguished from the latter, based upon Dasein's pragmatic use of things (Dreyfus, 1992, p. 129). Equipmentality—the referential ordering of things within a field of activity—thus for Dreyfus is 'a publicly available structure, that is also based in communal interaction and articulation' (Malpas, 2000, p. 219). Equipmentality is a technical term used by Heidegger to denote the relational totality and ordering of things, as 'ready-to-hand' or available, that structure a field of activity.

The central difficulty is that the early Heidegger derives spatiality from temporality and can only offer an impoverished sense of space. He is therefore unable to offer a consistent account of space or locatedness, which Malpas claims is directly tied to his inadequate treatment of the body. Rather than talking of space or spatiality, by contrast, Malpas suggests that we adopt the notion of *place* 'as a structure that encompasses . . . both spatial and temporal structures as well as structures deriving from the equipmental and the social' (Malpas, 2000, p. 222). Extending Heidegger's line of argument, Malpas explains that within technological modernity, the spatial ordering of things is disturbed so that the difference between the near and far becomes obliterated. Technological disclosedness or revealing, thus covers over things: 'it replaces the things themselves with images or representations . . . of things—that is, it re-presents things within a particular 'frame' and in a way that is abstracted from their original locatedness' (Malpas, 2000, p. 226). Malpas argues that the technological shift from locateness to dislocation, from things to representations, has a number of long-term and appalling consequences:

> Inasmuch as technology covers over the concrete locatedness of both human being and worldly object, it covers over the nature of both human and the thing. As a result, technology leads us to misunderstand the character of our own being-in-the-world as well as the mode of being of the things with which we are engaged. In this respect, inasmuch as technology removes us from our proper place, obliterating any proper sense of place, it also covers our own mortality—a mortality that can itself be viewed as essentially connected to the place-bound character of our being (Malpas, 2000, pp. 226–27).

While seeming to be amenable to human control, modern technology increasingly enframes us as resources, transforming the character of human experience, reducing it to re-presentation and narrowing our sensitivity to a small range of sensory and interactive modalities, rather than engaging the body and its multiple senses in its entirety (see also Malpas, 1999). These Heideggerian observations are of overwhelming importance to pedagogy and to critical pedagogical practices (see Peters, 2002c). They provide not only the basis for a philosophical account of the critical importance of space and the body to pedagogy and an implicit critique of a traditional pedagogy that has all but ignored the body (space) or privileged it over mind (atemporality), but also they contain within them pedagogical critique of a technological modernity aimed at the efficient delivery of information via a model of distance education. Let us examine this line of argument further by reference to the work of Hubert Dreyfus.

PLATONISM, BODY TALK AND NIHILISM:
DREYFUS' *ON THE INTERNET*

This section draws on a review of Dreyfus' work (see Peters, 2002a). Hubert Dreyfus' (2001) *On the Internet* is at one and the same time, philosophical, post-Nietzschean and also 'computer literate' or, better, computer sensitive. He begins and ends, (uncharacteristically for Dreyfus), by quoting Nietzsche on the body, from *Thus Spake Zarathrustra:* beginning—'Behind your thoughts and feelings, my brother, there stands a mighty ruler, an unknown sage—whose name is self. In your body he dwells; he is your body' and ending—'I want to speak to the despisers of the body. I would not have them learn and teach differently, but merely say farewell to their own bodies—and thus become silent.' Therein, is encapsulated Dreyfus' thesis on the Internet, as he succinctly sums it up in the final paragraphs:

> as long as we continue to affirm our bodies, the Net can be useful to us in spite of its ten-dency to offer the worst of a series of asymmetric trade-offs: economy over efficiency in edu-cation, the virtual over the real in our relation to things and people, and anonymity over commitment in our lives. But, in using it, we have to remember that our culture has already fallen twice for the Platonic/Christian temptation to try to get rid of our vulnerable bodies, and has ended in nihilism. This time around we must resist this temptation and affirm our bodies, not in spite of their finitude and vulnerability, but because, without our bodies, as Nietzsche saw, we would be literally nothing (Dreyfus, 2001, pp. 106–7).

It is a thesis as powerful as it is frightening, as simple and elegant as it is prophet-ic. The Net as a kind of technological *enframing* of being stands at the door. It con-tains both the danger and the saving power. If we allow it to transcend the limits of the body we will also allow it to abstract from our moods, our cultural location and belongingness, our finitude and vulnerability, our animality that helps comprise our linguistic and cultural identities, and also the meaning we give our lives. By leav-ing the body behind we will succumb to the same nihilistic impulses in our culture that began with Platonism and was repeated by Christianity. Dreyfus thus lines up behind Nietzsche, Kierkegaard, Heidegger and Merleau-Ponty, a group of philoso-phers who were dedicated to overcoming the dualisms ruling Cartesian thought and who argued for a phenomenology of the body.

The idea that the soul is distinct from the body has it roots in classical Greek philosophy and is found in Plato. For instance, in the *Meno,* Plato indicates that the soul acquires knowledge before it enters the body and thus all knowing consists in recollecting. Later, in the *Phaedo* and other dialogues Plato articulates the notion of Forms that are considered eternal, changeless and incorporeal. The Platonic dualism between the world of Forms and the world of mere appearances becomes one of the problem sets in the history of philosophy. Gilbert Ryle said that all Western philosophy consists in a series of footnotes to Plato and, indeed, one can detect in the history of contemporary philosophy the antagonism between Platonism and anti-Platonism as a dominant theme. Anti-Platonists or antifoundationalists is a convenient category that refers to a group of philosophers—phenomenologists, pragmatists and post-Nietzscheans—who want to give up on a set of dualisms (appearance/reality, body/mind, made/found, sensible/intellectual) that have dom-inated the history of Western philosophy. On the basis of these dualisms Platonists and Kantians have argued for an unchanging and ahistorical human nature that can serve as the foundation for universal moral obligations.

Platonism, thus, in educational philosophy stands for the elevation and privileging of the mind or intellect over the body: it stands for a host of optional metaphors that serve to dualize or bifurcate reason and emotion, metaphors, in their application and formalisation, have become the substance of educational practice. Perhaps, the most culturally deeply embedded dualism with which educational theory and practice must come to terms with is the mind/body separation. This dualism historically has developed as an instrument of 'othering': of separating boys from girls, reason from emotion, minorities from the dominant culture, and classes from each other. It nests within a family of related dualisms and remains one of the most trenchant and resistant problems of education in postmodernity.

The same underlying philosophical problem set is at issue in Dreyfus' *On the Internet*. The body is everything. Dreyfus argues 'loss of embodiment would lead to *loss of the ability to recognize relevance*' and, most importantly for learning, that 'Without involvement and presence *we cannot acquire skills*' (Dreyfus, 2001, p.7). In short, our bodies matter; they provide the 'source of our sense of our grip on reality' (Dreyfus, 2001, p. 7). He quotes Merleau-Ponty, thus: 'The body is our general medium for having a world.' Of course, Dreyfus is no stranger to Merleau-Ponty or to Heidegger or Kierkegaard, for that matter. His account of the acquisition of skill is indebted to Merleau-Ponty and his commentary on Heidegger (Dreyfus, 1991) has now become a standard. He is a long-standing critic of computer ideologies and, in particular, the cognitive science modelling of the brain on the computer in books like *What Computers Can't Do* and *What Computers Still Can't Do* (Dreyfus, 1992; see also Dreyfus, 1982). In *Mind over Machine* (Dreyfus & Dreyfus, 1986) he argued that where human beings begin learning a new skill by understanding and carrying out its rules as a novice, only to leave rules behind as they become expert, the best that a computer can attain is a sort of 'competence' that consists in carrying out the rules it has been taught, albeit very quickly and reliably. A version of this argument appears in *On the Internet*. Indeed, Dreyfus outlines the stages by which a student learns—novice, advanced beginner, competence, proficiency, expertise, practical wisdom. Dreyfus' major conclusion is that disembodied learning can only ever attain the stage of mere competence and will not achieve the stage of self-mastery or practical wisdom (see also Dreyfus & Dreyfus, 1985). Questions of space and the body, of the location and place of the learner and teacher, are, thus, crucially germane to the phenomenology of learning, as they determine questions of *locatedness, situatedness,* and, therefore, also broader notions of identity, at the personal, national and cultural levels.

FOUCAULT'S SPACES OF POWER

We are in an epoch where space takes for us the form of relations among sites. (Michael Foucault, 1994, IV, p. 754).

The analysis of space was always important to Foucault although he wrote little directly on this topic except for his essay 'Of Other Spaces' (Foucault, 1986b). Foucault was to maintain that space is inherently political and that is it is fundamental to any exercise of power. Under the influence of Heidegger, the French epistemologist Gaston Bachelard, and the movement of structuralism, more generally, Foucault provided us with a history of present that recast genealogy as a historical ontology, a form of *spatialised history*, rather than merely a history of space (Elden, 2001, p. 6). An equally important aspect of Foucault's analysis of space is his emphasis on the materiality of the body, which echoes Heidegger's criticism of Nietzsche, in that Foucault abandons 'the simple equation of the body with an 'I,' an 'ego' or a self.' By contrast, 'Foucault concentrates on the question of the body without the subjectivism; instead there is an investigation of how the subjection of the body forms the subject' (Elden, 2001, p. 104).

For Foucault, every social space is structured by power and invested with knowledge. In a late interview he remarks that in the eighteenth century there emerges a specific political discourse, which reflects upon architecture 'as a function of the aims and techniques of the government of societies' (Foucault, 1984, p. 239). Cities and buildings became spatial models for government rationality. They provided the basis for the exercise of social control and manipulation. The school, for example, is considered as a form of disciplinary architecture demonstrating at an abstract level the relation between educational space and a particular form of disciplinary political rationality that produces an *individualized* subject.

Foucault painstakingly documents the histories of different institutional spaces: the clinic, the prison, the school. In *Discipline and Punish,* for instance, Foucault observes how 'disciplinary power' depends upon 'a politics of space.'

A whole problematic then develops: that of an architecture that is no longer built simply to be seen (as with the ostentation of palaces), or to observe the external space (cf. the geometry of fortresses), but to permit an internal, articulated and detailed control—to render visible those who are inside it; in more general terms, an architecture that would operate to transform individuals: to act on those it shelters, to provide a hold on their conduct, to carry the effects of power right to them, to make it possible to know them, to alter them (Foucault, 1977, p. 72).

Disciplinary power based on the instruments of observation, judgement and examination are enabled by a carefully designed institutional architecture permitting total surveillance: the hospital building is organized as 'an instrument of medical action';

the prison is built as a 'space of confinement'; the school building is organized as a spatial mechanism for training of the individual, for individualization. He calls it 'a pedagogical machine' (p. 172).

In *Discipline and Punish,* the section on 'discipline' is organised into three sections, respectively 'docile bodies,' 'the means of correct training' and 'panopticism.' It includes an account of the ways that during the seventeenth and eighteenth centuries the disciplines became general formulas of domination. Foucault claims that this new political anatomy was evidenced in a multiplicity of often-minor processes at different locations that eventually coalesced into a general method:

> They [i.e., disciplinary techniques] were at work in secondary education at a very early date, later in primary schools; they slowly invested the space of the hospital; and, in a few decades, they restructured the military organization (Foucault, 1977, p. 138).

Foucault talks of disciplinary techniques in terms of 'the art of distributions,' (the monastic model of enclosure became the most perfect educational regime and 'partitioning' (every individual had his or her own place). 'The rule of *functional sites*' refers to the ways that architects designed space to correspond to the need to supervise and to prevent 'dangerous communication.' Foucault argues 'the organization of a serial space was one of the great technical mutations of elementary education' (Foucault, 1977, p. 147) that made it possible to supersede the traditional apprenticeship system where the pupil spends a few minutes with the master while the rest of the group remains idle.

Foucault also details 'the control of activities,' including the timetable, what he calls 'the temporal elaboration of the act' (e.g., marching), and the correlation of the body and the gesture (e.g., 'good handwriting . . . presupposes a gymnastics'), as well as other aspects. He writes:

> To sum up, it might be said that discipline creates out of the bodies it controls four types of individuality, or rather an individuality that is endowed with four characteristics; it is cellular (by play of spatial distribution), it is organic (by the coding of activities), it is genetic (by the accumulation of time), it is combinatory (by the composition of forces). And, in doing so, it operates four great techniques; it draws up tables; it prescribes movements; it imposes exercises; lastly, in order to obtain the combination of forces, it arranges 'tactics' (Foucault, 1977, p. 167).

He discusses the means of correct training in terms of 'hierarchical observation.' As he suggests 'the school building was to be a mechanism for training . . . a 'pedagogical machine,' normalizing judgement (Foucault, 1977, p. 172). The examination 'transformed the economy of visibility into the exercise of power,' introduced 'individuality into the field of documentation,' and 'surrounded by all its documentary techniques, . . . [made] each individual a 'case'' (Foucault, 1977, p. 187f). Most famously, Foucault, discusses 'panopticism'—a system of surveillance, based on

Jeremy Bentham's architectural figure, that operates by permitting the relentless and continual observation of inmates at the periphery by officials at the center, without their ever being seen.

Discipline and Punish is concerned with the operation of technologies of power and their relations to the emergence of knowledge in the form of new discourses, based around modes of objectification through which human beings became subjects. It is a theme that Foucault develops further in his work on the history of sexuality. Foucault asks:

> Why has sexuality been so widely discussed and what has been said about it? What were the effects of power generated by what was said? What are the links between these discourses, these effects of power, and the pleasures that were invested by them? What knowledge was formed as a result of this linkage? (Foucault, 1980a, p. 11).

It is in the course of his inquiries into sexuality and the proliferation of associated discourses that Foucault coins the term 'bio-power' considered as a kind of anatomo-politics of the human body and control of the population at large.

Hubert Dreyfus' (1996) begins his essay 'Being and Power: Heidegger and Foucault' with the following comparison between the two thinkers:

> At the heart of Heidegger's thought is the notion of being, and the same could be said of power in the works of Foucault. The history of being gives Heidegger a perspective from which to understand how in our modern world *things* have been turned into *objects*. Foucault transforms Heidegger's focus on *things* to a focus on *selves* and how they became *subjects*. And, just as Heidegger offers a history of being, culminating in the technological understanding of being, in order to help us understand and overcome our current way of dealing with things as objects and resources, Foucault analyzes several regimes of power, culminating in modern bio-power, in order to help us free ourselves from understanding ourselves as subjects (Dreyfus, 1996, p. 1).

In contrast to Platonism and in line with the trajectory of contemporary French philosophy Foucault emphasises the enfleshed subject, sensuous reason, and the embodied subject—a subject, not timelessly cast as an abstract universalism as with the Kantian ethical subject or *homo economicus* of neoclassical economics, but one that emphasizes the everyday contingencies of the self and its understanding as the site of a dissociated self—a body normalised, individualised and inscribed with the effects of power.

While Dreyfus does not provide a point of comparison between Heidegger and Foucault specifically in relation to space, he does provide a useful analysis of their respective notions of resistance in relation to technology and bio-power.

> Neither Heidegger nor Foucault think that we can resist techno/bio-power directly because what ultimately needs to be resisted is not particular technologies nor particular strategies but rather a tendency in the practices towards ever greater order and flexibility that produces

and sustains them. Thus the current understanding can only be resisted by first showing that it is not inevitable but is an interpretation of what it is to be, second by connecting our current style with our current discomfort and then by taking up marginal practices which have escaped or successfully resisted the spread of techno/bio-power (Dreyfus, 1996, p. 16).

Foucault, as Dreyfus explains, bases his notion of resistance on the self. His genealogical investigations and historical ontology leads him back to the ethics of self-mastery—a set of cultural practices of the self he finds in the writings of the Stoics that provide a basis to demonstrate that there are no universal necessities in human existence (that we could be otherwise), and, like Nietzsche, to question Christian asceticism, with its ethic of self-renunciation. In his last seminars given at Vermont and Berkeley in 1983, Foucault illustrates by reference to classical texts the form of an education, differently conceived at different times, based on truth-telling and a conception of self-mastery that integrates the *logos* with the *nomos* and the *bios* in practical ways that lead to a successful engagement with the world (see Peters, 2003). In terms of these variable practices of the self he is able to question the direction of our current practices, and to contemplate the possibility of resistance. In particular, he draws upon the question in antiquity of knowing how to govern one's life so as to give it the most beautiful form possible. Here the notions of the 'art of living,' 'care of the self' and 'aesthetics of existence' loom large and Heidegger's and Nietzsche's combined influence is again keenly felt, especially in the notion of life as a work of art. Ultimately it is in these 'practices of creativity' of the self that Foucault wants to ground the possibilities of resistance. Dreyfus comments:

> There is, nonetheless, an important kind of resistance these two thinkers [Heidegger and Foucault] share. Thinking the history of being, for Heidegger, and the genealogy of regimes of power, for Foucault, opens a space for critical questioning by showing that our understanding of reality need not be defined by techno/bio power—that we need not be dominated by the drive to order and optimize everything. They both show that we had a different relation to being and to power once, which suggests that we could have again. Thus an understanding of our historical condition weakens the hold our current understanding has on us and makes possible disengagement from the direction our practices are taking (Dreyfus, 1996, p. 16).

In one sense it could be argued that resistance for both Heidegger and Foucault is retrospective and based on a form of historical understanding that demonstrates that we could be otherwise than we are. Yet there are positive strategies and tactics of resistance as well to be gained from their work, which are important to mapping geographies of resistance in critical pedagogical practices. These forms of resistance crucially involve the body and the relations between the body and place, which also provide the ground for most discussions of identity, citizenship and the Other. Yet if we are to understand resistance in Foucauldian terms we must also understand that his conception of power *entails* resistance—resistance is a relation of power. Just as freedom is a necessary condition for relations of power, so it is for resistance.

Foucault does not accept the liberal juridical notion of power, which is grounded in sovereignty and opposed to authority. He understands power (and resistance) as something to be exercised rather than something to be possessed. Power is productive (as well as repressive), and it is diffuse, permeating the social body through multiple sites. On this model, then, where the very existence of power depends on points of resistance, critical pedagogical practices depend upon on an embodied engagement with the world, based on the ethic of self-mastery that seeks to 'recover' our own sense of place and the potential of modern technology to obliterate all difference.

GEOGRAPHIES OF RESISTANCE
IN CRITICAL PEDAGOGIC PRACTICES

In a recent essay John Morgan (2000) has argued for a 'critical pedagogy of space' where space is seen as a social construction. He suggests that 'space should not be seen simply as the product of capitalist social relationships, but tied up with other axes of power, such as gender, ethnicity and sexuality' and he ends by issuing the challenge to develop a critical pedagogy of space that reflects the multiple and contested nature of space (Morgan, 2000, p. 273). He emphasises, first, (and following the Marxian geographer, David Harvey, 'the way in which the production of space is linked with the exercise of economic power,' what in the context of globalisation Peters has called the 'postmodernisation of education.' He then considers space in relation to the school curriculum, especially geography, where he indicates 'different social groups may have distinct spatialities' (Morgan, 2000, p. 279), emphasising 'a shift away from the idea of space as homogenuous, continuous, objective, Cartesian and knowable, towards a view of space as fragmented, imaginative, unknowable and subjective' (Morgan, 2000, p. 281). He raises the possibility that 'a critical pedagogy of space might begin with an analysis of the gendered use of space in the classroom' and it might also pay attention to 'the experience of public space,' focusing on 'spaces of exclusion,' and 'geographies of resistance through which people deal with, and resist, oppressive practices' (Morgan, 2000, pp. 282–83). He concludes by suggesting that 'spaces as social texts' provide the opportunity for highlighting issues concerning identity formation in relation to questions of scale 'through the *body-home-community-city-region-national-global*' (Morgan, 2000, p. 286).

Morgan's account is a useful addition to the literature on space although it is restricted largely to the ways in which critical pedagogy might be encouraged in academic geography and depends in large measure on a 'geography of resistance' in the narrow disciplinary sense—how we might import new politicised notions of space into school geography. This is undoubtedly an important project but the notion of 'geographies of resistance' needs to be interpreted more broadly and not restricted to one subject in the curriculum where it has obvious application. Clearly, the themes *body-home-community-city-region-national-global* may be easily pursued in other parts of the arts/humanities curriculum—in history, English, social studies, and art as much as geography.

More importantly, there is a need for theorists and practitioners in critical pedagogy to address questions concerning critical *ontologies of space* by unpacking the notion of the body, construed both in terms of the historically privileged set of mind/body and its impact on learning theory (i.e., in terms of the individual learner) and in terms of collective notions (the student body). Here the contributions of Heidegger and Foucault are of paramount importance, not simply because they provide one trajectory for a consideration of the importance of space philosophically—from an essentialising ontology of being (Heidegger) to an historical ontology of ourselves (Foucault)—but also because Foucault's opus depends crucially upon spatial concepts that he has developed in relation to institutional spaces of enclosure (the prison, the school, the clinic, the factory), to *epistemes* (and the spatialisation of knowledge and their disciplinary formation), and to the transition from disciplinary societies to societies of control (involving the postmodernisation of education—see Peters, 2001h). Geographies of resistance are geographies of the body that are intimately tied to the politics of space, to locality and to identity and identity politics. Critical pedagogical practices considered in this sense may not, therefore, be related only to contents areas and their successful prosecuting in the classroom but may indeed more properly embrace lived practices and conditions of existence. Nowhere is this more important than in the current debate concerning distance education or education on the Internet for in this most politicised of spaces questions of globalisation, the body, and the politics of identity intersect in unexpected and novel ways.

PART THREE

Truth-Telling, Risk
AND Subjectivity

CHAPTER FIVE

Truth-Telling AS AN Educational Practice OF THE Self

My role—and that is too emphatic a word—is to show people that they are much freer that they feel, that people accept as truths, as evidence, some themes which have been built up at a certain moment in history, and that this so-called evidence can be criticized and destroyed. . . . All my analyses are against the idea of universal necessities in human existence.

MICHEL FOUCAULT, 'TRUTH, POWER, SELF: AN INTERVIEW WITH MICHEL FOUCAULT'

What is truth? A mobile army of metaphors, metonyms, anthropomorphisms, in short, a sum of human relations which were poetically and rhetorically heightened, transferred, and adorned, and after long use seem solid, canonical, and binding to a nation. Truths are illusions about which it has been forgotten that they are illusions, worn-out metaphors without sensory impact, coins that have lost their image and now can be used only as metal, and no longer as coins.

NIETZSCHE, 'ON TRUTH AND LIES IN AN EXTRA-MORAL SENSE'

INTRODUCTION

This chapter is devoted to an examination of Foucault's approach to truth-telling in relation to the changing practice of education. The first section briefly examines the notion of truth as Foucault uses it to investigate the sociopolitical sphere. The remainder of the chapter is given over to Foucault's six lectures entitled 'Discourse and Truth: The Problematization of Parrhesia' and subsequently edited by Joseph Pearson and published as a book, *Fearless Speech* (Foucault, 2001a). Foucault problematizes the practices of *parrhesia,* 'free speech' or truth-telling speech activities in classical Greek culture intent 'not to deal with the problem of truth, but with the problem of truth-teller or truth-telling as an activity' (Foucault, 2001a, p.169). Foucault outlines the meanings and the evolution of the classical Greek word *'parrhesia'* and its cognates, as they enter into and exemplify the changing practices of *truth-telling* in Greek society. In particular, Foucault investigates 'the use of *parrhesia* in specific types of human relationships' and 'the procedures and techniques employed in such relationships' (Foucault, 2001a, p. 107). Central to his analysis is the importance of education, how it was central to 'care of the self,' public life and the crisis of democratic institutions.

Although the Berkeley lectures continue and partly elaborate some of the themes concerning 'technologies of the self' that Foucault (1988a, 1988b) gave as lectures at the University of Vermont a year earlier in 1982 (see chapter 2), there are significant differences in the themes Foucault pursues, the way he pursues them and his characterization of the Platonic model. In the Vermont set he characterizes the Platonic model as 'defective' in that it is dualistic (teacher/pupil) and directed at knowing oneself rather than care for the self; in the more considered Berkeley lectures he treats the Socratic/Platonic model with greater sympathy, emphasizing that the tradition is not only the source of the search for truth (as in the truth value of a statement) but also of a critical philosophy based upon an understanding of the practices of truth-telling.

He claimed that truth-telling as a speech activity emerged with Socrates as a distinct set of philosophical problems that revolves around four questions: 'who is able to tell the truth, about what, with what consequences, and with what relation to power' that Socrates pursued in his 'confrontations with the Sophists in dialogues concerning politics, rhetoric and ethics' (Foucault, 2001a, p.170). Foucault points out the problematization of truth since the end of Presocratic times has created two major branches of Western philosophy—a 'critical' tradition and an 'analytics of truth' tradition that is primarily concerned with 'ensuring that the process of reasoning is correct in determining whether a statement is true (or concerns itself with our ability to access the truth)' (Foucault, 2001a, p. 170). He states that aligns himself with 'critical' philosophical tradition that is concerned 'with the importance of telling the truth, knowing who is able to tell the truth, and knowing why we should tell the truth' rather than the analytic tradition (Foucault, 2001a, p. 170). Foucault demonstrated that these practices link truth-telling and education in ways that are still operative in shaping our contemporary subjectivities, thus they are relevant in understanding the exercise of power and control of contemporary citizenship especially in situations where there is some risk for a person in telling the truth to a superior—a situation that clearly can occur in schools, in the student-teacher relationship and which certainly occurred for some youth in their antiwar activities in 2003 as shown in chapter 6.

In the Vermont set of seminars, the technology of the self is one of the four technologies described by Foucault, along with technologies of production (Marx), technologies of signs (Saussure), and technologies of domination. Foucault does not attempt to defend this fourfold typology or his indebtedness to Heidegger's conception of technology. Technologies of the self, for Foucault, is an approach to study the ethics of an individual whereby the individual can come to know himself as well as take care of himself—twin themes in the inherited Western ethical tradition associated with specific techniques of truth-telling practices that human beings apply to understand themselves. In his examination of classical Greek and early Christian texts Foucault distinguishes two models: the ('defective') pedagogical Platonic model based on the art of dialogue between teacher and pupil, which requires that the 'pupil' know himself so that he can participate in dialogue; and, the medical model which focuses on the presence of a continuous and permanent care of oneself. In terms of these two models analysed through various texts, Foucault demonstrates that the Senecan, Plutarchian and Pythagorean understanding of the self is different from the Platonic one. He later distinguishes ethical self-mastery of the Stoics based on *askesis* (a kind of training or exercise) from the self-renunciation of the early Christians where techniques of the self were exercised through the imposition of conditions and rules for particular self-transformations leading to salvation through confession, penance, and obedience.

To date, none of the many books on Foucault, which apply his methods to educational problems or issues, or directly address the relevance of his writings to the field of education, focus specifically on the question of truth in Foucault or refer to his Berkeley lectures. Yet these lectures demonstrate not only that Foucault did directly address education, but also that education was central to his elaboration of the theme of 'care of the self.'

FOUCAULT ON TRUTH: FROM *REGIMES* TO *GAMES* OF TRUTH

In his early work Foucault, treated truth as a product of the regimentation of statements within discourses that had progressed or were in the process of progressing to the stage of a scientific discipline. In this conception, the subject, historized in relation to social practices, is denied its freedom or effective agency. This early conception of Foucault's is to be contrasted with his later notion of the subject where freedom is seen to be an essential aspect of its constitution as in the concept of governmentality and in his studies of the history of sexuality. For the early Foucault, as he indicates:

'Truth' is to be understood as a system of ordered procedures for the production, regulation, distribution, circulation and operation of statements (Foucault, 1980a, p. 133).

In the progress of a scientific discipline, studying how the human sciences emerged, Foucault (1972, pp. 186–87), proposed four stages through which a science must develop. The following account is based on van Gigch's (1998) thoughtful essay. First, 'the discursive practices' begin to exhibit 'individuality and autonomy' from other discourses, although there is no attempt yet to systematize accumulated knowledge in the form of theory. Second, the emerging discipline begins to make claims of 'verification and coherence' for some of its pronouncements, which are formulated as laws, as yet unproven or justified. Third, propositions are regulated in terms of formal criteria for the production of 'true' statements and efforts are made to formalize the knowledge of the discipline into a systematic framework. Finally, the discipline moves beyond formalization to reach mature scientific status and is, accordingly, able to offer a proven methodology that demonstrates success in solving most problems exhibited by its domain. At this stage practitioners become professionals who provide valid solutions to a broad range of recognisable problems. With its institutional development and its own canon, the discipline becomes acceptable as a science also by those outside the discipline. It is at this stage that the discipline must question its own epistemological foundations, questioning both its own reasoning methods and how its reaches the truth, otherwise it will begin to repeat itself, lose its relevance, become useless and disappear, as other disciplines supersede it.

Thus, for Foucault (1972, p. 182–83) knowledge is, first of all 'A group of elements, formed in a regular manner by discursive practice' and 'The field of coordination and subordination of statements in which concepts appear, and are defined and transformed.' It is also 'That of which one can speak in a discursive practice, and which is specified by that fact,' emphasising that knowledge is not the sum of what is thought to be true, but rather the whole set of practices that are distinctive of a particular domain.

With the 'doubtful' human sciences human beings emerge as both subject and object of knowledge. In the context of the disciplines of the human sciences, Foucault investigates the internal relation of power and knowledge: power and knowledge directly imply one another, for there is no power relation without the corresponding constitution of a field of knowledge. The human sciences will be capable of distinguishing between true and false when they will 'free themselves from their involvement with power' (Dreyfus & Rabinow, 1983, p.116), that is, once it has overcome the problem of objectivity. Yet given that the human sciences are an integral part of the social practices, which they seek to investigate, it is doubtful whether they will ever achieve objectivity and, thus, attain the status of 'normal science' in Kuhn's sense of the term.

Thus, relations of power inhere in the human sciences for they cannot meet the objectivity criterion and 'scientists' are as much a product of the cultural practices that they investigate as their subjects. It is these power relations, which sustain and regulate the procedures by which statements in the discourses of the human sciences are regulated. In other words, 'regimes of truth' are the discursive productions of the human sciences.

The shift from 'regimes of truth' to 'games of truth,' McKerrow (2001, p. 7) claims, is indicative of the shift in Foucault's thinking concerning the agency of the subject and not of Foucault's notion of truth which remains essentially Nietzschean. I dispute this interpretation. The Nietzschean perspective on truth is not straight-forwardly the concept that governs Foucault's account of truth in the human sciences. McKerrow quotes a late interview with Gauthier (1988, p. 3) where Foucault says:

> I have tried to discover how the human subject entered into games of truth, whether they be games of truths which take on the form of science or which refer to a scientific model, or games of truth like those that can be found in institutions or practices of control.

And Foucault elaborates the concept of 'game' in the following way:

> when I say 'game' I mean an ensemble of rules for the production of truth. . . . It is an ensemble of procedures which lead to a certain result, which can be considered in function of its principles and its rules of procedure as valid or not, as winner or loser (Gauthier, 1988, p. 15, cited in McKerrow, p. 7).

In fact, Foucault in a little known paper delivered to a Japanese audience in 1978, takes up the concept of game in relation to analytic philosophy (and probably Wittgenstein's influential notion of 'language-games,' although his name is not mentioned) to criticise its employment without an accompanying notion of power. Arnold Davidson (1997b, p. 3) mentions a lecture 'La Philosophie analytique de la politique' in which Foucault (1978) makes an explicit reference to Anglo-American analytic philosophy:

> For Anglo-Saxon analytic philosophy it is a question of making a critical analysis of thought on the basis of the way in which one says things. I think one could imagine, in the same way, a philosophy that would have as its task to analyze what happens every day in relations of power. A philosophy, accordingly, that would bear rather on relations of power than on language games, a philosophy that would bear on all these relations that traverse the social body rather than on the effects of language that traverse and underlie thought (cited in Davidson, 1997b, p. 3).

In the rest of the quotation, Foucault goes on to make a series of implicit criticisms of analytic philosophy in that it refrains from asking questions concerning power relations and how they operate in language. Language in this conception 'never deceives or reveals' rather simply, as Foucault asserts, 'Language, it is played. The importance, therefore, of the notion of game.' Further on he makes the comparison: 'Relations of power, also, they are played; it is these games of power that one must study in terms of tactics and strategy, in terms of order and of chance, in terms of stakes and objective' (cited in Davidson, 1997b, p. 4). As he tried to indicate, discourse considered as speaking, as the employment of words, could be studied as strategies within genuine historical contexts, focusing upon, for example, the history of judicial practices or

> even the discourse of truth, as rhetorical procedures, as ways of conquering, of producing events, of producing decisions, of producing battles, of producing victories. In order to 'rhetoricize' philosophy (cited in Davidson, 1997b, p. 5).

'Games of truth,' as McKerrow (2001) correctly points out, signifies a changed sense of agency on the part of Foucault, who, investigating practices of self, becomes interested in questions of the ethical self-constitution of the subject and self-mastery, especially in his analysis of classical texts. Thus,

> Unlike Habermas who postulates an ideal speech situation wherein games of truth would have the best chance of success, Foucault is a realist . . . Instead of an absolutely free discourse community, the best one can attain is a community in which one commands the requisite rules of procedure, as well as the 'ethics, the ethos, the practice of self, which would allow these games of power to be played with a minimum of domination' (Gauthier, cited in McKerrow, 2001, p. 7).

This is a valuable comment for not only does it point to the idealism of Habermas' quasitranscendentalism but also signals the new possibilities inherent in an 'aesthetics of existence' where the self *learns* the obligations involved in 'care for the self.' This is clearly exemplified in Foucault's analysis of the meanings and practices of *parrhesia*.

PARRHESIA, EDUCATION AND PRACTICES OF TRUTH-TELLING

The Meaning and Evolution of *Parrhesia*

Foucault claims that the word *parrhesia* occurs for the first time in Euripides (c.484–407 BC) and then is used in the Greek world of letters from the end of the fifth century BC. Meaning 'free speech' positions the person who uses *parrhesia* as the one who speaks the truth. Foucault elaborates on how the meaning of the word as it evolves in Greek and Roman culture develops five major characteristics which Foucault summarizes as follows:

> Parrhesia is a kind of verbal activity where the speaker has a specific relation to truth through frankness, a certain relationship to his own life through danger, a certain relation to himself or other people through criticism . . . , and a specific relation to moral law through freedom and duty. More precisely, parrhesia is a verbal activity in which a speaker expresses his personal relationship to truth, and risks his life because he recognizes truth-telling as a duty to improve or help other people (as well as himself). In parrhesia, the speaker uses his freedom and chooses frankness instead of persuasion, truth instead of falsehood or silence, the risk of death instead of life and security, criticism instead of flattery, and moral duty instead of self-interest and moral apathy (Foucault, 2001a, pp. 19–20).

First, it is associated with *frankness: parrhesia* refers to 'a special type of relationship between the speaker and what he says' (Foucualt, 2001a, p. 12). The male pronoun is used here on purpose as the *parrhesiastes* is generally male and must know his own genealogy and status and is usually a male citizen (see Foucault, 2001a, p. 12). Unlike rhetoric, which provides the speaker with technical devices to help him persuade an audience, covering up his own beliefs, in *parrhesia*, the speaker makes it manifestly clear what he believes as he gives his own opinion.

Second, *parrhesia* is linked with *truth*. In the Greek, *parrhesia* is a speech activity where there is an exact coincidence between belief and truth. Foucault claims that 'the "*parrhesiastic* game" presupposes that the *parrhesiastes* is someone who has the moral qualities which are required, first, to know the truth, and secondly, to convey such truth to others' (Foucault, 2001a, p. 14). He points out that the *parrhesiastic* certainty about truth stands in contrast to Descartes' uncertainty about what he believes in before he obtains clear evidence since for the Greek 'truth-having is guaranteed by certain moral qualities' (Foucault, 2001a, p. 15).

Third, the moral courage of the *parrhesiastes* is evidence of his sincerity, for there is a clear risk or *danger* in telling the truth which may or may not be life-threatening. Often the danger is invoked because the *parrhesiatic* relationship is between the speaker and a man of more power and status. The compulsion or duty to sincerely and frankly tell the truth to a superior required moral courage because the *parrhesiastes* risks putting himself in danger and his life at risk for example in challenging a tyrant or a teacher or father.

Fourth, rather than demonstrating truth, the function of *parrhesia* was *criticism*, which could be directed either towards oneself or another. The *parrhesiastes* is someone who has the courage to tell the truth even though he may be putting his life at risk for the truth that the *parrhesiastes* speaks is capable of hurting or angering the interlocutor. *Parrhesia* is thus a form of criticism, directly either towards oneself or another, where the speaker is always in a less powerful position than the interlocutor. The fifth and last characteristic concerns *duty* for in *parrhesia* telling the truth is a duty.

Foucault analyzes the evolution of the *parrhesiastic* game in ancient classical Greek culture (from the fifth century BC) to the beginnings of Christianity in terms of three aspects. The first aspect was *parrhesia*'s opposition to rhetoric. The second was its political role. In the Athenian democracy (from the fourth century BC) *parrhesia* was not only 'an ethical and personal attitude characteristic of the good citizen,' but also a guideline for democracy (Foucault, 2001a, p.22). Subsequently in Hellenistic monarchies it was the sovereign's advisors' duty to help the king make decisions and prevent him from abusing his power. The third aspect was its importance in philosophy 'as an art of life (*techne tou biou*)' as exemplified in the life of Socrates and in 'the care of oneself (*epimeleia heautou*)' (Foucault, 2001a, pp. 23 and 24).

The opposition between *parrhesia* and rhetoric is clear in the Socratic-Platonic tradition (in both the *Gorgias* and the *Phaedrus*) where the difference is spelled out in terms of 'the *logos* which speaks the truth and the *logos* which is not capable of such truth-telling' (p. 6). In politics, *parrhesia* was not only an ethical characteristic of the good citizen but also a guideline for democracy. The Athenian constitution (*politeia*) guaranteed citizens the equal right of speech (*demokratia isegoria*), equal participation in the exercise of power (*isonomia*) and *parrhesia,* as a prerequisite for public speech both between citizens as individuals and as an assembly. With the rise of the Hellenistic monarchies *parrhesia* becomes centred in the relation between the sovereign and his advisors, whose duty it is to help the king in making decisions but also to prevent him from abusing his power.

As an art of life (*techne tou biou*) *parrhesia* is typical of Socrates, although Plato, while using the word several times, never refers to Socrates in the role of the *parrhesiastes.* Socrates, for instance, appears in the *parrhesiastic* role in the *Apology* and *Alcibides Major* where he demonstrates his care for others in their concern for truth and the perfection of their souls. As Foucault comments, 'Philosophical *parrhesia* is thus associated with the theme of the care of oneself (*epimeleia heautou*)' and he suggests that by the time of the Epicureans *parrhesia,* in terms of care of the self, 'was primarily regarded as a *techne* of spiritual guidance for "'the education of the soul'"' (Foucault, 2001a, p. 24). Foucault's friend and colleague at the Collège de France, Pierre Hadot, professor emeritus of the History of Hellenistic and Roman Thought, on whom Foucault relies for so much his interpretation of classical texts in his last years, takes Foucault to task for his reading of the 'care of the self' (see Hadot, 1995; 1997; also Davidson, 1997c).

THE EDUCATIONAL PRACTICES OF SOCRATIC *PARRHESIA*

Thus far, the chapter has followed Foucault's seminars chronologically. Next in order he problematizes some *parrhesiastic* practices in six tragedies of Euripides, *Phoenician*

Women: Hippolytus; The Bacchae; Electra; Ion and *Orestes*. He points out that in the first four plays, rather than being 'an important topic or *motif*' the precise context within which word appears 'aids our understanding of its meaning' whereas in '*Ion* and *Orestes* the notion assumes a very important role' (Foucault, 2001a, p. 27).

He argues that *Ion,* is a play that 'is entirely devoted to *parrhesia* since it pursues the question: 'who has the right, the duty, and the courage to speak the truth' (Foucault, 2001a, p. 27). He noted that in *Orestes,* there was a crisis in the function of *parrhesia* in democracy. Democracy threw up the discrepancy between having the right to speak freely where even bad, ignorant or immoral men had such a right and the ability to speak the truth in a way that benefited the city. Furthermore there was no legal means of protecting the *parrhesiaistes* from potential harm nor of determining who was able to speak the truth and because there also existed negative *parrhesia*—garrulousness and ignorant outspokenness. The first issue involved 'who was entitled to use parrhesia?' (Foucault, 2001a, p.72). The second involved 'the relation of *parrhesia* to *mathesis,* [learning or wisdom] to knowledge and education' because pure frankness or sheer courage had become insufficient as the means of establishing the truth (Foucault, 2001a, p.73). What was now required was a good education, intellectual and moral development and some sort of personal training. For reasons of space we shall not review or comment upon his analysis of *parrhesia* in Euripides or his discussion of '*parrhesia* and the crisis of democratic institutions,' where Foucault analyzes a form of *parrhesia,* as free speech, that may become dangerous for democracy itself. In this respect, Foucault examines an aristocratic lampoon against Athenian democracy attributed to Xenophon, Isocrates' 'On the Peace' and 'Areopagiticus,' and Plato's *Republic.*

In the fifth and sixth seminars Foucault devotes himself to an analysis of the philosophical form of *parrhesia* as *practices* used in specific types of human relationships (specified as Socratic, community life, public life, and personal relationships) and, in the final seminar, as the procedures and techniques employed in these relationships.

In time *parrhesia* shifted from the political domain to the philosophical and to the personal. Socratic *parrhesia* is a new form, different from political *parrhesia,* that began to emerge before Socrates. The new personal form that emerged was one that required education in order to achieve a prominent role in city affairs. Foucault analyzes the dialogue *Laches* ('On Courage') for the instance of *parrhesia* that occurs when two elderly men, Lysimachus and Melesias, express a concern about the kind of education they should give their sons. They are worried for, as they admit publicly, while they were both from noble families and their fathers were illustrious, they themselves achieved nothing special in their time. Clearly belonging to a noble family is not sufficient in itself to achieve a prominent city role. They realize that education is required, but what kind?

Foucault explains, at the end of the fifth century BC, educational techniques revolved around rhetoric (learning to speak before an assembly), various sophistic techniques and sometimes also a form of military training. At this time in Athens, when there was a debate about what constituted a good military education (the Athenian infantry soldiers were inferior to their Spartan counterparts), all the political, social and institutional concerns about education are related to the problem of *parrhesia:* in particular, how to recognize a truth-teller, or as Foucault expresses the issue:

> For if you are not well-educated, then how can you decide what constitutes a good education? And if people are to be educated, they must receive the truth from a competent teacher. But how can we distinguish the good, truth-telling teachers from the bad or inessential ones? (Foucault, 2001a, p. 35).

Lysimachus and Melesias consult Nicias, an experienced general, and Laches, who cannot agree on what constitutes a good education, turn to Socrates. Socrates reminds them that education concerns the care of the soul, and Nicias, in a passage that Foucault quotes from the dialogue, explains why he will play the *parrhesiastic* game with Socrates, allowing himself to be 'tested.' In analyzing Nicias' speech which depicts Socrates as a *parrhesiastes,* Foucault extracts the following characteristics of Socratic *parrhesia.* First, the game requires close proximity between the *parrhesiastes* and the interlocutor; second, it takes place in a personal, face to face context, where the listener is led by the Socratic *logos* into 'giving an account' (*didonai logon*) of himself and the kind of life he has lived. Foucault is at pains to point out that we should not read this through our Christian cultural lens as giving a 'confessional autobiography' or as a narrative of the historical events of your life. Rather, giving an account of one's life or *bios,* is a demonstration of

> whether you are able to show that there is a relation between rational discourse, the logos, you are able to use, and the way you live. Socrates is inquiring into the way the logos that gives form to a person's life; for he is interested in discovering whether there is a harmonic relation between the two (Foucault, 2001a, p. 97).

Foucault explains that Socrates' role is to determine 'the degree of accord between a person's life and its principle of intelligibility or logos' (ibid.), and as a result in such an examination, as Nicias explains,

> one becomes willing to care for the manner in which he lives the rest of his life, wanting now to live in the best possible way; and this willingness takes the form of a zeal to learn and to educate oneself no matter what one's age (Foucault, 2001a, p. 98).

It emerges that why Socrates is considered a good teacher, and why respected older men, citizens of Athens, are willing to submit themselves to Socrates, is the fact there is an ontological harmony between his words (*logoi*) and his deeds (*erga*). Foucault explains that there were four kinds of harmony, which Plato distinguishes as Lydian (too solemn), Phrygian (too tied to the passions), Ionian (too soft and effeminate), Dorian (courageous). The harmony between word and deed in Socrates' life is courageous: unlike the Sophist, Socrates, the *parrhesiastes,* can 'speak freely because what he says accords exactly with what he what he thinks, and what he thinks accords exactly with what he does.'

Foucault compares three contemporary forms of *parrhesia:* the problematization of *parrhesia* in the form of a game between *logos,* truth and *genos* (birth) in relations between the Gods and mortals (as portrayed in Euripides' *Ion*); the problematization of *parrhesia* involved in a game between *logos,* truth and *nomos* (law) in the realm of politics; and, the problematization of *parrhesia* in the game between *logos,* truth and *bios* (life) in the form of a personal teaching relationship. The problem for Plato and Socrates, is how to bring the latter two games into line with one another so that they coincide, i.e., 'How can philosophical truth and moral value relate to the city through the *nomos?'* This is a problem, Foucault tells us, that Plato explores in the *Apology,* the *Crito,* the *Republic* and in the *Laws.* And, indeed, Socrates in the dialogues of *The Last Days of Socrates* exemplifies *parrhesia* in both the political and philosophical domains, as someone who was courageous and willing to tell the truth, risking his life despite facing a death sentence pronounced by the Athenian city fathers. As Foucault comments 'even in the city ruled by good laws there is still a need for someone who will use *parrhesia* to tell the citizens what moral conduct they must observe' (Foucault, 2001a, p.104).

This new kind of philosophical *parrhesia,* which arises in Greco-Roman culture, Foucault characterizes, first, as 'a *practice* which shaped the specific relations that individuals have to themselves' (Foucault, 2001a, p. 106). Much of the philosophy that emerged with Socrates and Plato, and shaped the philosophical tradition that is still ours today and which defines the roots of our moral subjectivity, involved the playing of certain games of truth. The philosophical role involved three types of activity: the philosopher-teacher (our construction) assumed an *epistemic* role insofar as he had to teach certain truths about the world; the philosopher-teacher assumed a *political* role insofar as he took a stand towards the city, its laws and political institutions; and, the philosopher-teacher assumed a *therapeutic* or *spiritual* (our construction) role in that he took responsibility for and clarified the relationship between truth and one's style of life, or 'truth and an ethics and aesthetics of the self' (Foucault, 2001a, p. 106). Second, this new kind of philosophical *parrhesia* is conceived in a personal teaching relationship aimed at convincing someone he must take care of himself and of others, by *changing his life*—a conversion theme important from the fourth century BC to the beginnings of Christianity—rather than aimed at persuading citizens in the Assembly. Third, these new practices 'imply a complex set of connections between self and truth aiming to endow the individual with self-knowledge . . . to grant access to truth and further knowledge' (Foucault, 2001a, p. 107). Fourth, these new philosophical practices were dependent upon a range of techniques different from those developed earlier and linked to rhetoric and persuasive discourse. What is more these practices are no longer linked to the court but can be used in diverse situations.

Foucault goes on to problematize the new practices as they emerged in community and public and personal relationships. Foucault examines *parrhesia* in the community life of the Epicureans, the practice of *parrhesia* in public life through the example of the Cynic philosophers (including, critical preaching, scandalous behaviour and 'provocative dialogue'), and the *parrhesiastic* game in the framework of personal relationships, from examples taken from Plutarch and Galen. Limitations of space do not permit us to review or examine Foucault's analysis of these practices, rather, we comment upon Foucault's examination of the techniques of *parrhesia*, Foucault's concluding remarks, and conclude, by offering some general comments of the importance of Foucault's method and studies for the discipline of education. It is important, however, to note that Foucault, provides a reading of a fragmentary Greek text by Philodemus (with the help of the Italian scholar, Marcello Gigante) which helps him to make some observations about the practice of *parrhesia* in Epicurean community life, and in particular, the important distinction between two categories of teachers and two types of teaching, which 'became a permanent feature of western culture' (Foucault, 2001a, p. 114). As he says: 'With the Epicurean schools, however, there is the pedagogical relation of guidance where the master helps the disciple to discover the truth about himself, but there is now, in addition, a form of 'authoritarian' teaching in a collective relation where someone speaks the truth to a group of others' (Foucault, 2001a, p. 114).

We shall deal in summary fashion with what Foucault calls 'techniques of the *parrhesiastic* games,' where he focuses upon the techniques employed in truth-games 'which can be found in the philosophical and moral literature of the first two centuries of our era' (Foucault, 2001a, p. 142). Foucault's interest in comparing Greek *askesis* and Christian ascetic practices is, of course, to a large extent governed and closely related to his reading of Nietzsche, especially the *Genealogy of Morals*. In the third essay 'What do Ascetic Ideals Mean?,' Nietzsche suggests that (Christian) ascetic ideals arose to give meaning to human suffering, under the perspective of *guilt*—a kind of will to nothingness, injurious to health and life, but, nevertheless a willing. As he says 'man would sooner have the void for his purpose than be void of purpose' (Nietzsche, 1956, p. 299).

These techniques indicate a shift from the classical Greek conception of *parrhesia* where the game was 'constituted by the fact that someone was courageous enough to tell the truth to *other people*' to 'another truth game which now consists in being courageous enough to disclose the truth about *oneself*' (Foucault, 2001a, p. 143 [italics in original]). This new kind of truth game of the self requires *askesis,* which, while the root for 'ascetic,' denotes a kind of practical training or exercise directed at the art of living (*techne tou biou*). The Greek conception of *askesis* differs significantly from Christian ascetic practices in that its goal is 'the establishment of a specific relationship to oneself—a relationship of self possession and self-sovereignty'—rather than the Christian renunciation of the self (Foucault, 2001a, p. 144). That is, the crucial difference consists in the Greek ethical principle of *self-mastery* versus that of Christian *self-renunciation.* Thus in this series of lectures, Foucault continues the arguments he put up in *Technologies of the Self* (1988b) that Christian asceticism involved detachment from the world, whereas Greco-Roman moral practices were concerned with 'endowing the individual with the preparation and the moral equipment that will permit him to fully confront the world in an ethical and rational manner' (Foucault, 2001a, p. 144)—a cry that is taken up by various citizenship education curricula in our contemporary world.

Foucault examines the differences between the practices of these new truth games involving an examination of culture. He refers in turn to Seneca's *De ira* ('On Anger'), Seneca's *De tranquillitate animi* ('On the Tranquillity of the Mind'), and the Discourses of Epictetus, emphasizing that despite the differences these practices share an implied relation between truth and the self very different from what is found in the Christian tradition. These practices he examines exhibit a shift in the relationship between master and disciple as the master no longer discloses the truth about the disciple, but rather the disciple takes on this responsibility as a duty toward himself. It is not enough to say that this personal relation of self-understanding derives from the general principle 'know thyself' (*gnothi seauton*) for the 'relationships which one has to oneself are embedded in very precise techniques which take the form of spiritual exercises—some of them dealing with deeds, others with states of equilibrium of the soul, others with the flow of representations, and so on' (Foucault, 2001a, p. 165). Finally, what is at stake in these practices is not the disclosure of a secret but 'the relation of the self to truth or to some rational principles' (Foucault, 2001a, p. 165). These exercises constitute what Foucault calls an 'aesthetics of the self.'

In his 'Concluding remarks,' Foucault states that 'My intention was not to deal with the problem of truth, but with the problem of truth-teller or truth-telling as an activity.' He expands this idea into the following point:

> What I wanted to analyze was how the truth-teller's role was variously problematized in Greek philosophy. And what I wanted to show you was that Greek philosophy has raised the question of truth from the point of view of the criteria for true statements and sound

reasoning, this same Greek philosophy has also raised the problem of truth from the point of view of truth-telling as an activity (Foucault, 2001a, p. 169).

Truth-telling as a speech activity emerged as a distinct philosophical problem which Socrates pursued in his confrontations with the Sophists in dialogues concerning politics, rhetorics, and ethics. He adds as a further expansion:

> And I would say that the problematization of truth which characterizes both the end of Presocratic philosophy and the beginning of the kind of philosophy which is still ours today, this problematization of truth has two sides, two major aspects. One side is concerned with insuring that the process of reasoning is correct in determining whether a statement is true (or concern [sic] itself with our ability to gain access to the truth). And the other side is concerned with the question: what is the importance for the individual and for the society of telling the truth, of knowing the truth, of having people who tell the truth, as well as knowing how to recognize them (Foucault, 2001a, p. 170).

One side he characterises the great philosophical tradition concerned with how to determine the truth-value of a statement, which he describes as the 'analytics of truth.' The other side, 'concerned with the importance of telling the truth, knowing who is able to tell the truth, knowing why we should tell the truth,' Foucault explains as the roots of the 'critical' tradition in the Western philosophical tradition and he describes his own purpose in the seminars in precisely those terms 'to construct a genealogy of the critical attitude in the [sic] Western philosophy' (Foucault, 2001a, pp. 170–71).

Foucault ends with a note defending his notion of 'problematization' of practices. It is not a form of 'historical idealism,' 'not a way of denying the reality of such phenomena' rather 'The problematization is an 'answer' to a concrete situation which is real.' It is not a 'representation' or 'an effect of a situation,' but rather a creation that explores the relation between thought and reality 'to give an answer—the original, specific, and singular, answer of thought—to a certain situation' (Foucault, 2001a, pp. 171–73).

CONCLUSION: FOUCAULT AND THE PROSPECTS FOR *PARRHESIASTICAL* EDUCATION

What can we conclude from this brief exposition and analysis? We think we can make some quite significant conclusions. First, in the set of lectures entitled 'Discourse and Truth,' delivered at Berkeley a year before his death, we see Foucault at his best, utilising Nietzschean genealogy to problematize the practices of *parrhesia* in classical Greek culture—a set of practices, culturally speaking, that are deepseated for the West. These practices that link truth-telling, on the one hand, and education, on the other, are not only the roots of our present-day cultural practices and conceptions, but they are still operative in shaping our subjectivities and, therefore, also still relevant in understanding the exercise of power and control in contemporary life.

Second, Foucault's problematization of *parrhesia* and especially his investigation of what he calls Socratic *parrhesia*, provides a genealogical analysis which demonstrates the cultural significance of truth-telling as a set of educational practices, strongly wedded to the Socratic beginning of the Western philosophical tradition, and, therefore, also to the West's cultural self-image or self-understanding. Foucault excavates from a variety of sources in classical literature, with the lightness of the palaeontologist's brush, a series of conceptual, historical and practical relations that link education and philosophy through truth-telling. Perhaps, more importantly, he links this *parrhesiastical* form of education to democracy, in a way that turns historical ideals into living practices. There is much more that we could develop from this thought: perhaps, the analysis of the ways in which today our schools, bent on teaching students generic skills as preparation for the knowledge economy, have deviated from our historical models and begun to shed the concern for truth and truth-telling in favour of entrepreneurship.

Third, the six lectures he gives in Berkeley demonstrate Foucault's direct concern for education and educational practices. In these lectures we see the full intellectual weight of Foucault settled on educational issues rather than having to infer, deduce or apply his genealogical insights or methods to education. And in relation to this point, fourth, we might begin to understand, in terms of Foucault's analysis of the human sciences—indeed of his epistemological model for becoming a science—that education has a history and that 'the history of non-formal thought had itself a system' (Foucault, 1973, p. x) capable of revealing a *'positive unconscious* of knowledge' (p. xi) but that it is incapable of becoming a science, as recent national research planning in the US and UK now demand, until it meets the 'objectivity criterion.'

Fifth, we see a very different Foucault in these six lectures than we do in, say, his neo-structuralist period when he was writing *Archaeology of Knowledge* or *The Order of Things*, especially when it comes to truth-telling, for the lectures reveal how Foucault thought that the 'critical' tradition in Western philosophy—the tradition concerned with the importance of telling the truth, rather than truth as the criteria for determining the truth-value of a statement (as we might express it today)— begins precisely at the same time as the 'analytics of truth' with the end of pre-Socratic philosophy and the institutionalisation of philosophy in the Athenian academies. This genealogy of the critical attitude in philosophy is to be traced to the same beginnings that all Western contemporary philosophy is heir to. Foucault's attitude here does not smack of the same antagonism he displayed earlier against analytic philosophy.

Sixth, with his genealogical investigations of the critical attitude in Western philosophy, Foucault delivers us both a fresh reading of the Socratic tradition and the role of education in relation to cultivating practices of truth-telling that subsequently became the basis for the West's cultural and philosophical self-definition. He provides us with the outline of a Nietzschean programme of philosophical research that seeks to question the genealogy of educational ethics. We should remember that Nietzsche, whose *Genealogy of Morals* clearly provides Foucault with a model, also gravitates back to Socrates as an archetype of the philosopher as cultural physician or sets the conditions for culture and the creation of new value. In more concrete terms, in terms of Foucault's Berkeley lectures we might discover anew the continuing relevance of the Socratic tradition. Let us briefly elaborate.

One of the most vexing questions in contemporary philosophy is the question of the relation between the philosopher and his or her work: in more precise terms the possibilities of the genre of philosophical biography. It stands at the door of questions concerning philosophical genres and philosophy as a kind of writing, especially with the emergence of the form of confession as an autobiographical philosophical genre in the work of Augustine and Rousseau, and thus helps to broach a wider set of questions concerning the relation between philosophy and literature that have become a standard reference in the work of thinkers as diverse as Stanley Cavell and Jacques Derrida. As James Conant comments, in contemporary thought we are offered an apparent deadlock:

> we are offered a forced choice between reductivism and compartmentalism—an understanding of an author's work is to be found wholly outside his work (in the external events of his life) or an understanding of the work is to be sought by attending solely to what lies wholly within the work (and the life is held not to be part of the work) (Conant, 2001, p. 19).

The case of Socrates, as the fountainhead of Western philosophy, provides an interesting example precisely because he did not *write* anything. As Conant (2001, pp. 19–20) writes: 'Socrates' life is his work and his work is his life . . . there is no understanding of his philosophy apart from an understanding of the sort of life he sought to live.' And Conant turns to Pierre Hadot, Foucault's colleague at the Collège de France, in order to explain how and why philosophy, during the Hellenistic and Roman eras, was 'a way of life,' where philosophy was a mode of existing-in-the-world and the emphasis fell on the transformation of the individual's life through *philo-sophia* as the love of wisdom. On this conception, one which motivated the late Foucault in his studies of the classical texts, 'a philosopher's life is the definitive expression of his philosophy' (Conant, 2001, p. 21) and his writings are merely the means to facilitate work on the self.

Yet this conception of philosophy as an ethical form of life is not restricted to an understanding of Socrates or to truth-telling practices that invest Socratic *parrhesia*. It can be argued that it is central also to understanding some of the inherited forms of modern philosophy and modern philosophers themselves such as Nietzsche and Wittgenstein (see Peters and Marshall, 1999; Peters, 2000; Peters, 2001c). It may not be too far-fetched to argue that this problematic could act as a framework for entertaining Foucault's own life and philosophy and the question of ethical self-constitution that concerned him late in his life or that it offers great prospects for a rehabilitation of Socratic *parrhesia*—of *parrhesiastical* education—in philosophy of education as a possible innovative research program for a form of applied professional ethics in education.

CHAPTER SIX

Risk AND THE Ethics OF Subjectivity

Parrhesia in Action

INTRODUCTION

Foucault's focus is on questions of subjectivity and the shaping and regulation of identities, on a relational self where intersubjectivity becomes central—a self that acknowledges and is constituted by difference and the Other. This chapter focuses on Foucault's notion of *parrhesia* by providing three examples of *parrhesia* in action in educational contexts.

If, as was discussed in chapter 2, modern technology produces different kinds of subjects—subjects who do not simply objectify and dominate the world through technology, but who are constituted by technology—then modern communication technology is an aspect of globalization that enables youth to construct the self in new ways. Foucault's two notions of technologies of domination and technologies of the self (1988b) can be used as a means for investigation of the constitution of postmodern youth under the impact of globalization.

The first example is an analysis of new kinds of youth who are constituted in response to globalization, the mass media, information technology and consumer society. From being seen as focused predominantly on style and lifestyle, many youth throughout the world became politically radicalised in response to the 2003 war against Iraq. Many such youth were using the Internet not only to find information about the war, but also to communicate with each other. In the UK, in particular, despite the influence of some formal curriculum, for example citizenship education, much of the information, communication and organisation for youth anti-war protests took place outside the classroom and through the Internet and text messaging. An example of this kind of project can be seen in the way in which the Hands Up for Peace campaign, which is detailed later in the chapter, was organised by youth. We argue that teachers now need to pay attention to the ways that youth construct themselves in a globalized postmodern world in relation to the Other, and in response to threats to the security of their world—threats that currently include terrorism and war.

The second example is of a disclosure made within school to a school counselor. This disclosure, which is not at all uncommon, about sexual abuse examines the risks and courage involved for one girl in making such a disclosure and how this example is therefore a form of truth-telling or *parrhesia*.

The third example highlights the risky situation that educational researchers may encounter and the issue of whistle-blowing they may feel duty-bound to undertake.

GLOBALIZATION AND POSTMODERN YOUTH: RISKING POLITICAL IDENTITY

This example poses a set of questions: Does globalization encourage an apolitical apathetic youth that is focused primarily on issues of style and lifestyle in a consumer society? Does it enable a greater understanding and empathy with the Other and in turn more altruistic and politicised constructions of youth? Are youth reactions to the threats of terrorism and war simply youth acting rationally in terms of self-interest, as a means of protecting themselves from the negative consequences of terrorism and war or is this an example of *parrhesia* in action in the modern day context?

Government educational goals for young people often refer to the type of person they are trying to form or construct in terms that are variations on the philosophical theme of a 'good' citizen. In pedagogy, educational policy and cultural and sociological theory the category 'youth' tends to be used as a 'universal.' The totalising effect of this is to negate any sense of difference or of multiple identities that reflect gender, sexuality, ethnicity, culture, class, etc. when talking about youth. Under postmodernity, many of our assumptions and 'truths' about youth that have been theorised within the dominant discourses of psychology and sociology have become outmoded. In fact, discourses 'psychologising adolescence' and 'sociologising youth' have constructed standard, if not, universal models of youth that have become widely used in pedagogical and educational discourses (Besley, 2002a, 2002b, 2006).

New kinds of youth are constituted in response to the impact of globalization, the mass media, information technology and consumer society (Giroux, 1990, 1996, 1998; Luke, 2000; Luke & Luke, 2000). It is also arguable that youth globally have now begun to construct their identities in response to terrorism and the Iraq war. While not wanting to essentialise or universalise, we need to begin to recognise the differences in the way youth constitute their identities in response to both terror and war, whereby there are likely to be markedly different constructions for youth in different Western nations, depending on the official stance taken and information presented in the media, for example, in the USA and UK compared with European, and Australasian youth.

For Muslim youth worldwide, the reactions have been similarly mixed. American and British Muslims have had particularly difficult issues of identity to resolve concerning the forced choice of country versus religion, having to decide which took precedence in their understanding of personal identity. Many Muslims saw the Iraq conflict as a continuation of the centuries old crusades and wars between Christians and Muslims, of Westerners invading, not liberating an Arab country and were consequently encouraged to believe that this was jihad, a holy war. Some took it much further, as evidenced by the London terrorist bombings in July 2006, perpetrated by four British Muslim young men from middle class families who had been persuaded to join militant groups, becoming suicide bombers. On the other hand, many more moderate Muslim youth abhorred the outwelling of violence in the name of Islam, emphasising that Islam is a peaceful religion and rejecting fundamentalist forms of Islam. Many Muslims were outraged at the cultural inappropriateness of male soldiers frisking female civilians after US troops were killed by two women suicide bombers in Iraq. Yet, even the opinions of Iraqi exiles about the war were contradictory, some horrified at the invasion of their country, while others welcomed the overthrow of Saddam Hussein, a brutal dictator.

Apart from locational and cultural differences, gender differences seem to also come into play, for example, in the UK many of the youth protests were led by young women (e.g., Hands Up For Peace & Scottish youth antiwar protests, as evidenced on the BBC programme, *Frontline Scotland,* 6 May 2003). By contrast, some boys became very hawkish, gung-ho and excited by a 'real' war happening rather than simply a video-game, impressed by the 'shock and awe' of the munitions used. They related very positively to seeing men in combat action on TV in ways that contributed to their construction of what it is to be a man. This conveniently ignored the fact that the US armed forces actually include some women, who were seldom shown on TV except the likes of 19-year-old Private Jessica Lynch who was luckily rescued by gallant Special Forces. The media did not focus to such an extent on any rescue of male soldiers, in the process, unthinkingly reinforcing traditional notions of women being weak and inept enough to get caught and needing to be rescued by men who put their lives at risk. Moreover, for those closely associated on each side with the tragedies and traumas of terror and war be they victims or soldiers and their families (many soldiers are teenagers, from age 18 upwards), constructions of identity will obviously differ. Consequently, pedagogies that deal with difference and identities are required in schools, not some blanket one-sided approach.

Globalization tends to destabilize local ethnic identity at the same time as it accelerates cultural contact, intermarriage and the development of hybridised multicultural ethnic communities (Besley, 2003a). With the emergence of new cultural hybridities many youth identify themselves as cultural or ethnic blends having multiple identities, of being part of and between many different worlds where they navigate a sea of texts where each attempts to position and define them as they construct their identities (Luke, 2000). Such 'texts' include written, aural and visual technologies, all of which produce our culture(s). More than simply texts, these are extratextual, multiple technologies that youth learn to use and negotiate and even to create as they have done with developing text messaging (texting). In terms of global identities, the UK Qualifications Curriculum Authority (QCA) website on "Respect for all: valuing diversity and challenging racism through the curriculum" provides both some general guidance and specific ways for teachers to use appropriate resources, presenting a broad and balanced view of cultures, challenging assumptions, understanding globalization and creating an open climate in the classroom. However, it is somewhat alarming that the emphasis should be *in* the classroom for this seems to ignore ways of dealing with such issues beyond the classroom, surely one of the important goals of education for diversity and living in a multiethnic society where cultures influence each other. It notes that "the emphasis is a somewhat anthropological stance, on the Other *within* the UK—on minorities themselves with limited engagement of situations *beyond* the UK" (http://www.qca.org.uk/ca/inclusion/respect_for_all/guidelines.asp, accessed 6 April 2003). Simply opting for a broad and balanced view of cultures that challenges assumptions does not sufficiently acknowledge the dominant culture and its generally Anglo-centric viewpoint

New information and communication technologies emphasise individualism since using a computer or mobile phone is overall a solitary activity that does not generally require the presence of another (e.g., using an iPod, playing a computer game, writing an e-mail, or text message does not require the presence of another at the other end as does a phone call or a conversation). 'Texting' is a new form of communication that youth (rather than adults) particularly favor, becoming almost a new language in itself with new signs and codes. Global telecommunications technologies are simultaneously technologies of sign, of domination and of the self—clearly interlinked, overlapping and reinforcing each other as Foucault (1988b) pointed out in 1982 prior to the advent of such new mass technologies. New technologies are encouraging engagement with consumer culture and the uptake of new and the latest 'cool' brands as youth construct the self in the marketplace—maybe buying online e.g., through Amazon or E-Bay. Yet as well as having solitary aspects, these same global technologies enable communication (e.g., through chat rooms, discussion boards, text messaging, blogs) with others throughout the world and the development of virtual communities (e.g., Myspace.com). In virtual communities, which are by their very nature 'disembodied,' identity is by no means straightforward. Those occupying such space are freed from constraints of the body—one's, age, gender, sexuality, ethnicity, interests and abilities, so they can create and present multiple virtual identities if they wish. Whereas in the physical, embodied world we can readily ascertain various signs and cues to another's identity and display signs to identify ourselves, in virtual communities, consisting of information or content rather than matter, the 'truth' of who we are can easily be masked and deceptions can occur. In worst case scenarios, criminal intent involving grooming young people to then meet a person and engage in sexual activity, sexual abuse, kidnapping or worse may be involved. However virtual identity cues emerge via certain styles of e-mail address, signature and subcultural forms of language used by personas within the community. Such new literacies are certainly not taught in schools, but are vital if young and vulnerable people are not to be deceived in such online sites.

Such new technologies also create both a sense of alienation and of boredom with schools and teachers who can no longer compete with such 'exciting' technologies (Giroux, 1990). Many youth get online without learning what are seen as 'the basics' (reading, writing & arithmetic). Contrary to developmental stage/readiness hierarchies that many educators seem to recommend, the critical literacies they now need involve new forms of analysis of the world that enable them to navigate and critique online texts and their relations with extratextual practices.

In the postmodern, globalised era, as the market logic penetrates the social fabric ever more deeply, youth have become consummate consumers in a culture of consumption (Baudrillard, 1998; Corrigan, 1997; Jameson, 1983; Ritzer, 1998). Style and identity have become inextricably mixed and hybridised such that youth self-constitution is played out in terms of international global styles that are clearly influenced by the logics of fashion, advertising, music, the cult of celebrity, video games and the plethora of multimedia sites. Such hybridisation involves negotiating both the local and the global that intrude, impose and are interconnected spatially, temporally and culturally—assembling identities in the global marketplace on the basis of one's local cultural predispositions. Hence, postmodern theorising has emphasized dual cultural processes of constructing youth identities first, through the global marketplace as an aspect of the culture of advanced consumerism and second, through the agency of youth themselves. 'Youth' is highlighted as a socio-cultural construction based on concepts of style, and lifestyle, reflecting Foucault's notion of the 'aesthetics of existence' and of making one's life a work of art. This has potential to become a new sociology of youth that emphasizes an aesthetics of self and questions of self-stylisation that follows both Nietzsche and Marx (Besley, 2003a; Best & Kellner, 2003; Foucault, 1990). A sociology based on an aesthetics of existence has conceptual strengths that help to unpick and unpack processes of what might be called a 'consumption of the self'—that is, patterns of self-constitution in consumer culture centred on 'investments' in the self at important points in one's lifetime. This is what we call the new prudentialism a concept that elucidates an actuarial rationality determining points, patterns and levels of self-investment (see chapter 8). At the same time it is not clear how much such a new sociology can interpret recent anti-war protest and struggles by youth in both Western and non-Western contexts. Clearly a principle of political agency and self-constitution—maybe even political self-education—is required to analyse recent protests by youth.

The atrocities of 9/11 shook up a somewhat complacent Western world such that subsequently many young people became fearful of the possibilities of future terrorism—something new for most Western youth, albeit not for many other young people elsewhere in the world. In response to threats of terrorism and the 2003 Iraq war, throughout the world many youth have proven themselves to be concerned about much more than just style and lifestyle choices. In the UK they have become markedly and even radically politicised, as young Zoe Pilcher noticed:

> It is now normal for me to overhear 14-year-olds discussing the pros and cons of military intervention, on the bus on the way home from school. Badges carrying anti-war slogans, such as "Not In My Name" are appearing on the lapels of school blazers and ties. It is common to turn on the television and see students under the age of 18 defying their teachers, waving banners and megaphones, and protesting in Parliament Square. . . . (http:// argument.independent.co.uk/low_res/story.jsp?story=389745&host=6&dir=140, Zoe Pilger, Generation Apathy has Woken Up, *The Independent*, 23 March 2003).

As 2002 proceeded, once war with Iraq became a possibility and then a probability, many commentators and youth alike, worried that such a war would potentially create hundreds of new terrorists from among the ranks of angry, disaffected, politicised, radicalised, fundamentalist Islamist Arab youth. Others worried at the shift in geopolitics and the changing balances of power and about the UN possibly becoming irrelevant. For various reasons, many people, including youth, oppose war as a solution to the world's problems.

On 15 February 2003, with the Iraq war imminent, there were large antiwar demonstrations throughout the world. In the UK, huge demonstrations were held in many cities and thousands of British school students joined approximately 800,000 in Glasgow on February 15 and 1 million on London in antiwar protests prior to the war. In Glasgow the Scottish Coalition for Justice Not War, which included trade unions, the Muslim Association of Britain, and Scottish Campaign Against Nuclear Disarmament, organised a protest that marched through the centre of town to the Scottish Exhibition and Conference Centre where the Labour Party's annual conference was being held. As part of a comparative international research project, a team led by Catherine Eschle and Wolfgang Rüdig from University of Strathclyde, Glasgow, conducted a survey at the 15 February protest that involved the distribution of postal questionnaires during the march plus over 400 face-to-face interviews both before and after the march. Their preliminary analysis of these interviews revealed that the majority of protesters came from similar political and social groupings to those on other peace marches; from a mainly secular, highly educated and professional background. The Scottish Muslim community was strongly represented. Conservative voters, manual workers and those with little formal education were largely absent. What was particularly noticeable was the number of young people (22% were 17–24) including school students who were demonstrating—a much higher proportion compared with the Scottish Census. Clearly the Iraq war had mobilised young adults (http://www.strath.ac.uk /government/awp/demo.html).

One example is The Hands Up For Peace campaign which was 'designed, funded and implemented entirely by young people to demonstrate their opposition to an unjust war in Iraq' and provides one example of a protest initiative taken by school children in the UK (http://www.messengers.org.uk). From their inner-city London comprehensive school common room, a group of students with coursework requirements, GCSE and A-Level exams looming asked, 'If two middle aged men can start a world war how many young people would it take to stop it?' They argued, 'it's not just exams that will determine our future, it's the decisions made by Bush and Blair. As young people we know that we are to inherit a future shaped by our leaders. We know that unless we stop this coming war, the blood that is spilled will be left on our hands' (http://www.messengers.org.uk). Significantly, they painted their banner on the school stage without the knowledge of teachers, and harnessed the technology of the Internet (e-mails, website, Hotmail account) amongst other means (an assembly, leaflets, badges and posters) to gain widespread UK and global support from other youth, therefore it seems appropriately respectful to give these young people their own voice about what they did and the instructions they provided so others could contribute. From the photos, it appears that most of the participants were girls. This extract displays that they not only had considerable empathy for others and obviously concern for themselves and the world to come, but also a high degree of technological literacy. They had become politicised sufficiently to take action without recourse to teachers—an example of political self-education that, considering they were a group of students, could even be considered to be group self-education that in effect constituted new identities for the participants.

Other young people left school during the day to attend antiwar marches, which, in some instances, were instigated by them (e.g., in Edinburgh on March 19 school children staged street-theatre of a mass 'die-in'; and likewise in London). Press releases from the StopWar organisation website provided evidence of hundreds of school students in antiwar protests (see Press Release, March 5 2003, http://www.stopwar.org.uk/release). Once war broke out there were further protests:

> School students disrupted many city centres, stopping traffic. Four thousand school students massed in Parliament Square in London. In Liverpool, police were called to remove protesters including many school children who blocked the Mersey tunnel. Many hundreds of schools were affected across the UK (press release 20 March, http://www.stopwar.org.uk/release).

In an article entitled, "Voices of tomorrow don't wait to protest," Geraldine Bedell, wrote in *The Observer,* 23 March 2003:

> On the balmy early spring afternoon the day after the war started, more than 500 children massed on the lawns of their school in south London. They had permission to go home half an hour early, but had chosen to stay and wave placards, listen to speeches and read the poems they had written for peace.

> The protest was indicative of the impact the war has had already on a generation commonly deemed benignly apathetic about politics. Representatives of every year at Graveney School, a large comprehensive in Tooting with no previous history of political activism, addressed the crowd in speeches of an impressively high quality. They ranged over the Palestinian question, the role of the International Court of Justice, analyses of contemporary imperialism, and, from a Muslim girl, an explanation of the misconceptions of the Islamic idea of jihad. . . . (http://education.guardian.co.uk/Print/0,3858,4631332,00.html *The Observer,* 23 March 2003)

Despite the influence of some formal curriculum lessons, much of the information, communication and organisation would have taken place outside the classroom and through the Internet and text messaging as for example with the Hands Up For Peace campaign. Many teachers were alarmed to find that youthful students took their citizenship lessons and civic responsibilities seriously enough to take action in protest against the Iraq war. Many teachers and adults were worried at the rapid wildfire-like spread of school student protest action. Not surprisingly considering the conservatism of some teachers who do not see youth as being media-savvy or mature enough to have informed opinions, as being unduly swayed by propaganda from antiwar groups and who think that the classroom-based education they provide is the be-all-end-all of life, they were considered truant by teaching authorities and teacher unions. Dea Birkett pointed out in *The Guardian*, Tuesday March 25, 2003,

> The recent child-led anti-war demonstrations throughout the country have been condemned by teaching unions and the police, with some schools arguing that the curriculum provides appropriate channels for children to express their beliefs without leaving school: "Treat it as normal truancy and take appropriate action," said the Secondary Heads Association" (http://education.guardian.co.uk/Print/0,3858,4632153,00.html).

For example, sixteen-year-old sixth-former, Sachin Sharma was suspended from Prince Henry's Grammar School, Otley for urging pupils to walk out in protest over war in Iraq, pointedly noting that 'the majority of our school does not have democratic rights. They have no means to express themselves, and they don't have a voice in real terms. The only way we can, as minors, express ourselves is through demonstration' (http://education.guardian.co.uk/Print/0,3858,4632153,00.html, Dea Birkett, 'It's their war too,' *The Guardian*, 25 March 2003).

A representative of the Educational Institute of Scotland (a teacher's union, see: http://www.eis.org.uk/latest.htm) appeared on TV suggesting that parents should be jailed for letting their children truant (something that had happened to a solo-mother in Oxford, England, in 2002 whose child was a persistent truant). Such comment was in marked contrast to reaction from East Dumbartonshire Council, Scotland, that permitted its workers time off to protest (ironically schools come under the control of such local authority councils in both the UK and Scotland, which has a separate education system). The significance of being suspended for what some schools constructed as encouraging other students to 'truant' was in stark contrast to how the pupils conceived of their action to promote peace not war. The attitude of some schools to current pressing issues of our world does not show great moral leadership. If we are societies that actually value peace we need to encourage youth to critically engage with media that includes the messages that politicians and their spin doctors are trying to make the public believe.

Ironically, it was because youth had been perceived as disaffected and politically apathetic, that government and schools had introduced citizenship curricula (and modern studies in Scotland) partly designed to engage them in the political process, but when they actually take a political stand, youth are generally condemned—a Catch-22 situation. It seems that many schools are only interested in their young people *talking* about, but not acting upon such issues and curricula.

There were some general warnings about terrorist threats with particular concern about the vulnerability of London and the Tube (which subsequently came horribly true in July 2006). Prior to war and in response to terrorism warnings, some people stocked up with water and other essential foods, but there seemed to be nothing on the scale of fear that the media had promulgated in the USA during February 2003 when various supplies (e.g., duct tape) became scarce. The pedagogic response to the war varied throughout the UK and Scotland. Geraldine Bedell, in *The Observer*, 23 March 2003 posed a pertinent question, 'While thousands of teenagers march against the war, others fear Saddam is about to bombard them with nerve gas. Amid all the division and confusion, what do parents and teachers tell a generation brought up on computer battle games?' (http://education.guardian.co.uk/Print/0,3858,4631332,00.html). Whether or not schools should encourage pupils to form and express their own political views and if the current curriculum allowed for this became key questions that schools answered very differently. Some schools focused on a standard curriculum, largely ignoring the war. In contrast, other schools made space available for discussion trying at the same time to avoid scaring students who were understandably afraid of the consequences of war and of potential terrorism. In London, for example Alfred Salter School often started the day with 'Metro time'—a half-hour when children picked out news stories from a free paper and discussed the issues raised, e.g., the UN and its future role; comparing America and Saddam Hussein as bullies (http://education.guardian.co.uk/Print/0,3858,4632153,00.html).

Prior to hostilities beginning, the National Union of Teachers urged schools to be ready to deal with any increase in bullying and racism, especially anti-Semitism and Islamophobia as a result of the Iraq war, pointing out that such issues can be addressed through the new citizenship curriculum, which requires students to be taught about national and religious identities and social justice, which provides an opportunity to discuss the war (see: http://www.nut.org.uk/). However, once war began one of the consequences was the development of virulent anti-Americanism in the Middle East even in moderate Muslim states friendly to the USA (e.g., Morocco and Egypt) and in Europe amidst fears that hundreds of fundamentalist Islamic youth have been radicalised and are likely to become terrorists in the future (see BBC1, Panorama, *'The Race to Baghdad'* 6/04/2003: http://news.bbc.co.uk/nol/shared/spl/hi/programmes/panorama/transcripts/racetobaghdad.txt). Furthermore, some considering the multicultural nature of many UK schools (e.g., in London about 30% of the population is considered 'ethnic,' i.e., people of colour &/non-British—see *The Observer Review*, 6 April 2003: 5) classes will have students with family and friends engaged in the hostilities on both the British side and the Iraqi side, or who are Islamic. So ways of dealing with such differing ideas, values and emotions need to be found.

Schools must be relevant to the outside world and engage students in issues that affect them and which they care about—so when the major issues are war and terrorism understandably there are innumerable questions such as: Why war? Why now? How else could we do things? How is this liberation when it is an invasion? The USA calls this war 'Operation Iraqi Freedom' but why did no one ask the Iraqi people if bombing was the price they were prepared to pay for liberation from Saddam? What is the difference between guerrilla warfare, terrorism and suicide bombing? What is a just and moral war and an illegal one? Is this about oil and unfinished Bush family politics? Does Iraq still have weapons of mass destruction? How can we understand competing patriotisms and nationalism? Who should manage the peace? Which component of our identity and values (if any) takes priority—being British, Christian, Islamic, Jewish, atheist, Iraqi, Pakistani, Scots, European, male, female, black, white, Asian? Is it incumbent upon Western liberal democracies to tell the people the truth? Etc.

Pedagogies that study difference, cultural identity and citizenship have contributed to the radicalisation of youth and to how youth construct their identities to a certain extent, but cannot take full credit. With many youth having computers at home now and with the huge uptake of mobile phones and text messaging as the latest communication trend among youth, students learn (with or without the help of schools) to negotiate and use new ICT technologies and develop new literacies of text messaging and the Internet. They use these mediums for much more than chat and arranging social events, to access information about the issues and questions about war within or outside the classroom (Lankshear & Knobel, 2003). While many youth are media savvy, well aware of the ways and ruses the media target markets them and able to construct understandings of the world that acknowledge power relations and possible exploitation, others especially poorer students who are less likely to have home computers remain on the wrong side of the digital divide. Many years ago, Marshall McLuhan argued that the information level was higher outside the classroom than inside it. Considering the current age of technological sophistication of many youth McLuhan's thesis could be added to in a variety of ways. Not only is the level or amount of information higher, it is also more diverse, more open to indoctrination without the authority of the teacher, and comprised of multiple sources of differing quality. Certainly, traditional news broadcast media provide a technological transmission that cannot be easily equalled in the classroom. Access to information is also higher outside the classroom for some groups especially if there is access to home computers. Also access to information is self-governed by youth rather than controlled (unless parents chose to censor it through various means) hence the new media and ICT tends to decentre the authority of the teacher.

The curriculum in some UK schools (and certain teachers) especially via subjects such as media studies, citizenship, history, liberal studies, etc., can be given credit for teaching students to 'know' about and empathise with different cultures and identities, to analyse texts, to be concerned about values such as tolerance, peace and cooperation. Citizenship education is a government priority in the whole of the UK. The Qualifications Curriculum Authority (QCA), which is the official curriculum organisation for UK (except Scotland), issued 'General guidance for teachers: Respect for all: valuing diversity and challenging racism through the curriculum' (http://www.qca.org.uk/ca/inclusion/respect_for_all/guidelines.asp).

In Scotland a paper by Learning and Teaching Scotland, 'Education for Citizenship in Scotland' forms the basis for a national framework for education for citizenship from age 3 to 18 (see http://www.ltscotland.com/citizenship/). The aim is

> to teach pupils respect for self and one another and their interdependence with other members of their neighbourhood and society and to teach them the duties and responsibilities of citizenship in a democratic society . . . to work towards a more inclusive society where inequities are addressed effectively and cultural and community diversity is celebrated. Ways and means are being sought to tackle disaffection and disengagement from society and, more broadly, to address issues of social injustice and of personal identity (http://www.ltscotland.com/citizenship/).

Unlike the QCA's document, the Scottish one does not mention racism, but neither specify peace or war, instead the documents, especially the Scottish one, are couched in very general terms (full critique is beyond the scope of this paper). Other official organisations provide further curriculum assistance, e.g., Development Education Association (DEA) e-noticeboard on the War in Iraq provides some web Resources for UK schools (http://www.dea.org.uk).

Furthermore many students have developed literacies, critical thinking skills and reasoning that enable them to analyse and decode the whole gamut of advertising, PR, spin and propaganda of politicians, military spokespersons and a plethora of commentators in the 2003 Iraq war. Students have learned how to decipher the multiple meanings of current politico-war language: e.g., collateral damage, benign invasion, regime change, friendly bombs, cluster bombs, daisy cutters, shock and awe, precision guided munitions, surgical strikes, mouse-holing, friendly fire, and illegal combatants, etc. Once schools teach students to resolve conflict and bullying through negotiation or mediation rather than fighting and violence, many see this as preferable a way of addressing international crises. Unsurprisingly when US foreign policy under the Bush regime shifted to the notion of 'pre-emptive strike' and military action, many youth saw this as an aggressive action akin to bullying. This became increasingly apparent since Iraq clearly had far more limited military technology than either the USA or Britain. The incongruency between what is taught in schools and the behavior that the adults who hold powerful political leadership positions display in relation to other countries was not lost on many students.

The newly politicised youth generation in the UK have become acutely aware of geopolitics and the new world order. Unlike the Cold War days, with its nuclear threat and notion of maintaining a balance of power between the USA and USSR, the world is, arguably, now unipolar, with the USA's immense military, technological and economic power leaving it as the only superpower that furthermore is now dominant in popular culture. Not only has English become the lingua franca, but *American* English is increasingly gaining supremacy. Altogether this constitutes an American hegemony that is hard to resist, despite being much resented, especially when President Bush simplistically asserts that people/countries are either with us or against us. There is increasing worry that after this current war, we face a series of wars maybe for decades against states that threaten our security—Syria, Iran and North Korea have already been mentioned by Bush and Rumsfeld as part of an 'axis of evil.' Some worry that rather than the Iraq war making the world safer as Bush and Blair maintain, quite the reverse will happen, especially considering the anger that has been generated within the Arab world and the continued problems between Israel and the Palestinians.

Schools and teachers now need to pay more attention to the ways that youth construct themselves rather than to the traditional academic discourses which retain 'truths' that are becoming increasingly challenged and outdated (Besley, 2002c). In the globalised postmodern world, through tapping into ICT and new associated literacies, many youth are now producing the self through constructing identities that address the Other. These include understandings of difference in culture, power, politics, gender, class, values and ideals—identities that are relational, at the same time as they are individual at a particular historical moment. As the historico-cultural context changes so to are their constructions of identity likely to change. Youth actions especially in response to the Iraq war indicate an example of choice-making in producing the self through the moral choices—a relational self where intersubjectivity has become central, a self that acknowledges and is constituted by difference and the Other. Therefore Foucault's notion of technologies of the self becomes central in ethically constituting the self in relation to the Other as the production of selves/identities is constructed through the social apparatus where clearly the curriculum and ICT technologies play a part.

Arguably many of the youth who protested the Iraq war were involved in a form of *parrhesia* because their actions clearly involved the five criteria of frankness, truth, danger, criticism and duty—in telling the truth to someone of a higher status. In the process, many students exposed themselves to considerable risk—risk of punishment that included suspension from school for some. Foucault demonstrated that *parrhesia* links truth-telling and education in ways that are still operative in shaping our contemporary subjectivities, thus they are relevant in understanding the exercise of power and control and of contemporary citizenship especially in situations where there is some risk for a person in telling the truth to a superior—a situation that clearly can occur in schools, in the student-teacher relationship and which certainly occurred for some youth in their antiwar activities in 2003.

THE DANGERS OF DISCLOSING SEXUAL ABUSE IN SCHOOL

> There's a widespread notion that children are open, that the truth about their inner selves just seeps out of them. That's all wrong. No one is more covert than a child, and no one has greater cause to be that way. It's a response to a world that's always using a tin-opener on them to see what they have inside, just in case it ought to be replaced with a more useful type of tinned foodstuff (Høeg, P, 1993: 44).

This example uses one teenager's story to examine the potential risk for students in disclosing sexual abuse to school counselors. It is argued that this sort of disclosure is a form of *parrhesia* since there is considerable risk associated with the compulsion many young people have to tell the truth about themselves. It harnesses the narrative of Fay (not her real name)—a 13-year-old Pacific Island girl (to preserve anonymity and confidentiality, her actual ethnicity is deliberately obscured by the use of general terminology, 'Pacific Island') in a class at a multicultural, co-educational high school in a large New Zealand city. The example briefly describes salient aspects of the story Fay disclosed of sexual abuse by her stepfather, and the counselor's reflections on the actions taken to explore some of the dilemmas that arise for the young person when they disclose sexual abuse. The focus is on the ethics and the politics of telling and the impact on the young person who has been abused: Why tell? Who to tell? When to tell? Does age of the child affect this? What are the ramifications of telling? It invokes a *'meta-telling'* in the form of a narrative (or case study) that is in effect a further telling of the story for professional purposes.

Despite assurances of confidentiality, once the authorities are told many people end up knowing and although school and social work policies may set out procedures, a rigid application of these can result in further harm and risk for the young person. While not dismissing the effects of the abuse on the whole family system, this example is premised in the understanding that the child is the central figure, and that a genuinely child-centred approach is needed to prevent re-victimising the child by the very procedures that are designed for protection, help and healing.

Many societies and the professionals who might have challenged the existence of sexual abuse of children and youth have responded with denial, silence and repression. Freud initially revealed and subsequently denied that many of his female patients had faced unwanted sexual experience or sexual abuse (Masson, 1989). Because his theory was unacceptable and was consequently rejected by profession-al colleagues at the time, Freud recanted, replacing it with a theory that seduction experiences described were expressions of children's sexual fantasies rather than real-ity, an Oedipus complex. Perhaps if he and others had felt free enough or had the courage to act as *parrhesiastics*, they would have spoken freely and told the unpalat-able truth about what they found so that sexual abuse would have begun to be addressed much earlier.

In Western societies, the veil of silence was only lifted with the rise of femi-nism in the 1970s when the stories that women began relating during consciousness-raising sessions started revealing abuse that had happened to them as children (see Bagley & King, 1990; Bass & Davis, 1988; Doyle, 1990). In the light of subsequent research, feminists argue that sexual abuse is a function of the inferior status of women and children and of male socialisation within patriarchal social structures. In the family the perverse exercise of patriarchal power over females and children results in the high level of sexual violence and abuse practised by fathers, male kin and kin substitutes with having a stepfather more than doubling the risk of a girl's being sexually abused (Brownmiller, 1976; de Francis 1969; de Young, 1982; Finkelhor, 1984; Gruber & Jones, 1983; Herman & Hirschman, 1977; Jacobs, 1984; Nelson, 1982; Parks, 1990; Rush, 1980; Russell, 1983; Ward, 1984). A pre-ponderance of personal accounts, case studies and ethnographic literature of the sto-ries of people who have been sexually abused as children show many commonalties that underline a number of important findings in the professional literature (Bagley & King, 1990; Bass & Davis, 1988; Doyle, 1990). These include a difficulty in telling that involves complex feelings of fear, shame, ignorance, loss of self-esteem and indi-cate that better and earlier education could help children avoid and resist sexual attacks. Sexual abuse can have different and contrary impacts on victims whereby some may act out sexually while others withdraw to protect or disguise the tortured centre of self. Consequent feelings of helplessness, moral defeat and confusion in human relationships and in sexuality can often brand victims as easy prey for future predators. In sum, the abuse disrupts or destroys childhood, diminishes adolescence and can devastate adult mental health and one's sense of self and identity.

Fay's Narrative

Fay was the child from her mother's previous relationship and lived with her European stepfather and several younger step-siblings. All the children were born in New Zealand. Fay's mother and grandparents had immigrated from a Pacific Island where traditional values predominated and extended families lived together, but in New Zealand the grandparents lived separately but nearby. Fay accepted Western values more so than her mother and grandparents yet treated her European step-father as any male in a traditional, patriarchal, Pacific Island family, as 'head' of the house whose word was law, as sanctioned by both cultural and religious norms, even though the family was not church-going.

Following a class lesson about sexual abuse taken by the counselor, Fay tearfully disclosed that in the past her stepfather had abused her in her bedroom once mother had gone to work at night. She emphasized that it had now finished, but had started when she was 10 years old and was absolutely terrified about anyone, especially her family being told. She became angry, threatening to deny everything, to pretending that she had made it up and take whatever punishment (probably a 'hiding'—a beating) came her way if the authorities were informed without her consent. Her worst fear was that this would break up the family, something for which she didn't want to be held responsible. She worked out very quickly what she would lose. Her mother would be furious with her for breaking up her marriage; her siblings would hate her for causing their father to leave; the family would be shamed in front of other friends and relatives and all of them would suffer financially. This was a massive burden for any thirteen-year-old girl to bear.

The first concern was for her immediate safety, if the abuse was continuing. The second was that the younger children might be in danger. If the counselor did not believe that she was telling the truth, there would clearly be a case of serious and immediate danger to herself and others, consequently the counselor's ethical and legal responsibility would be to act in the interests of child safety and protection by informing the authorities, overriding any concerns about breaching confidentiality (see *NZAC Handbook*, 1995 & 2000 for the then Code of Ethics). The child protection agency was the New Zealand Children and Young Person's Service (CYPS as it was then known) as legally set out in the Children, Young Persons & their Families Act (1989) and its amendments of 1995. These outlined how child abuse was to be reported and placed child protection duties on the Department of Social Welfare which was responsible for the care and protection of children and young people and ensuring that their welfare and interests were paramount.

If Fay was telling the truth and the abuse was actually in the past, the counselor did not need to inform CYPS because there was no mandatory reporting of past sexual abuse in New Zealand. Following considerable public debate the New Zealand government had opted to emphasise education and voluntary reporting rather than mandatory reporting and so *Breaking the Cycle: an Interagency Guide to Child Abuse* was published along with a set of National Interagency Protocols (NZCYPS, 1995; 1996; see Besley, 2003c). The school's policy covered different procedures to follow in situations of *past* and of *current* abuse that were consistent with the law and with procedures of a sexual abuse counseling service.

Because the counselor felt reasonably reassured that the abuse was in the past, she agreed to not tell immediately, but to work things through with her about how this would be done later. Nevertheless it was made clear that before long both the authorities and her mother would need to be told because as a young person she was still under her mother's care and responsibility. Furthermore, the counselor pointed out that it was important that her stepfather was called to account and that some appropriate therapy could be provided for the family—something beyond the brief of a school counselor and something that the authorities could fund and provide. She thought this would be okay in the future once she'd got her head around it. After a few weeks, Fay agreed for the counselor to inform CYPS at the same time as she told her mother because she reasoned that she knew how best to handle her mother. Fay and her family were subjected to the formal processes of CYPS and made an evidential video (see New Zealand Children & Young Persons Service, 1995 & 1996). She reported that her mother was furious, but she was believed and luckily the younger siblings had not been abused. The stepfather pleaded guilty in court but was not imprisoned. He was removed from the family home, ordered to undergo sexual abuse counseling and through a legal protection order, was forbidden from contact with Fay. Fay and her mother were entitled to individual and joint sexual abuse counseling at a specialist agency funded by the state's Accident Compensation Commission (ACC). However, two months later they expressed dissatisfaction with this counseling and stopped attending. They seemed to shift blame from the threat within the family to the counseling agency, which they saw as a powerful external threat to the stability and security of the family. Fay opted to return to counseling at school without the family knowing, but because the school counselor was not a specialist sexual abuse counselor nor registered with ACC, it was arranged for Fay to attend specialist counseling outside school fortnightly for the next year. Both Fay and this counselor chose to keep the school counselor informed as the person on the spot at school if any problems arose.

However, not only was the stepfather formally removed from the family, but also, following an informal family agreement, Fay was removed. The legal protection order required that the stepfather must not come into contact with Fay, yet legally he could not be denied seeing the younger children for whom family visits were important. To comply with the court order and enable his visits to the family Fay was sent to live with her mother's parents, ostensibly to look after them and to concentrate more on her schoolwork. This was the official, face-saving story the family told relatives and friends. The younger children were not told the truth because they were considered to be too young to understand the unpleasant reality that their father had been convicted of sexual abuse. Therefore they believed that Fay had done something wrong and was the cause of their father's leaving them, so they questioned her about this. She discussed this painful situation in counseling but was adamant that it was best to collude with the fabrication, continuing to sacrifice herself for the greater good of the family. She worried about how they would react when they eventually learned the truth about their father and about growing up with a lie. In effect she had 'lost' her immediate family and had little contact with her siblings or with her mother, with whom things remained tense. Fay had become a scapegoat, but said she was prepared take it in her stride because she was relieved that the abuse had stopped and would not happen again.

A year later when the temporary legal protection order was due to become permanent, Fay came under another round of intense family pressure. She wanted the order continued and was adamant about continuing counseling despite opposition from the extended family who thought she should be over it by then. The lawyer assigned by the Court (known as 'counsel for child') was vehemently supportive of her wishes and rights to both legal protection and counseling. The pressure subsided after the lawyer spoke with the adult family members about how they had tended even inadvertently to blame Fay. Two years later at her fortnightly counseling sessions Fay reported that she'd been helped to deal with her continued feelings of anger towards her stepfather and her mother, of guilt, of worthlessness and not deserving better in relationships. Her relationship with her mother had become more difficult because she sensed her mother saw her as a 'Lolita.' Furthermore Fay resented her mother's strong and largely continuing tie with the stepfather and so did not feel she was properly supported. These barriers may well have diminished with some joint therapy but neither agreed to this.

We argue that this sort of disclosure *is* a form of *parrhesia* because it clearly involved the five criteria of frankness, truth, danger, criticism and duty—in telling the truth to someone of a higher status—the school counselor. It is a form of personal *parrhesia* that focused on the self and the where the young person displayed courage in disclosing the truth about herself and her family. In the process, the student exposed herself to considerable risk—to being interviewed and questioned by family and friends and a whole range of professionals: counselors, CYPS social workers, lawyers, police, the judge in Court; to repeatedly telling her story (and the untrue official family one); to not being believed by others; to change or even lose family relationships; to financial loss; to experiencing a whole range of negative emotions; to being an object of curiosity and possibly fun, ridicule and shame if peers worked out what was going on and so on. It is not surprising that several times Fay wished she'd never told. To a certain extent it was directed at the art of living (*techne tou biou*)—at making living with an unpalatable truth more comfortable—yet the result was certainly not entirely satisfactory for the girl. She certainly gave an account of herself and her situation in a personal, face-to-face context. Although Foucault warned that such an account was not to be confused with a confessional autobiography or narrative of the historical events of one's life, this sort of disclosure is much more than simply an autobiography for it required frank speech, truth-telling, courage to face a whole range of probable risks and potential personal danger as well as a sense of duty or compulsion to do so, since the stepfather's abuse was an anathema to her. It may well be that the subsequent development of Christian notions of confession—something that he explored in *Technologies of the Self* (Foucault, 1988b) were partly derived from the personal and autobiographical forms of *parrhesia*. Nevertheless, it is clear that education can indeed be a risky business, so no wonder young people are wary about telling the truth about themselves and being opened up like a can as Peter Høeg points out in the opening quote.

WHISTLE-BLOWING AND THE ETHICAL CONSTITUTION OF EDUCATIONAL RESEARCHERS

In the late 20th century, neoliberal, managerialist notions of accountability, professionalization and effectiveness have led to the development of ethical codes—a form of applied professional ethics that provides pragmatic, regulatory guidelines for individual action and standards of practice that reflect societal and organizational belief systems. Such codes enable a profession to gain status, power, and public credibility. They usually involve both practical or mandatory ethics (behavior that must be complied with to ensure safe practice, to avoid censure, malpractice, or conflicts of interest and often complaints or disciplinary procedure) and sometimes philosophical or aspirational ethics. Yet being an ethical educational researcher goes beyond simply adherence to ethical codes. If an educational researcher stumbles upon serious misconduct he/she may feel a duty to inform relevant authorities, in effect becoming a whistle-blower—a truth-telling practice which is an example of what Foucault problematizes as *parrhesia* or free speech. Such an action may well be personally and professionally transformative. In reflecting on their research and its impact on both their subjects and on themselves, researchers are involved in truth-telling practices that constitute the self and which may involve 'confession' of the self and self-regulation, as Michel Foucault's work on subjectivity discusses (Foucault, 1977, 1980a, 1986, 1988b).

Truth telling pervades our institutions: friendship (we rely on our friends to tell us the truth); journalism (the highest standards are those to do with accuracy and reliability of reported information); and education (the pedagogical relationship insofar as it involves the transmission of knowledge is also dependent on truth). Scientific research is based around truth criteria (rules of evidence) for testing the veracity of claims and theories. Truth also figures as a set of social conventions (obligations) that govern the behaviour of the researcher both in her relationship to her subjects and to members of the scientific community, e.g., in their commitment to the pursuit of truth, Hammersley (1990) argues that researchers should open their work to academic scrutiny so that judgements can be made about the validity of findings and errors detected.

Clearly, the four questions of *parrhesia*, *prima facie*, would seem to have a ready application to educational research and might even serve as a general heuristic for emphasising the development of a critical attitude in becoming an educational researcher. First, *who is able to tell the truth?* This question has a range of possible applications concerning not only the educational researcher but also the subjects of research. There is an important power/knowledge asymmetry that we must recognise between the researcher and the researched. Despite the recent attention to the 'voice' of the researched, especially in forms of qualitative, participatory and empowering research, the editorial decisions of whose voices are represented and to what extent, whatever the professed aims of research, are predominantly still made by the researcher. Thus, the question of *who* is able to tell the truth has a double aspect; first in relation to the communicative relationship between the researched and the researcher (what the researched decides to tell or confide in the researcher); second, how the researcher represents this information and how she editorialises, selects, highlights and presents as 'data.' This is further complicated by the fact that the former relationship (i.e., between researcher and researched) is private and often confidential, anonymous and 'protected' in some sense, while the relationship of the researcher's report, study or findings are generally public. So there is an important and often unacknowledged public/private dynamic in research that invests epistemological concerns with issues power.

About what? Again there are decisions to be made, choices on both sides of the research divide, even with the most democratic forms of inquiry. What truths can be told and what withheld? Of course, this question presupposes that the truth are 'all on the surface' waiting to be identified, rather than deep, implicit, disguised, hidden or manufactured. For example, in the controversy over Margaret Mead's ethnographic research about growing up in Samoa it has been claimed that her informants simply made up the stories they thought that Mead wanted to hear. There is a great deal more to be said about this feature of *parrhesia* as it applies to educational research including all the techniques and methods researchers use to shape their problems and the responses/answers they receive.

With what consequences? Here attention is drawn to the effects of research as a form of truth-telling not only on the researcher and the researched but also on the research community, the institutions that are involved and in some cases the wider public. These truth-telling effects may of course be positive or negative; they may be beneficial or harmful for the parties involved and when we come to the final item of the quartet *with what relation to power?* Clearly, power relations are involved with each of the three dimensions above.

It needs to be noted that in problematizing *parrhesia* that Foucault is using a dynamic concept in describing and analysing a set of cultural practices that have shifted over time. Foucault demonstrates this by reference to the shifting histori-cal nature of the concept with Euripides, what he calls Socratic *parrhesia* evident in the Platonic dialogues, and later Christian confessional practices, although he specifically warned that the Socratic *logos* 'giving an account of your life or *bios*' was not a 'confessional autobiography' or narrative of the historical events of your life. Rather, it was used 'to demonstrate whether you are able to show that there is a rela-tion between rational discourse, the logos, you are able to use, and the way you live' (Foucault, 2001a, p. 97). What is important here is that we might learn from him even if there is not an exact correspondence between historical forms of *parrhesia* and current practices of educational research. Insofar as educational research con-cerns practices of truth-telling we can utilise Foucault's analysis to provide some insights into the power/knowledge relations that constitute educational research as a form of truth-telling.

It is to the five components of the *parrhesiastic* relationship as it would apply in the ethical self-constitution of educational researchers that our attention now turns: frankness, truth, danger, criticism and duty. The centrality of truth in rela-tion to the self is developed through using 'others' as an audience—intimate or pub-lic—in a form of performance that allows for the politics of confession and (auto)biography.

In performing *parrhesia* an educational researcher might become what we commonly call a whistle-blower—a person from within an organization who reveals information to prevent or stop what he/she believes to be some practice that is sig-nificantly wrong within that organization (McNamee, 2001). On the one hand, such an expression of dissent and accusation of wrong-doing can be seen as a challenge to authority and even perhaps, of being disloyal to the organization. On the other hand, it may be seen as an act that requires considerable moral courage and personal risk or danger in telling some unpleasant or unpalatable truth, in effect, it requires *parrhesia*.

Mike McNamee (2001) examines and critiques the five conditions or justifications in the standard theory of whistle-blowing as outlined by Davis (1996). The first condition is that the policy or product of the organization to which the potential whistle-blower belongs, would seriously harm the public. The second requires that the whistle-blower reports the threat of harm to an immediate superior, but concludes that no effective action will be taken. The third requires that all (or as many) other internal procedures within an organization must be exhausted, 'as the danger to others and her own safety make reasonable' (p.431). For Davis, the fourth and fifth conditions are obligatory. Fourth, the whistle-blower has (or has accessible) evidence that 'would convince a reasonable, impartial observer that her view of the threat is correct' and fifth, he/she 'has good reason to believe that revealing the threat will (probably) prevent the harm at reasonable cost (all things being considered)' (p. 431).

If the first three of these conditions are satisfied, then whistle-blowing is morally justified according to the standard theory. Davis's position emphasizes using internal procedures within an organization before invoking external measures such as public exposure. Yet as McNamee points out 'the very mechanisms and ethos of the institution may well display sexist, racist or other unethical dimensions which might lead a reasonable person to conclude that the internal mechanisms (or lack of them) are themselves part of the problem' (McNamee, 2002, p. 431). McNamee rejects Davis's fourth criteria as a 'throw-back to a naïve view of science and a rationalist conception of ethics' where the impartial observer is therefore a 'non-starter' for today's understanding of research. He also rejects as even more problematic the 'consequentialist calculation of costs and benefits' in Davis's fifth criteria, arguing that the utilitarian notion of weighing costs and benefits runs counter the meaning of the very notion of moral obligation to treat people respectfully and to not be harmed (p. 431).

What sorts of things might compel an educational researcher to invoke *parrhesia?* The most obvious would occur if children inadvertently disclose criminal activity by themselves, their peers or their family members—such things as: fraud, theft, embezzlement; benefit fraud; child abuse—physical and sexual; neglect; drug use/dealing; prostitution; pornography; intent or actual harm of others, even murder, etc. In considering that such discoveries are outside the boundaries of the research, rather than disclosing them, a researcher may decide to turn a blind-eye—in effect colluding or lying by omission, especially if the illegal activity was judged to be relatively minor. On the other hand, if the discovery was of serious misconduct and harm to others, surely the only responsible course of action would be to disclose it.

While using *parrhesia* as a whistle-blower is unlikely to endanger an educational researcher's life in Western countries today, it is certainly a highly risky activity for the researcher. It may mean that he/she falls foul of the educational establishment—either the institution being researched and/or the body funding the research, and/or the researcher's employer. In an era when educational institutions are particularly concerned about how the public views them, publication of unpalatable criticism and truths may be vehemently rejected. It may mean that the researcher is unable to obtain further research contracts if his/her criticism is seen as uncomfortably critical by such authorities and in turn, he/she may be informally blacklisted, and thereby prevented from earning an income from educational research.

McNamee (2001) points out the deontological and consequentialist moral ambiguities in whistle-blowing theory and poses a scenario that explores the complexities involved in deciding what action to take, considering that harm may occur to innocent parties—we suggest calling this 'collateral damage.' While applying the guidelines of a code of ethics or of practice may eliminate the worst excesses of professional misconduct by educational researchers, it is not enough. Acting in the best interests of the greater good may mean harming certain innocent individuals so some degree of weighing the potential damage for all concerned is needed. The researcher must take into account the particular circumstances that are involved and seek to minimize harm to all parties concerned. It may even be that doing nothing is not simply turning a blind-eye to protect one's own interests, but something that takes courage. However, as McNamee (2001, p. 439) warns, 'if you want to do educational ethnography and/or action research in educational contexts, you must first decide how you will cope with dirty hands. You may sometimes have to blow the whistle.'

Foucault's discussion of the care of the self, whereby truth-telling and confession form only a part, provides a philosophical approach that offers educational researchers a very useful theory of power and also a Kantian-like basis for ethics based upon the way in which choices we make under certain conditions create who we become. Foucault's main aspects of the self's relationship to itself point to various ways that people can ethically constitute themselves (ethical self-constitution) by ethical work that a person performs on their self with the aim of becoming an ethical subject; the way in which individuals relate to moral obligations and rules; and the type of person one aims to become in behaving ethically. One element that might be derived from Foucault is the importance of 'writing' and 'reading' the self alongside conversational or dialogical forms and 'talking' or confessing the self as an educational researcher reflects on his/her professional work. Therefore becoming an ethical educational researcher goes beyond the protocols of codes of ethics, requiring truth-telling practices and personal and professional integrity such that it can constitute and possibly transform the researcher's professional and personal self.

PART FOUR

Governmentality— Governing THE Self

CHAPTER SEVEN

Understanding THE Neoliberal Paradigm OF Education Policy

The political, ethical, social, philosophical problem of our days is not to liberate the individual from the State and its institutions, but to liberate ourselves from the State and the type of individualisation linked to it.

FOUCAULT, 'THE SUBJECT AND POWER'

Power is exercised only over free subjects, and only insofar as they are free.

FOUCAULT, 'THE SUBJECT AND POWER'

INTRODUCTION

In his governmentality studies in the late 1970s, Foucault held a course at the Collège de France on the major forms of neoliberalism, examining the three theoretical schools of German ordoliberalism, the Austrian school characterised by Hayek, and American neoliberalism in the form of the Chicago School. Among Foucault's great insights in his work on governmentality was the critical link he observed in liberalism between the governance of the self and government of the state—understood as the exercise of political sovereignty over a territory and its population. He focused on government as a set of *practices* legitimated by specific rationalities and saw that these three schools of contemporary economic liberalism focused on the question of too much government—a permanent critique of the state that Foucault considers as a set of techniques for governing the self through the market. Liberal modes of governing, Foucault tells us, are distinguished in general by the ways in which they utilise the capacities of free acting subjects and, consequently, modes of government differ according to the value and definition accorded the concept of freedom. These different *mentalities* of rule, thus, turn on whether freedom is seen as a natural attribute as with the philosophers of the Scottish Enlightenment, a product of rational choice making, or, as with Hayek, a civilizational artefact theorised as both negative and antinaturalist.

Foucault's account of German *ordoliberalism*, is a configuration based on the theoretical configuration of economics and law developed at the University of Freiberg by W. Eucken and F. Böhm that views the market contingently as developing historically within a judicial-legal framework. The economy is thus based on a concept of the Rule of Law, anchored in a notion of individual rights, property rights and contractual freedom that constitutes, in effect, an economic constitution. German neoliberal economists (Müller-Armack, Röpke, Rüstow) invented the term 'social market economy' which shared certain features with the Freiburg model of law and economics but also differed from it in terms of the 'ethics' of the market (as did Hayek in *The Constitution of Liberty*). This formulation of the 'social market economy' proved significant not only in terms of the postwar reconstruction of the (West) German economy but through Erhard, as Minister and Chancellor, became important as the basis of the EEC's and, later, EU's "social model."

The object in this chapter is to understand the neoliberal paradigm of education policy and our approach to this question is premised on Michel Foucault's lectures on the notion of governmentality and recent work undertaken by neo-Foucauldians. By neo-Foucauldian we refer mainly to the British and Australian neo-Foucauldians (for example, Gordon, 1991; Burchell, 1993; Rose, 1993), as distinct from both the French and U.S. neo-Foucauldians, and as exemplified in a recent edited collection called *Foucault and Political Reason* (Barry et al., 1996).[1] This approach centers on Foucault's concept of governmentality as a means of mapping the 'history of the present' and understands the rationality of government as both permitting and requiring the practice of freedom of its subjects. In other words, government in this sense only becomes possible at the point at which policing and administration stops; at the point at which the relations between government and self-government coincide and coalesce. As Barry and his colleagues argue, in this sense, the emphasis is centered upon 'the extent to which freedom has become, in our so-called free societies, a resource for, and not merely a hindrance to, government' (Barry et al., 1996, p. 8).

This perspective is taken for several reasons. First, a neo-Foucauldian approach to the sociology of governance avoids interpreting liberalism as an ideology, political philosophy, or an economic theory and reconfigures it as a form of governmentality with an emphasis on the question of *how* power is exercised. Second, such an approach makes central the notion of the *self-limiting state* which, in contrast to the administrative (or police) state, brings together in productive ways questions of ethics and technique, through the responsibilization of moral agents and the active reconstruction of the relation between government and self-government. Third, it proposes an investigation of neoliberalism as an intensification of an economy of moral regulation first developed by liberals, and not merely or primarily as a political reaction to big government or the so-called bureaucratic welfare state of the postwar Keynesian settlement. Indeed, some who adopt this approach see welfarism as an aberrant episode that has little to do with liberalism per se. Fourth, the approach enables an understanding of the distinctive features of neoliberalism. It understands neoliberalism in terms of its replacement of the natural and spontaneous order characteristic of Hayekian liberalism with '*artificially* arranged or contrived forms of the free, *entrepreneurial*, and *competitive* conduct of economic-rational individuals' (Burchell, 1996, p. 23). And, further, it understands neoliberalism through the development of '*a new relation between expertise and politics*,' especially in the realm of welfare, where an actuarial rationality and new forms of prudentialism manifest and constitute themselves discursively in the language of 'purchaser-provider,' audit, performance, and 'risk management.'

Foucault's overriding interest was not in 'knowledge as ideology,' as Marxists would have it, where bourgeois knowledge, say, modern liberal economics was seen as false knowledge or bad science. Nor was he interested in 'knowledge as theory' as classical liberalism has constructed disinterested knowledge, based on inherited distinctions from the Greeks, including Platonic epistemology and endorsed by the Kantian separation of schema/content that distinguishes the analytic enterprise. Rather Foucault examined *practices* of knowledge produced through the relations of power.[2] He examined how these practices, then, were used to augment and refine the efficacy and instrumentality of power in its exercise over both individuals and populations, and also in large measure helped to shape the constitution of subjectivity.

Fundamental to his governmentality studies was the understanding that Western society professed to be based on principles of liberty and the Rule of Law and said to derive the legitimation of the State from political philosophies that elucidated these very principles. Yet as a matter of historical fact, Western society employed technologies of power that operated on forms of disciplinary order or were based on biopolitical techniques that bypassed the law and its freedoms altogether. As Colin Gordon (2001, p. xxvi) puts it so starkly, Foucault embraced Nietzsche as the thinker 'who transforms Western philosophy by rejecting its founding disjunction of power and knowledge as myth.' By this he means that the rationalities of Western politics, from the time of the Greeks, had incorporated techniques of power specific to Western practices of government, first, in the expert knowledges of the Greek tyrant and, second, in the concept of pastoral power that characterized ecclesiastical government.

It is in this vein that Foucault examines government as a practice and problematic that first emerges in the sixteenth century and is characterized by the insertion of economy into political practice. Foucault (2001b, p. 201) explores the problem of government as it 'explodes in the sixteenth century' after the collapse of feudalism and the establishment of new territorial States. Government emerges at this time as a general problem dispersed across quite different questions: Foucault mentions specifically the Stoic revival that focused on the government of oneself; the government of souls elaborated in Catholic and Protestant pastoral doctrine; the government of children and the problematic of pedagogy; and, last but not least, the government of the State by the prince. Through the reception of Machiavelli's *The Prince* in the sixteenth century and its rediscovery in the nineteenth century, there emerges a literature that sought to replace the power of the prince with the art of government understood in terms of the government of the family, based on the central concept of 'economy.' The introduction of economy into political practice is for Foucault the essential issue in the establishment of the art of government. As he points out, the problem is still posed for Rousseau, in the mid-18th century, in the same terms—the government of the State is modelled on the management by the head of the family over his family, household and its assets.[3]

It is in the late sixteenth century, then, that the art of government receives its first formulation as 'reason of state' that emphasizes a specific rationality intrinsic to the nature of the state, based on principles no longer philosophical and transcendent, or theological and divine, but rather centred on the *problem of population*. This became a science of government conceived of outside the juridical framework of sovereignty characteristic of the feudal territory and firmly focused on the problem of population based on the modern concept which enabled 'the creation of new orders of knowledge, new objects of intervention, new forms of subjectivity and. . . . new state forms' (Curtis, 2002, p. 2). It is this political-statistical concept of population that provided the means by which the government of the state came to involve individualization and totalization, and, thus, married Christian pastoral care with sovereign political authority. The new rationality of 'reason of state' focused on the couplet *population-wealth* as an object of rule, providing conditions for the emergence of political economy as a form of analysis. Foucault investigated the techniques of police science and a new bio-politics which tends to treat the 'population' as a mass of living and co-existing beings, which evidence biological traits and particular kinds of pathologies and which, in consequence, give rise to specific knowledges and techniques (Foucault 1989, p. 106, cited in Curtis, 2002).

As Foucault (2001b) comments in 'The Political Technology of Individuals,' the 'rise and development of our modern political rationality' as 'reason of state,' that is, as a specific rationality intrinsic to the state, is formulated through 'a new relation between politics as a practice and as knowledge' (p. 407), involving specific political knowledge or 'political arithmetic' (statistics); 'new relationships between politics and history,' such that political knowledge helped to strengthen the state and at the same time ushered in an era of politics based on 'an irreducible multiplicity of states struggling and competing in a limited history' (p. 409); and, finally, a new relationship between the individual and the state, where 'the individual becomes pertinent for the state insofar as he can do something for the strength of the state' (p. 409). In analysing the works of von Justi, Foucault infers that the true object of the police becomes, at the end of the eighteenth century, the population; or, in other words, the state has essentially to take care of men as a population. It wields its power over living beings, and its politics, therefore has to be a biopolitics (p. 416).

Foucault's lectures on governmentality were first delivered in a course he gave at the Collège de France, entitled *Sécurité, Territoire, Population,* during the 1977–78 academic year. While the essays 'Governmentality' and 'Questions of Method' were published in 1978 and 1980, respectively, and translated into English in the collection *The Foucault Effect: Studies in Governmentality* (Burchell et al., 1991), it is only in 2004 that the course itself has been transcribed from original tapes and published for the first time (Foucault, 2004a), along with the sequel *Naissance de la biopolitique: Cours au Collège de France, 1978–1979* (Foucault, 2004b), although both books remain to be translated.[4] The governmentality literature in English, roughly speaking, dates from the 1991 collection and has now grown quite substantially (see, for example, Miller and Rose, 1990; Barry et al., 1996; Dean, 1999; Rose, 1999).[5] As a number of scholars have pointed out Foucault relied on a group of researchers to help him in his endeavours: François Ewald, Pasquale Pasquino, Daniel Defert, Giovanna Procacci, Jacques Donzelot, on governmentality; François Ewald, Catherine Mevel, Éliane Allo, Nathanie Coppinger and Pasquale Pasquino, François Delaporte and Anne-Marie Moulin, on the birth of biopolitics. These researchers working with Foucault in the late 1970s constitute the first generation of governmentality studies scholars and many have gone on to publish significant works too numerous to list here. In the field of education as yet not a great deal has focused specifically on governmentality.[6]

Gordon (2001, p. xxiii) indicates three shifts that took place in Foucault's thinking: a shift from a focus on 'specialized practices and knowledges of the individual person' 'to the exercise of political sovereignty exercised by the state over an entire population'; the study of government as a *practice* informed and enabled by a specific rationality or succession of different rationalities; and, the understanding that liberalism, by contrast with socialism, possessed a distinctive concept and rationale for the activity of governing. Liberalism and neoliberalism, then, for Foucault represented distinctive innovations in the history of governmental rationality. In his governmentality studies Foucault focused on the introduction of economy into the practice of politics and in a turn to the contemporary scene studied two examples: German liberalism during the period 1948–62, with an emphasis on the Ordoliberalism of the Freiburg School, and American neoliberalism of the Chicago School. The section on Foucault's reading of German neoliberalism and the emergence of the 'social market' has significance not only for understanding the historical development of an economic constitution and formulation of 'social policy' (and the role of education policy within it), but also for the development of the European social model, more generally, and the continued relevance for Third Way politics of the 'social market economy.'

First, this chapter sets the scene with a brief review of Foucault's notion of 'governmentality' and the critical Kantian tradition, second, it looks at three versions of neoliberalism, third it details the elements of neoliberal governmentality, fourth, it analyses Foucault's account of German neoliberalism and the birth of biopolitics; fiinally it ends with a brief look at a set of historical relationships between American neoliberalism, the Chicago School and human capital theory.

FOUCAULT, GOVERNMENTALITY AND THE CRITICAL (KANTIAN) TRADITION

Foucault (1991a) coins the term 'governmentality' (government rationality) to mean *mentalities of rule* and, historically, to signal the emergence of a distinctive mentality of rule that he alleged became the basis for modern liberal politics. He begins to examine the problematic of government by analysing the *series: security, population, government,* maintaining that there is an explosion of interest on the 'art of government' in the sixteenth century which is motivated by diverse questions: the government of oneself (personal conduct); the government of souls (pastoral doctrine); the government of children (problematic of pedagogy) (Foucault, 1991a).

He maintains that there was an explosion of interest in the 'art of government' in the in the late sixteenth and early seventeenth centuries that crystallises for the first time around the notion of 'reason of state,' understood in a positive sense:

the state is governed according to rational principles which are intrinsic to it and which cannot be derived solely from natural or divine laws or the principles of wisdom and prudence;
the state, like nature, has its own proper form of government, albeit of a different sort
(Foucault, 1991a, p. 97).

By the term 'governmentality' Foucault means three things:

1. The ensemble formed by the institutions, procedures, analyses, and reflec-
    tions; the calculations and tactics that allow the exercise of this very spe-
    cific, albeit complex, form of power, which has as its principal form of
    knowledge political economy and as its essential technical means appara-
    tuses of security.
2. The tendency which, over a long period and throughout the West, has
    steadily led toward the pre-eminence of this type of power that may be
    called government over all other forms (sovereignty, discipline, etc.) result-
    ing, on the one hand, in the formation of a whole series of specific govern-
    mental apparatuses, and, on the other, in the development of a whole
    complex of *savoirs*.
3. The process, or rather the result of the process, through which the state of
    justice of the Middle Ages, transformed into the administrative state dur-
    ing the fifteenth and sixteenth centuries, gradually became 'governmental-
    ized.' (Foucault, 1991a, pp. 102–3)

In elaborating these themes Foucault emphasizes not only *pluralized* forms of government but also its *complexity* and its *techniques*. Our modernity, he says, is characterized by the governmentalization of the state. He is interested in the question
of *how* power is exercised. In outlining the three aspects of governmentality he is
implicitly providing a critique of the contemporary tendencies to overvalue the problem of the state and to reduce it to a unity or singularity based on a certain
functionality.

> At the intersection of two competing tendencies—state centralization and a logic of disper-
> sion—the problematic of government can be located; a problematic that poses questions of
> the *how* of government and seeks 'to articulate a kind of rationality which was intrinsic to
> the art of government without subordinating it to the problematic of the prince and of his
> relationship to the principality of which he is lord and master' (Foucault, 1991a, p. 89).

In charting this establishment of the art of government, Foucault thus identifies the introduction of 'economy'—that is, 'the correct manner of managing goods
and wealth within the family'—into political practice as the essential aspect of the
establishment of the art of government in the sixteenth century (see Foucault,
1991a, p. 92). This usage of political economy remained stable into the eighteenth

century; it signified 'wise government of the family for the common welfare of all,' although the word no longer stood for a form of government but rather designated a field of intervention (p. 92).

In line with this analysis, Foucault, defines governmentality in terms of a specific form of government power based upon the 'science' of political economy (see Redman, 1997), which, over a long period, he maintains has transformed the administrative state into one fully governmentalized, and led to both the formation of governmental apparatuses and knowledges or *savoirs*. The rejection of state-centred analyses—has emerged from the governmentality literature as it has become a more explicit problematic.

By understanding mentalities of rule in the genealogical sense in which it was intended (see O'Malley, 1998), we are less to likely to develop a highly rationalised account of neoliberalism based upon a set of abstract characteristics producing 'ideal knowledges'—a kind of rationalisation trap that Boris Frankel (1997) argues that the Anglo-Foucauldians have fallen into in marking out the second order construct of 'advanced liberalism.' We turn to Foucault to indicate how he fits into the *critical* tradition of Kant with its accent on the history of systems of thought[7] and to indicate briefly why we think this approach is important to understanding both the neoliberal paradigm of education and social policy (Peters, 2001), and the new forms of prudentialism it has encouraged, along side the 'responsibilization of the self'—turning individuals into moral agents and the promotion of new relations between government and self-government, as a basis of an individualised 'social insurance' and risk management programme.

One thing that follows from defining Foucault as part of the critical tradition is that we can get some purchase on his theoretical innovations: his impulse to historicize questions of ontology and subjectivity (against the abstract category of the Cartesian-Kantian subject) by inserting them into systems or structures of thought/discourse. Thus governmentality is developed and played out against these tendencies.

Burchell indicates that Foucault's account of classical liberalism occupies a position in relation to a set of discourses about government, which has its beginnings both in the 'reason of state' (*ragione di stato*) literature of the later-Italian Renaissance, and in the emergence of the 'science of police' (*polizeiwissenschaft*) in seventeenth-century Germany (Burchell, 1997, p. 375). He goes on to argue:

> It is here, Foucault argues, that the modern art of governmental reasoning emerges, out of a series of doctrines which insist that the exercise of state authority has its own distinctive form of internal political reason (reason of state), and that this reason can be turned into a kind of science (police) (Burchell, 1997, p. 375).

Burchell indicates the way in which liberalism on Foucault's accounts stands in ambiguous relation to this literature and tradition; it is both heir and critique.

Here the notion of 'economy' enters into political science in two ways: it speaks of a form government, informed by the precepts of political economy, on the one hand, and, on the other, of a government concerned to economise its own efforts and costs, where government has become its own problem. It is in the latter sense, established as a distinctively modern form or style of government by Adam Smith that we can speak properly of the *critique of state reason.*

From the mid 1970s through to the early 1980s Foucault shifts his understanding of power relations, under the influence of an interpretation of Friedrich Nietzsche's will-to-power (and, perhaps also Wittgenstein's notion of language-games)[8], to view power relations in terms of *strategic games* between liberties. As he says:

> It seems to me we must distinguish between power relations understood as strategic games between liberties—in which some try to control the conduct of others, who in turn try to avoid allowing their conduct to be controlled or try to control the conduct of others—and the states of domination that people ordinarily call 'power.' And between the two, between games of power and states of domination, you have technologies of government ... (Foucault, 1997, p. 300).

Foucault, in *historized* Kantian terms, speaks of governmentality as implying the relationship of the self to itself (and to others), referring explicitly to the problem of *ethical self-constitution and regulation.* Governmentality is thus defined as the set of practices and strategies that individuals in their freedom use in controlling or governing themselves and others. Such an analytics of power bypasses the subject of law, or the legal concept of the subject, that is demanded by an analysis of power based upon the institution of political society. Foucault's point is that if you can conceive of the subject only as a subject of law, that is, as one that either has rights or not, then it is difficult to bring out the freedom of the subject and ethical self-constitution in games of freedom. In Foucault's account the relationship of the self to the self is a possible point of resistance to political power, and it is the historic role of critical philosophy to call into question all forms of domination and (deriving from the Socratic injunction) to 'Make freedom your foundation, through mastery of yourself.' 'The task according to Foucault,' write the editors of *Foucault and Political Reason* (Barry et al., 1996, p. 8), 'was not to denounce the idea of liberty as a fiction, but to analyse the conditions within which the practice of freedom has been possible.'

On this basis we accept the theoretical promise of the problematic made explicit by the so-called Anglo-Foucauldians. Let us quickly summarise: first, a neo-Foucauldian approach to the sociology of governance avoids interpreting liberalism as an ideology, political philosophy or an economic theory to reconfigure it as a form of governmentality with an emphasis on the question of *how* power is exercised.

Second, such an approach makes central the notion of the self-limiting state, which in contrast to the administrative (or 'police') state, brings together in a productive way questions of ethics and technique, through the 'responsibilization' of moral agents and the active reconstruction of the relation between government and self-government. Third, it proposes an investigation of neoliberalism as an intensification of an economy of moral regulation first developed by liberals and not merely or primarily as a political reaction to 'big government' or the so-called bureaucratic welfare state of the postwar Keynesian settlement. Indeed, as Andrew Barry and his fellow editors (1996) point out, some who adopt this approach the era of postwar welfarism as an aberrant episode that has little to do with liberalism *per se*. Fourth, the approach enables an understanding of the distinctive features of neoliberalism. It understands neoliberalism in terms of its replacement of the natural and spontaneous order characteristic of Hayekian liberalism with '*artificially* arranged or contrived forms of the free, *entrepreneurial* and *competitive* conduct of economic-rational individuals' (Burchell, 1996, p. 23). And, further, it understands neoliberalism through the development of '*a new relation between expertise and politics*' (ibid.), especially in the realm of welfare, where an actuarial rationality and new forms of prudentialism manifest and constitute themselves discursively in the language of 'purchaser-provider,' audit, performance, and 'risk management' (O'Malley, 1996).[9]

THREE VERSIONS OF NEOLIBERALISM

Colin Gordon (1993) traces three versions of neoliberalism that were given some attention by Foucault in his course of lectures at the Collège de France during 1979, not coincidentally, also the date of the election of Margaret Thatcher to power in Britain. Foucault mentioned the versions of neoliberalism that took root in postwar West Germany (*Ordoliberalen*) under the government of Helmet Schmidt, the United States (where economics was dominated by the Chicago School) and Valéry Gisgard d'Estaing's France. Gordon suggests that three ideas come together in this lecture course:

> First, Focuault shifts the focus of his own work from specialized practices and knowledges of the individual person, such as psychiatry, medicine, and punishment, to the exercise of political sovereignty by the state over an entire population. Second, he addresses government itself as a practice—or succession of practices—animated, justified, and enabled by a specific rationality (or, rather, by a succession of different rationalities). In the context of modern Europe, this leads him to particularly attentive analyses of liberalism and neoliberalism. Lastly, he advises his audience that socialism lacks a distinctive concept and rationale for the

activity of governing, a fact that places it at a damaging disadvantage in confronting its contemporary adversary (Gordon, 2001, p. xxiii).

These new forms of governance identified by Foucault do not represent an innocent return to liberalism's main articles of faith. In other words, the historical revival of liberalism in the present is not simply an exercise in nostalgia that represents a simple and naive return to past principles. There are major differences between past and present forms of liberalism. Neoliberalism, in other words, displays an innovative interpretative strategy in restyling basic principles to accommodate new exigencies. What they have in common, as Burchell (1993, p. 270) claims, 'is a question concerning the extent to which competitive, optimizing market relations and behaviour can serve as a principle not only for limiting governmental intervention, but also for rationalizing government itself.'

Gordon attributes to *Ordoliberalen* the capacity to generate new meanings to the market considered as a form of governmentality. He emphasizes, for instance against Hayek, that under this form of neoliberal governmentality the market is no longer thought of as a natural or spontaneous institution. Rather the market is seen as an evolving social construct that must be protected and that requires, therefore, a positive institutional and juridical framework for the game of enterprise to function fully. As Burchell clearly indicates, forms of neoliberalism differ from earlier forms of liberalism:

> [T]hey do not regard the market as an already existing quasi-natural reality situated in a kind of economic reserve in a space marked off, secured and supervised by the State. Rather, the market exists, and can only exist, under certain political, legal and institutional conditions that must be actively constructed by government (1993, pp. 270–71).

For early liberalism the limitation of government was tied to the rationality of the free conduct of governed individuals themselves. For neoliberalism, by contrast, 'the rational principle for regulating and limiting governmental activity must be determined by reference to *artificially* arranged or contrived forms of the free, *entrepreneurial* and *competitive* conduct of economic-rational individuals' (Burchell, 1993, 271). Burchell depicts neoliberalism, following the work of Donzelot, as promoting 'an *autonomization* of society through the invention and proliferation of new quasieconomic models of action for the independent conduct of its activities.' He concludes by suggesting that 'the generalization of an 'enterprise form' to *all* forms of conduct . . . constitutes the essential characteristic of this style of government: the promotion of an enterprise culture' (Burchell, 1993, pp. 274–75).

As Gordon (1991, p. 42) comments, the major problem for *Ordoliberalen* 'is not the anti-social effects of the economic market, but the anti-competitive effects of society.' All three versions of neoliberalism to which Gordon refers are, to a greater or lesser extent, committed *to institutionalizing the game of enterprise as a generalized principle for the organization of society as a whole.* In all versions this feature is seen to take the form of a kind of individualism that involves fashioning one's life as the enterprise of oneself: the individual becomes, as Gordon notes, 'the entrepreneur of himself or herself' (p. 44). This notion is traced in terms of the French version's emphasis on the care of the self, especially in relation to the right to permanent retraining. It also surfaces in the United States in the human capital interpretation of work, by which work is construed in terms of two components, a genetic endowment and an acquired set of aptitudes that are produced as a result of private investment in education and the like.

Gordon views the American version of neoliberalism based on a version of human capital the most radical because it proposes 'a global redescription of the social as a form of the economic.' His interpretation is worth quoting at some length:

> This operation works by a progressive enlargement of the territory of economic theory by a series of redefinitions of its object, starting out from the neo-classical formula that economics concerns the study of all behaviors involving the allocation of scarce resources to alternative ends. Now it is proposed that economics concerns all purposive conduct entailing strategic choice between alternative paths, means and instruments; or yet more broadly, *all rational conduct* (including rational thought, as a variety of rational conduct); or again, finally, all conduct, rational or irrational, which responds to its environment in a non-random fashion or 'recognizes reality' (Gordon, 1991, p. 43).

The progressive enlargement is based on the behavioral postulate known as *homo economicus:* the modern rediscovery of the main tenant of classical liberal economics, that people should be treated as rational utility maximisers in all of their behavior. In other words, individuals are modeled as seeking to further their own interests (defined in terms of measured net wealth positions) in politics as in other aspects of behaviour.

On this basis, neoliberal governments have argued for a minimal state that has been confined to the determination of individual rights construed in consumerist terms and for the maximum exposure of all providers to competition or contestability as a means of minimizing monopoly power and maximizing consumer influence on the quality and type of services provided. Neoliberalism depends on the development of a set of practices of self-government whereby the individual learns to refashion himself or herself as the entrepreneur of oneself—the 'enterprising self'—and so learns the fiduciary art of restyling the self through various forms of personal investment and insurance in a range of welfare fields—health, education, retraining—that are necessary both as a safeguard against risk but also as the preconditions for participation in the competitive society.

ELEMENTS OF NEOLIBERAL GOVERNMENTALITY

First this section summarises the main elements of neoliberal governmentality in terms of Figure 1 below, before elaborating the essentials of the neoliberal paradigm of education policy by focusing on human capital theory—a highly influential form of American neoliberalism originated by Theodore Schultz and systematically developed by Gary Becker—and the notion of the entrepreneurial self. This way we can begin to see how neoliberalism as a form of governance applies to the area of education policy and also how central education policy has become to neoliberalism.

Figure 1. Elements of Neoliberal Governmentality

1. **Classical liberalism as a critique of State reason.** A political doctrine concerning the self-limiting State where the limits of government are related to the limits of State reason, i.e., its power to know. This constitutes a permanent critique of the activity of rule and government.
2. **Natural versus contrived forms of the market.** Hayek's notion of natural laws based on spontaneously ordered institutions in the physical (crystals, galaxies) and social (morality, language, market) worlds has been replaced with an emphasis on the market as an artefact or culturally derived form and (growing out of the callaxy approach) a *constitutional* perspective that focuses on the judicio-legal rules governing the framework within the game of enterprise is played.
3. **The Politics-as-exchange innovation of Public Choice theory ('the marketisation of the State').** The extension of Hayek's spontaneous order conception (callactics) of the institution of the market beyond simple exchange to complex exchange and finally to *all processes of voluntary agreement* among persons. This has been described as the 'economic imperialism' of the Chicago School, i.e., where economic models are imported to explain non-market behaviour.
4. **The relation between government and self-government.** Liberalism as a doctrine which positively requires that individuals be free in order to govern. Government is conceived as the community of free, autonomous, self-regulating individuals with an emphasis on the 'responsibilisation' of individuals as moral agents. It also involves the neoliberal revival of *homo economicus,* based on assumptions of individuality, rationality and self-interest, as an all-embracing redescription of the social as a form of the economic. Finally, this element highlights all forms of *capitalization of the self,* including human capital in its statist, corporatist and private or individual investment forms.
5. **A new relation between government and management.** The rise of the new managerialism, 'New Public Management' which implies a shift from *policy* and *administration* to *management.* It also involves the emulation of private sector management styles, an emphasis on 'freedom to manage' and the promotion of 'self-managing' (i.e., quasi-autonomous) individuals and entities, giving rise to the privatisation and individualisation of 'risk management' and the development of new forms of prudentialism.
6. **A 'degovernmentalisation' of the State (considered as a positive technique of govern-**

ment). Government 'through' and by the market, including promotion of consumer-driven forms of social provision (health, education, welfare), 'contracting out' and privatisation.

7. **The promotion of a new relationship between government and knowledge.** 'Government at a distance' developed through relations of forms of expertise (expert systems) and politics, especially the development of new forms of social accounting embodying an actuarial rationality. Also the development of referendums and intensive opinion polling made possible through the new information and computing technologies.

8. **An economic theory of democracy ('the marketisation of democracy').** There is an emerging structural parallel between economic and political systems—political parties have become entrepreneurs in a vote-seeking political marketplace where professional media consultants use policies to sell candidates as image products and voters have become passive individual consumers. In short, democracy has become commodified at the cost of the project of political liberalism and the state has become subordinated to the market.

9. **The replacement of 'community' for 'the social.'** The increasing decentralisation, 'devolution' and delegation of power/authority/ responsibility from the centre to the region, the local institution, the 'community.' The emergence of the 'shadow state' and the encouragement of the informal voluntary sector (and an autonomous civil society) as a source of welfare and 'social capital.'

10. **Cultural reconstruction as deliberate policy goal ('the marketisation of 'the social").** The shift away from the welfare state and the so-called culture of dependency towards the development of an 'enterprise culture' involving the privatisation of the public sector and the development of quasimarkets, together with the marketisation of education and health. The development of a curriculum of competition and enterprise as the basis for the enterprise culture.

11. **Low ecological consciousness.** The advent of 'green capitalism' and 'green consumerism' based on a linear as opposed to ecological modernisation epitomised in 'no limits to growth' and market solutions to ecological problems (Giddens).

12. **Promotion of a neoliberal paradigm of globalisation.** The political promotion by governments and international policy agencies (IMF, World Bank, WTO) of world economic integration based on 'free' trade and a free or self-regulating financial international system with no capital controls.

We do not have the space to discuss in any detail the topic of neoliberal governmentality but rather will restrict ourselves here to exploring the element referred to as *the relation between government and self-government*, although the analysis which follows explicitly draws upon other elements (especially 5 to 10) and, implicitly, draws upon Foucault's philosophical understanding that defines the driving ethos of advanced forms of liberalism as a *critique of State reason*.

GERMAN NEOLIBERALISM AND THE BIRTH OF BIOPOLITICS

Naissance de la biopolitique (Foucault, 2004b) consists of thirteen lectures delivered by Foucault at the Collège de France (10 January–4 April 1979). It is helpful to see this course in the series of thirteen courses he gave from 1970 to 1984. The first five courses reflected his early work on knowledge in the human sciences, concerning punishment, penal and psychiatric institutions.[10] The remaining eight courses focused squarely on governmentality studies, with a clear emphasis also on the problematic (and hermeneutics) of the subject and the relation between subjectivity and truth.[11] Even from this list of courses it becomes readily apparent that the question of government concerns Foucault for the last decade of his life and that for his governmentality studies, politics were inseparable in its modern forms both from biology—biopower and the government of the living—and truth and subjectivity. It is important to note that these same concerns in one form or another enter into Foucault's formulations in *Naissance de la biopolitique*.[12]

In the first lecture, having dealt with the question of method and reviewed the preceding year, Foucault signals his intention to pursue the question of how the introduction of political economy served as an internal (and defining) principle limiting the practice of liberal government. In the second lecture, he considers French radical jurisprudence and English utilitarianism as emerging solutions to the problem of the limitation of the exercise of public power. He begins to specify the novel features of the art of liberal government as consisting in three related aspects: the constitution of the market as a form of truth and not simply a domain of justice; the problem of the limitation of the exercise of public power; and the problem of equilibrium in the internal competition of European states. With Adam Smith and the Physiocrats he charts the birth of a new European model based on the principle of the 'freedom of the market' that surfaced with discussion of international trade, rights of the sea, and perpetual peace in the 18th century. This section focuses more heavily on lectures 4–8 in the course because they concern German neoliberalism and may be, therefore, more of interest to my German colleagues. They also contain the bulk of the references to Hayek. Lectures 9 and 10 focus on American neoliberalism, and lectures 11 and 12 investigate the model and history of *homo economicus* and the notion of civil society.[13]

Foucault begins the fourth lecture with a discussion of 'fear of the State' or State phobia which had surfaced in the 1920s with the calculation debate of Mises and anti-Socialist sentiments of the Austrian School and which came to a head in Germany after the World War II with the experience of National Socialism, postwar reconstruction and the development of the Keynesian interventionist welfare state in Britain and Roosevelt's New Deal in the US. (Foucault also mentions the opposition between Keynes at Cambridge and Hayek at the London School of Economics. Hayek was recruited by the Director, Lionel Robbins in the early 1930s). In the context of postwar reconstruction Foucault details the Marshall Plan, adopted in 1948, and the Scientific Council set up in 1947 in Germany with the function, in the Anglo-American zone, of undertaking the reconstruction and administration of the economy. The Council comprised representatives of the Freiburg School (W. Eucken, F. Böhm, A. Müller-Armack, L. Miksch, A. Lampe, O. Veit and others) as well as members of the Christian Socialists. Much of his analysis of postwar Germany in these early years focuses on the role of Ludwig Erhard (1897–1977).

Erhard drafts the memorandum of war financing and debt consolidation and later as a member of the Bavarian Cabinet becomes Minister of Economics responsible for currency reform. As deputy of the Christian Democrats he is instrumental in introducing the politico-economic concept of the 'social market economy' and becomes Minister of Economics in the first Adenauer government in 1949. He later becomes a council member of the Coal and Steel Community, Governor of the World Bank, appoints Müller-Armack as Secretary of State at the Economics Ministry in Bonn from 1958 to 1963, plays a strong role in the EEC, and eventually is elected as the Federal Chancellor of the CDU in 1963 and remains so until 1967.[14] Foucault's emphasis is on the concept of the 'social market economy' which Erhard established in 1948, fundamentally changing the West German economy, and with it the whole of postwar society. The social market economy was coined by the national economist Müller-Armack to define an economic system based on the free market principles, aimed at guaranteeing economic efficiency and social justice with a high degree of individual freedom. The crucial aspect for Foucault's governmentality studies is that the social market economy was devised as an economic system combining market freedom with social equilibrium, where the government played a strong regulatory role by creating a juridical-legal framework for market processes that both secured competition and ensured social equity.

In the fifth lecture Foucault begins to outline the German programme of neoliberalism by reference to the theoreticians, Eucken, Böhm, Müller-Armark and Hayek. Eucken was cofounder of the *ordoliberalen* Freiburg School with the jurists, Böhm and Hans Großmann-Doerth, who were united in their concern for constitutional foundations of a free economy and society, an approach that combined law and economics. Foucault notes that Eucken knew and met with Husserl and a footnote (fn 2, p. 125) in the text refers to a paper that discusses the phenomenological roots of German ordoliberalism. They were concerned to provide an institutional framework for the competitive order based on transparent rules for the efficient functioning of a private market economy embodied in the concept of 'complete competition,' which involved State monitoring of monopolies and antitrust laws. Other aspects of the *ordoliberalen* framework included monetary stability, open markets, private property and ownership of the means of production, and freedom of contract between autonomous economic agents, including liability for one's commitments and actions.

The ordoliberal Freiburg School, as Vanberg (2004, p. 2) usefully notes, while certainly part of the foundations on which the social market economy was created and generally subsumed under the rubric of *German neoliberalism*, also exhibited differences with neoliberal economists such as Müller-Armack, Röpke and Rüstow.

For the Freiburg School the market order, as a nondiscriminating, *privilige-free* [sic] order of competition, is in and by itself an *ethical* order. As far as the need for 'social insurance' is concerned, the Freiburg ordoliberals recognized that the competitive market order can be, and should be, combined with a system of minimal income guarantees for those who are, temporarily or permanently, unable to earn a living by providing saleable services in the market. They insisted, though, that such social insurance provisions must be of a nondiscriminating, privilege-free nature, and must not be provided in ways—e.g., in the form of subsidies or other privileges granted to particular industries—that corrupt the fundamental ethical principle of the market order, namely its privilege-free nature. Müller-Armack, by contrast, regards the market order as an economically most efficient order, but not as one that has inherent ethical qualities. It is a 'technical instrument' that can be used by society to produce wealth, but it does not make itself for a 'good' society. It has to be made 'ethical' by supplementary policies, in particular 'social' policies. The important point is that in Müller-Armack's case, these supplementary 'social provisions' that are supposed to make the market economy—beyond its economic efficiency—ethically appealing are not constrained, as they are for the Freiburg ordoliberals, by the proviso that they must not be in conflict with the privilege-free nature of the rules of the game of the market. Vanberg (2004) argues that the constitutional approach of the ordoliberals distanced itself from laissez-faire economics and is closely modelled by James Buchanan's constitutional economics. Vanberg also notes differences that occurred in discussions at the Mont Pelerin Society between Eucken and Mises. While Eucken knew Hayek since the early 1920s, Vanberg argues that ordoliberalism was a German invention that was not influenced by Anglo-Saxon influences or the Austrian School.[15]

Foucault proceeds to discuss obstacles to political liberalism that had beset Germany since the 19th century, including economic protectionism, the socialism of the Bismarckian State, the role of WWI and economic reconstruction, a type of Keynesian rigidity, and the political economy of National Socialism. The neoliberal critique of National Socialism and State phobia is the starting point for an extension of this critique to both the New Deal in the US and Beveridge's Welfare State in the UK, that is, to the growth and development of the power of the State, and to standardization and massification as infringements of individual liberty defined through competition. Foucault claims that German neoliberalism enjoyed a novel relationship with classical liberalism through its constitutional theory of pure competition.

Lectures 4, 5 and 6 are devoted exclusively to 'le néolibéralisme allemande' and Foucault in the last of these three lectures is concerned to discover what distinguishes neoliberalism from classical liberalism. He responds by arguing that the problem of neoliberalism is knowledge (*savoir*) of how to exercise global political power based on the principles of a market economy and he suggests that a major transformation occurred with the association between the principle of the market economy and the political principle of laissez-faire that presented itself through a theory of pure competition. Pure competition emerged as the formal structure of property that neoliberals saw as means for regulating the economy through the price mechanism.

He traces problems of government in this period in relation to monopolies and political society. He also examines the emergence in postwar Germany of what he calls 'politique de société' or *Gesellschaftspolitik*, which we translate as 'social policy,' and the ordoliberal critique of the welfare state (l'économie de bien-être), where society is modelled on the enterprise society, and enterprise society and the good society come to be seen as one and the same.

The second aspect of social policy according to these German neoliberal thinkers is the problem of right in a society modelled on economic competition of the market which Foucault explores in lecture 8 by reference to a text by Louis Rougier and the idea of a legal-economic order, the question of legal intervention in the economy, and the development of the demand for a judiciary. The concept of order (*Ordnung*) is *the* central concept in the Freiburg School as it is at the basis of an understanding of *economic constitution*, or the *rules of the game*, upon which economies or economic systems are based. Eucken insisted that 'all economic activity necessarily takes place within an historically evolved framework of rules and institutions' and that one improves the economy by improving the economic constitution or the institutional framework within which economic activity takes place (Vanberg, 2004, p. 6). This was, in effect, the attempt to create conditions 'under which the 'invisible hand' that Adam Smith had described can be expected to do its work' (Vanberg, 2004, p. 8). The major historical step for German neoliberals was the shift from feudalism to a civil law society where people enjoyed the same rights and status under the law and thus, had the *freedom to contract* with one another. This, in essence, represented their conception of free market economy, which was based on the natural order of free competition where all players met as equals and voluntary exchange and contract enabled coordination of economic activity.

GERMAN NEOLIBERALISM AND THE BIRTH
OF THE EUROPEAN SOCIAL MODEL

Foucault's prescient analysis in 1979 of German neoliberalism focused on the Freiburg School of ordoliberalism as an innovation in the rationality of government by devising a conception of the market order based squarely on the Rule of Law. This conception, and its related versions in both German neoliberalism (after Müller-Armack and others) and Austrian economics going back to Mises and Hayek, was responsible for a form of constitutional economics that invented the 'social market economic' and shaped *Gesellschaftspolitik* or 'social policy,' as an ethical exception to the rules of the market game. The challenge for scholars, especially in the German context or those with the language skills that permit them to analyse formations of German 'social policy' is to provide the genealogical investigation of the change of values and shifting meanings underlying the the development of educational policy as part of 'the social,' and later its shift to being at the centre of economic policy, especially in the decade of 1980s and 1990s when Third Way and EU policies constitute education policy as an aspect of the 'knowledge economy.'

Foucault's analysis, formulated in the years 1978–79, and then developed in a series of subsequent themes as 'the government of the living,' 'subjectivity and truth,' and 'the government of self and others,' took up an account of the practices neoliberal governmentality as a set of novel practices introduced as a form of economic liberalism, that operated on the premise of of a critique of 'too much government,' what Foucault describes as a permanent critique of State reason. Foucault would not have been unaware of the rise of a particular form of politics refrred to as the New Right, which under both Thatcher and Reagan, combined elements of neoliberalism and neoconservativism in a contradictory formulation wielded together through 'great' statesmanship.

In this new neoliberal climate established at a popular level in an Anglo-American model that attained global ambitions under various guises through the old Bretton Woods institutions, the IMF and World Bank, and other formations like the 'Washington consensus,' the notion of the 'social market economy,' originally developed through German neoliberalism, offered some new hope as the basis of Third Way economic policies and, more generally, as the basis for the European social model (see, e.g., Joerges & Rödl, 2004).

In the United Kingdom, Chancellor Gordon Brown's foray into the discussion of the role and limits of the market in the context of globalisation has helped launch a new debate. In the BBC4 series *The Commanding Heights: The Battle for the World Economy* (2003) based on the book by Daniel Yergin and Joseph Stanislaw, Gordon Brown, who heads up the key policy-making IMF committee, told Yergin:

> The problem for the Left in the past was that they equated the public interest with public ownership and public regulation, and therefore they assumed that markets were not in the public interest . . . [Markets] provide opportunities for prosperity, but equally they're not automatically equated with the public interest.

He went on to say:

> The idea that markets must work in the public interest, the idea that governments have a responsibility for the level of employment and prosperity in the economy, the idea that governments must intervene on occasions—these are increasingly the ideas of our time.

> In an age of consumerism, a fundamental question is to what extent, if at all, the 'citizen-consumer'—a market-democracy hybrid of the subject—can shape privately funded public services in ways other than through their acts of consumption and whether acts of consumption can genuinely enhance the *social* dimensions of the market (see Peters, 2005c).

AMERICAN NEOLIBERALISM, THE CHICAGO SCHOOL[16]
AND HUMAN CAPITAL THEORY

The 'Chicago School' is, perhaps, the most influential form of American neoliberalism. As the approach of the Department of Economics at the University of Chicago, the 'Chicago School' is associated with a strong 'free market' libertarianism, yet over its hundred year development it has passed through different phases. It was only in its later post-WWII phases—first under Milton Friedman, and later, Gary Becker and others—that the Chicago School developed into an 'imperialistic' form where economics was deemed to provide a *unified* approach to the study of human behaviour and neoclassical economics was applied to social issues, including education.

The University of Chicago was founded by the oil magnate John D. Rockefeller in 1892 and in this early period there was little to distinguish the Department as a school. It really began to take on a distinctiveness under the influence of Frank H. Knight and Jacob Viner, who were theoreticians (in the Austrian and Marshallian senses) rather than empiricists, like most other economists of the time. We can refer to this phase, after its establishment period, as the First Chicago School (1920–1945). The school at this time included the mathematically oriented economists Oskar Lange, Henry Schultz and Paul H. Douglas who together followed the Lausanne School. At this stage the School differed considerably from what it was to become in the later periods. In particular, the first Chicago School set itself against the prevailing positivist methodology in economics and, under Knight, argued for a confined role for economic analysis. The School during this period was in favour of interventionist policies and entertained strong doubts about the efficiency claims of *laissez-faire* policies. Yet, nevertheless the School held firmly to the major tenets of neoclassical theory, rejecting alternative paradigms, particularly the Keynesian revolution in macroeconomics. During the 1940s the department lost Schultz, and the other leading economists (Viner, Lange and Douglas) left for other universities or for political life.

The postwar years 1945–1960 saw an injection of new blood including Jacob Marschak, the development economists, Gregg Lewis and Bert F. Hoselitz, and the agricultural economists, Theodore W. Schultz, D. Gale Johnson and Walter Nicholls. It was Marschak who in the late 1960s and thereafter introduced the theory of information into economics through Shanon's formalisation of information and theory of communication. Schultz was important in basing an account of development on a theory of human capital during the early 1960s, emphasizing that investment in education led to economic growth. In was not until the early 1960s that the department began to develop into a second School under the leadership of George J. Stigler and Milton Friedman, both avowed Marshallians. The second School stood committed to neoclassical economics and strongly against the concept of market failures. Indeed, in this period Chicago was the only department that rejected Keynesianism.

It was this School that began a renaissance of neoclassical economics, extending the paradigm in search theory (Stigler), human capital theory (Gary Becker) and transaction cost theory (Ronald H. Coarse). It was this School that was largely responsible for the criticisms of its 'imperialist' ambitions and, in particular, 'the application of economic reasoning to areas traditionally considered the prerogative of other fields such as political science, legal theory, history and sociology.' Neoclassical price theory was extended into business and finance. Stigler, Coarse and Buchanan, among others, extended neoclassical economics into political science and institutional theory. Robert W. Fogel and Douglas C. North proposed a neoclassical reading of economic history, while Richard Posner and William M. Landes of the Chicago Law School extended neoclassical economics into legal theory. Finally, Gary Becker and Jacob Mincer adapted neoclassical economics to sociological issues, giving education, family, and marriage an economic interpretation.

The second School, developed under Friedman during the 1960s and 1970s, became the strongest advocate of monetarism in macroeconomics and perhaps the fiercest antagonist of Keynesian economics, finding in monetarism the theoretical and empirical means to question and roll back interventionist policies. Monetarism has since given way to a more mathematically rigorous so-called New Classical economics in the 1970s (Robert E. Lucas). The third Chicago School (1970s to today), together with monetarism (1960s) and new classical macroeconomics (1970s), we can add to the New Institutionalism, New Economic History and Law-and-Economics movements.[17] The New Institutionalism refers

> to the collection of schools of thought that seek to explain political, historical, economic and social institutions such as government, law, markets, firms, social conventions, the family, etc. in terms of Neoclassical economic theory. New Institutionalist schools can be thought of as the outcome of the Chicago School's 'economic imperialism'—i.e. using Neoclassical economics to explain areas of human society normally considered outside them (http://cepa.newschool.edu/het/schools/newinst.htm).

A number of strands of the Chicago schools have been important in education reform, from Friedman's emphasis on 'freedom to choose' and his strong advocacy of vouchers, to the public choice theory of Gordon Tullock and James Buchanan, principal-agency theory and transaction cost analysis—all of which have been important as the theoretical underpinning to what many have called New Public Administration (or new managerialism) and its extension into education policy through the doctrine of self-management (see Peters in De Alba et al., 2000).

The Chicago Schools' contribution to the economics of information and knowledge has been drawn upon as a legitimation for the restructuring of science and higher education policy (insofar as the latter concerns the production of research knowledge). The economics of information was pioneered by Jacob Marschak (and coworkers Miyasawa, and Radner), and George Stigler who won the Nobel Memorial Prize for his seminal work in the 'economic theory of information,' whereas Fritz Machlup's (1962) groundwork and development of the economics of the production and distribution of knowledge became the early blueprint for the 'postindustrial society,' the 'service economy' and, most recently, the 'knowledge economy' (see Peters, 2001c).

Of greatest importance, perhaps, for education reform has been human capital theory developed by Schultz and Becker. Becker went to the University of Chicago for graduate work, meeting Friedman in 1951, and coming under the influence of Gregg Lewis (his use of economic theory to analyse labor markets) and Schultz's pioneering research on human capital. He also was strongly influenced by Aaron Director's applications of economics to antitrust problems, and industrial organization more generally, and L. J. Savage's research on subjective probability and the foundation of statistics. His PhD thesis was published as his first major book

The Economic Approach to Human Behaviour in 1957 (Becker, 1976) in which he laid out the essentials of his approach as follows:

> The heart of my argument is that human behavior is not compartmentalized, sometimes based on maximizing, sometimes not, sometimes motivated by stable preferences, sometimes by volatile ones, sometimes resulting in optimal accumulation of information, sometimes not. Rather, all human behavior can be viewed as involving participants who maximize their utility from a stable set of preferences and accumulate an optimal amount of information and other inputs in a variety of markets. If this argument is correct, the economic approach provides a united framework for understanding behavior that has long been sought by and eluded Bentham, Comte, Marx, and others (Becker, 1976, p. 14).

As he explains it in his Nobel Prize autobiography:

> The book contains the first systematic effort to use economic theory to analyze the effects of prejudice on the earnings, employment and occupations of minorities. It started me down the path of applying economics to social issues, a path that I have continued to follow (Becker, 1992).

The Economic Approach to Human Behaviour pursued a range of topics, including: competition and democracy, crime and punishment, the allocation of time in the household, irrational behavior, and economic interpretations of fertility, marriage and social interactions. While the book was favorably reviewed as he records 'it had no visible impact on anything.' Becker was soon to take up an appointment at Columbia combined with one at the National Bureau of Economic Research and his book on human capital Becker (orig. 1964, 1993) was the outgrowth of his first research project for the Bureau. It was at Columbia that he began a workshop on labor economics and began a research collaboration with Jacob Mincer on human capital.

Becker returned to Chicago in 1970 after the student rebellion of 1968 and his dissatisfaction with the 'incompetence' of the administration at Columbia University in handling the crisis. He opposed the student protests and believed 'that Columbia should take a firm hand and uphold the right to free inquiry.' At Chicago he continued to work on the family and in 1983, after accepting a joint appointment in the Sociology Department at Chicago, began an interdisciplinary seminar on rational choice in the social sciences with James Coleman—a seminar which provided much of the conceptual grounding for work on social capital.

As Becker himself testifies, his work applying economic theory to social issues was not well received by many in the profession, and it has only been since the early 1980s that his work on human capital has received strong approval from politicians and policymakers. From the gestation of his economic approach to social issues to the development of his book on human capital was a mere seven years (1957 to 1964), yet it was not for another twenty years before his analysis of human capital developed in relation to human capital became the reigning orthodoxy. As he writes in the Preface to the third edition of *Human Capital,*

> In the recent presidential campaign, both President Clinton and former President Bush emphasized the importance of improving education and skills of American workers. They did not even shy away from using the term 'investing in human capital' to describe the process of improving the quality of the work force. A dozen years ago, this terminology would have been inconceivable in a presidential campaign (Becker, 1993, p. xix).

Broadly speaking, as Becker explains in the Ryerson Lecture (added to the 1993 edition):

> Education and training are the most important investments in human capital. My book showed, and so have many other studies since then, that high school and college education in the United States greatly raise a person's income, even after netting out direct and indirect costs of schooling, and after adjusting for the better family backgrounds and greater abilities of more educated people (Becker, 1993, p. 17).

In a period of roughly thirty years human capital theory has become the basis for education policy in most Western countries. Historically, we might see this as part of the rise of individualism in the liberal West and a commitment to the assumptions of individuality, rationality, and self interest that govern neoclassical economic theory.

CHAPTER EIGHT

Enterprise Culture AND THE Rise OF THE Entrepreneurial Self

INTRODUCTION

The notion of 'enterprise culture' emerged in the United Kingdom as a central motif in political thought under Margaret Thatcher's administration and continued in modified form under Tony Blair and New Labour. In Thatcher's neoliberalism, the promotion of the entrepreneurial self represents a shift away from the Keynesian welfare state to notions upheld by the neoliberal state. The move was a profound cultural shift, from a rights-based welfare model of the citizen to a deliberate attempt at cultural restructuring and engineering based upon the neoliberal model of the entrepreneurial self—a shift characterized as a moving from a 'culture of dependency' to one of 'self-reliance.' On this model, the citizen-consumer, based on the rejuvenation of *homo economicus*, positions the individual to calculate the risks and so invests in his/herself at critical points in the learning life cycle. In education this shift takes the form of the 'enterprise education,' together with the associated 'enterprise curriculum.' Utilizing a Foucauldian perspective, this chapter analyzes 'the generalization of an "enterprise form" to all forms of conduct' and the way in which the promotion of enterprise culture has become a style of governance characteristic of both neoliberalism and Third Way politics (Burchell, 1993, p. 269).

This chapter focuses upon a 'new prudentialism' in education that focuses on an entrepreneurial self that 'responsibilizes' the self to make welfare choices based on an actuarial rationality. It is a form that seeks to 'insure' the individual against risk, since in this instance the State has transferred this risk to the individual. Such moves constitute new types of subjectivity—nothing less than what/how we become human beings. This chapter focuses on a more limited objective; that of tracing difference in social prudentialism in education and the shift in forms of social insurance through education from one welfare regime to another.

First, the chapter provides an introduction to an analysis of the 'risk society,' emphasizing the way in which risk management has become a form of social regulation and policy development in education. This begins by focusing on the theme of the 'responsibilizing of the self' as one of the distinctive means of neoliberal governance of welfare and education—a theme referred to as the development of the 'entrepreneurial self.' Second, the chapter provides a brief analysis of Foucault in relation to the Kantian tradition to outline the theoretical approach adopted. Third, the chapter develops a notion of actuarial rationality in relation to the different styles of risk management characterising the provision of public services in the welfare state on the one hand and the neoliberal state, on the other. The chapter examines this form of governance more fully through the rise of enterprise culture and enterprise education during the Thatcher years. It also suggests that this form of neoliberal thinking underlies New Labour policies and Third Way politics. Finally, the chapter utilises Foucault's notions of governmentality and the ethics of self-constitution, as a basis to explore dimensions of the entrepreneurial self and a new prudentialism in education and the emergence of the self-consuming 'citizen-consumer.'

EDUCATION, RISK AND SOCIAL REGULATION

If anything, the original thesis concerning the 'risk society' articulated by Ulrich Beck (1992) has taken on a new imperative after 9/11, especially in relation to questions of security at all levels—national, personal and institutional. This is clearly evident in the growth of risk management and risk management education programs, especially since the perceived growing vulnerability of public institutions like schools. Some schools in the USA, for example, have introduced security systems based on the latest iris-recognition technology. Beck was the first to put the notion of risk on the sociological agenda focusing on environmental, health and personal risk. The transition for Beck is not from 'industrial society' to 'post-industrial' or 'post-modern society' but to 'risk society' where the driving logic is no longer class politics as an organising principle, but rather socially manufactured risk and risk management. No longer are inequalities of wealth and income paramount (although such inequalities remain), the chief problems are now environmental hazards, which cut across traditional inequalities. As he explains: 'Risk may be defined as a systematic way of dealing with hazards and insecurities induced and introduced by modernization itself' (Beck, 1992, p. 21). He elaborates: 'In contrast to all earlier epochs (including industrial society), the risk society is characterized essentially by a lack: the impossibility of an external attribution of hazards. In other words, risks depend on decisions, they are industrially produced and in this sense politically reflexive' (Beck, 1992, p.183). In 'risk society' Beck argues societal courses of action or policies based on calculated risk have been deliberately taken based on the assumption and paradigm of our technological mastery over nature. While Beck coined the term, Giddens (1990; 1991) usefully relates the analysis of 'risk' to the concept of 'security.' Modernity for Giddens is a double-edged process for while it has greatly increased individual choice (and freedom) it has done so at a cost which points not only to the 'globalisation of risk' (such as nuclear war or changes in the international division of labour) but also in terms of 'institutionalised risk environments,' that is, new risks arising from the nature of modern social organizations.

In the field of education, there has been also some talk of 'risk.' Arguably, notions of 'at-risk youth' and 'nation at risk' predate Beck's and Giddens' uses of the term. 'Nation at Risk' was the title that the US National Commission on Excellence in Education set up by the Secretary for Education, T. H. Bell, under the chairmanship of David Pierpont Gardner, in 1981. The Commission choose to point to a new 'Imperative for Educational Reform' (its subtitle). The risk is conceived as a national one, calculated against the future of America's pre-eminence as a world leader both economically and technologically. It is a multinatured risk that places an onerous burden on education as the basis for the nation's future economic and technological competitiveness.

> Our Nation is at risk. Our once unchallenged pre-eminence in commerce, industry, science, and technological innovation is being overtaken by competitors throughout the world. This report is concerned with only one of the many causes and dimensions of the problem, but it is the one that undergirds American prosperity, security, and civility. We report to the American people that while we can take justifiable pride in what our schools and colleges have historically accomplished and contributed to the United States and the well-being of its people, the educational foundations of our society are presently being eroded by a rising tide of mediocrity that threatens our very future as a Nation and a people. What was unimaginable a generation ago has begun to occur—others are matching and surpassing our educational attainments (http://www.ed.gov/pubs/NatAtRisk/risk.html).

The report focuses on the competitive element comparing the US in terms of efficiency to Japan, South Korea and Germany in producing capital goods. The risk is perceived as being not only tied to loss of position in the production of strategic goods but also the 'redistribution of trained capability throughout the globe' that this signifies. The report goes on to emphasise an early view of the knowledge economy and the crucial role of education within it, stressing concepts of 'excellence' and the 'learning society':

> Knowledge, learning, information, and skilled intelligence are the new raw materials of international commerce and are today spreading throughout the world as vigorously as miracle drugs, synthetic fertilizers, and blue jeans did earlier. If only to keep and improve on the slim competitive edge we still retain in world markets, we must dedicate ourselves to the reform of our educational system for the benefit of all—old and young alike, affluent and poor, majority and minority. Learning is the indispensable investment required for success in the 'information age' we are entering (http://www.ed.gov/pubs/NatAtRisk/risk.html).

Fifteen years later in 1998 the same rhetoric is revived in a document entitled *A Nation Still at Risk: An Education Manifesto* (http://edreform.com/pubs/manifest.htm) signed by Jeanne Allen (President of The Center for Education Reform) and thirty-five prominent Americans, including school superintendents, US Department of Education officials, businessmen, members from State House representatives, education commissioners, charter schools project managers, university staff, researchers and policy analysts from thinktanks (like Diane Ravitch from the Brookings Institute), and leaders of various project supporting 'standards' and 'excellence' in education.

The risk posed to 'tomorrow's well-being' by 'educational mediocrity' is now defined as 'economic decline' and 'technological inferiority.' The Report reads: 'Large numbers of students remain at risk. Intellectually and morally, America's educational system is failing too many people.' The Report suggests the Excellence Commission had the right diagnosis but was naïve as to the cure. 'The real issue is power,' the Report advises and the way the 'power-brokers' and 'bureaucrats' hold on to power. It goes on to state: 'It should now be clear to all that the era of the big-government monopoly of public education needs to end . . . ' The nature of the risk is spread by a failed public system of education that penalises 'children of the poor and minorities.' The guiding principles and strategies for changes are clear: public education must be deregulated; it must staffed and delivered in new ways; 'a vast transfer of power is needed from producers to consumers'; 'There must be an end to paternalism; the one-size-fits-all structure; and the condescending, government-knows-best attitude. Every family must have the opportunity to choose where its children go to school'; but in order to exercise their power wisely 'education's consumers must be well-informed about school quality.' The main renewal strategies mentioned are: '*standards, assessments and accountability*' on the one hand, and '*pluralism, competition and choice,*' on the other (italics in original).

The document proceeds to outline the risk management regime for the US education system in terms of 'ten break-through changes for the 21st century' including the now familiar, 'national academic standards,' 'standards-based assessment' and 'tough accountability systems,' alongside 'school choice,' charter schools, deregulat-ed teacher force, differential teacher pay systems, and 'essential academic skills.' Policy observers and practitioners in the United Kingdom will recognise much of the rhetoric and the national risk management strategy as that of the Blair admin-istration's approach to education policy in its second term and as reflecting more generally the change of ethos in public service philosophy and provision.

RISK MANAGEMENT AND ACTUARIAL RATIONALITY: FROM WELFARE STATE TO CULTURES OF CONSUMPTION

The elements of the programme of risk management can be described in terms of the shift from the Keynesian welfare state and compulsory social insurance to neoliberalism (or culture of consumption) and a form of private insurance construct-ed through choice. Within this new regime (re/de)regulation represents an inten-sive juridification—a legal liberation and optimism based upon confidence in rules. On this model the well-governed society is committed to the coherence of a frame-work of rules, that is, a codification, where the government increasingly steps back from actual involvement in state activities, now devolved to agencies, institutions or regions. Government assumes the metaposition of rule maker. In this political environment the economic, the constitutional and the legal or juridical forms of advanced liberalism overlap in the construction of the citizen-consumer. Increasingly, alongside the 'empowerment of consumers'—simultaneously their individualisation and their responsibilization—is the belief in the efficacy of rules and the distrust of expert knowledges. These knowledges (and discourses) grew up with the welfare state—evident in the 19th century census as an instrument of gov-ernmentality—and began to exist increasingly independent of the state. Neoliberalism, considered as a risk management regime, involves the distrust of expert knowledges, especially those traditionally involved with the welfare state such as social workers and teachers. Under neoliberalism there is a shift to the creation of a uniform structure of expert knowledges based on the calculating science of actu-arialism and accountancy ('the audit society'). 'The social' is promoted as that which is capable of being governed—traditionally, the regulation of 'the poor' and 'pauperisation.' 'Work' and 'unemployment' have become fundamental modern categories of social regulation.

In this sense neoliberalism can be seen as an intensification of moral regulation based on the radical withdrawal from government and responsibilization of indi-viduals through economics and it emerges as an actuarial form of governance that promotes an actuarial rationality through the encouragement of a political regime of ethical self-constitution as consumer-citizens. 'Responsibilization' refers to modern forms of government of the self where individuals are called upon to make choices about lifestyles, their bodies, their education and health at critical points in the lifecycle—birth, 'starting school,' 'going to university,' 'first job,' marriage, retirement. 'Choice' assumes a much wider role under neoliberalism: it is not simply 'consumer sovereignty' but rather a moralisation and responsibilization—a regulated choice-making transfer responsibility from State to the individual in the social market. Its specific forms have entailed a tearing up of labour law under the welfare state and an emphasis upon more privatised forms of welfare often involving tougher accountability mechanisms and security/video surveillance. The 'risk society' is put in place through actuarial mechanisms and there is an emphasis on all forms of insurance as a means of reducing risk to the individual (in areas of employment, education, accident, security, retirement). In one sense, this is the primary link between government and the government of the self, which is promoted in its relation to choice making through cybernetic and information systems. Neoliberalism has a suspicion of autonomous forms of self-regulation. Actuarialism is a mobilisation of one predominant structure of expert knowledge and an interrogation of the autonomy, which accompanies other expert knowledges of teachers, social workers (traditional forms under the welfare state). Prudentialism refers to the new form of insurance against risk, which is 'forced' onto individual as consumers in the social market. The mode of 'forced choice' which encourages a 'responsibilization' Peters calls 'actuarial rationality' as in making consumer choices concerning education as a service individual consumers in effect become actuaries calculating the risks of their own self-investments.

In this view modernity is characterised by a statist view based on contract. Keynesian welfarism is an interlude before returning to a form of statism and its distinctive forms of legal regulation involving a recontractualization of social relations through the market, but not simply a two-party (buyer/seller) contract but rather a juridification of society in, for example, a contractualization of the university based on user fees and privatised student loans where the issue becomes 'are students (or parents or funders) getting their money's worth?' This contractualization mirrors legal forms, that is, a proceduralization requiring notification, complaint in writing, personal redress, etc., presupposed in the move to a litigation model.

The regulation of risk takes place through insurance and the responsibilization of the individual consumer who increasingly is forced to become responsible for one's own safety, health, employment and education. We might called this a prudentialization of social regulation—we are made to be prudent (as part of a wider moral discourse) and risk management of the social hazards facing us in modernity is based on the self-constituting prudential citizen under economic and contractual conditions.

Much of the change of regime emphasizing risk, while not always properly theorized, has been usefully taken up in the UK by an ESRC (Economic and Social Research Council) research programme entitled 'Cultures of Consumption' (see: www.consume.bbk.ac.uk). The Executive Summary for the programme begins:

> Consumption has returned to the centre of public affairs, government policy making, and intellectual life in recent years, In Britain as well as more globally. Consumption and related issues of consumers' rights and interests, consumer culture and consumer policy inform today [sic] major debates about the future of democracy and the nation-state, wealth and welfare, economic governance, the role of new technologies and the environment, and the changing relationship of commerce and culture in contemporary societies. (See revised specification at: http://www.consume.bbk.ac.uk/about.html).

The AHRB/ESRC research programme contextualizes itself by reference to the UK government's White Paper released in 1999. In his Foreword, the then Secretary of State for Trade, Stephen Byers, asserted that in putting consumers centre stage the government had recognised 'for the first time that confident, demanding consumers are good for business.' The opening up of global markets and the spread of electronic commerce bring opportunities and challenges for consumers and for business. In its White Paper, Modern Markets: Confident Consumers, the Government has set a new agenda:

- to promote open and competitive markets
- to provide people with the skills, knowledge and information they need to become demanding consumers
- to encourage responsible businesses to follow good practice
- to avoid burdening those businesses with unnecessary regulation
- to protect the public from serious trading malpractice and unsafe products.
- The White Paper will benefit all consumers but the Government will focus in particular on the needs of those with less developed consumer skills, those who are socially excluded and those on low incomes who can least afford to make a bad purchase. (http://www.dti.gov.uk/consumer/whitepaper/overview.htm).

Clearly, the White Paper presages issues concerning Third Way policy concerning the consumer as a new social actor in the PFI (Private Finance Initiatives), public/private partnerships that are now redesigning consumer-driven public services and attempting to encourage a better alignment between consumption and citizenship. These consumer-driven public services signify the end of one-size-fits-all and large monolithic institutions and the move towards smaller, more flexible customised public services with also greater public accountability harnessed to a set of more workable democratic relationships between the market, consumer advocacy, and public policy.

Much of what shapes education policy finds its general parameters within the shifting regime of social regulation based on the quasimarket and the neoliberal forms of the so-called social market that is strongly favored by Third Way politics. At the same time it is important to recognise implications of neoliberal governmentalism characterizing Third Way policies in a variety of policy initiatives including 'professional learning communities,' the emphasis on assessment in teacher education, 'developmentally appropriate' practices, inclusion, school report cards, data-driven management and forms of managerialism.[1] It is also evident in the concept of enterprise culture and the promotion of entreprenurialism per se that permits a range of public private partnerships (PPP) in the funding of new schools in Britain and a host of schemes revolving around 'education for work' and the new vocationalism.

Thus, Frank Trentmann examining new perspectives on consumption that go 'beyond consumerism' and the received view based on 'the definition of an acquisitive individualist mentality as the defining feature of modern consumer behaviour and, since this originated in the West, a view of expansion that looks from the epicentre (West) outwards.' (Trentmann, 2002, p. 6). The acquisitive model of consumerism which forms the basis of traditional left-wing approaches such as the Frankfurt School's research into mass society or Horkheimer and Adorno's investigation of the culture industry, as Trentmann argues, tends to rule out a priori or to obscure the politics of consumption where 'new sites of consumption,' for instance, 'offered opportunities for an emancipation of the self' (p. 7) (especially for 'middle-class women [who] defined a new sense of bourgeois feminine identity,' p. 18) or modes of consumption which do not centre on the purchase of goods. Trentmann suggests that 'consumption in the late twentieth century has become as much about services, experiences, and citizenship as about the acquisition of goods' (Trentmann, 2002, p. 9). Trentmann also draws attention to the fact that historians (and social scientists more generally) have been slow to investigate 'the changing interface between politics and consumption' (Trentmann, 2002, p. 22), which is particularly ironic given the significance of the shift from production to consumption in understanding advanced liberal societies for New Labour and third Way politics. Trentmann usefully offers a corrective to methodological assumptions that favour the individual as the core of modern consumer society. Both economic historians, operating with the neoclassical notion of the rational utility maximiser, and culturalists (sometimes poststructuralists) tend to operate with such deeply individualist explanations that often prevent an understanding of when 'consumption has been a political site for collective mobilisation concerning civil society, democracy, and global justice' (Trentmann, 2002, p. 23). This criticism is valid, although at the same time we must remember that predominant modes of economic analysis and of policy development have been framed in terms of neoclassical economic theory that works from the revival of *homo economicus* with its assumptions of rationality, individualism, and self-interest. Thus while collective behaviour is not ruled out, the tendency at both the level of analysis and policy has been to encourage understanding of collective behavior in terms of simple aggregation. It is no wonder that social science and the humanities should note and follow these tendencies.

NEOLIBERAL GOVERNANCE OF WELFARE AND EDUCATION: RESPONSIBILIZING THE SELF

The prevalence of the doctrine of the self-limiting state in many Western states, including the United Kingdom, has manifested itself in terms of neoliberal welfare and education policies through an intensification of moral regulation rather than through an overall reduction of levels of welfare and education spending in real terms. During the 1980s the United Kingdom and other English-speaking countries saw the reduction of the state's trading activities enacted through privatization programs and the 'downsizing' of the public sector. This neoliberal limiting of the State's role decreased its power to mediate in the market to achieve the traditional welfare goal of full employment or of equality of opportunity in education. Precisely at the point when neoliberals were attempting conceptually to remoralize the link between welfare and employment and to 'responsibilize' individuals for investing in their own education, neoliberal governments began to dismantle arrangements for State arbitration in the labor market, substituting individualized employment contracts, and exposing workers to the vagaries of the market. This policy move must be mapped against the growth of a recalcitrant and permanent underclass, of those who are structurally disadvantaged in terms of access to an increasingly specialized and highly segmented labor market. Intergenerational unemployment now seems an entrenched feature of most Western states, with both a femininization and a casualization of the labor force and, often, high rates of youth unemployment, especially in depressed urban areas. Many commentators have discussed the potential de-skilling effects of the new information technologies and the redundancy of the unskilled, the semiskilled, and manual laborers in face of greater computerization and automation of both blue-collar work and service industries.

At the same time, there has been a cumulative shift in the tax burden away from corporations toward individual wage earners. Indirect forms of taxation (such as a goods and services tax) and the flat tax structure introduced by some OECD countries have ended up favoring corporations and high-income groups at the expense of low- to middle-income groups. The shift to indirect forms, particularly consumer taxes, is seen by policymakers as a way to retain revenue levels in face of an ageing population and labour force. This move has both politicized and encouraged political support among different constituencies, notably among middle-income earners, for policies designed to reduce levels of income tax—in fact, more broadly, for viewing a high income-tax level as undue state interference—in exchange for a privatized welfare system in which individuals, through user charges, vouchers, and forms of personal insurance, are forced to take care of themselves. The state has only been able to begin the process of writing itself out of its traditional responsibilities concerning the welfare state through twin strategies of a greater individualization of society and the responsibilization of individuals and families. Both are often simultaneously achieved through a greater contractualization of society, and particularly by contracting-out state services.

A genealogy of the entrepreneurial self reveals that it is the relationship, promoted by neoliberalism, that one establishes to oneself through forms of personal investment (for example, user charges, student loans) and insurance that becomes the central ethical component of a new individualized and privatized consumer welfare economy. In this novel form of governance, responsibilized individuals are called upon to apply certain management, economic, and actuarial techniques to themselves as subjects of a newly privatized welfare regime. In this context Burchell's remark made in the context of a Foucauldian analysis of neoliberalism that an 'enterprise form' is generalized to all forms of conduct and constitutes the distinguishing mark of the style of government, could not be more apt (Burchell, 1996, p 275). At one and the same time enterprise culture provides the means for analysis and the prescription for change: education and training are key sectors in promoting national economic competitive advantage and future national prosperity. They are seen increasingly as the passport for welfare recipients to make the transition from dependent, passive welfare consumer to an entrepreneurial self. In the past, so the neoliberal argument goes, too much emphasis has been placed on social and cultural objectives and insufficient emphasis has been placed on economic goals in education systems. Henceforth, the prescription is for greater investment in education and training as a basis for future economic growth. Such investment in human skills is underwritten by theories of human capital development and human resources management. The major difference from previous welfare state regimes is that education, increasingly at all levels but more so at the level of tertiary education, is no longer driven by public investment but, rather, by private investment decisions. The uptake of education and training grants by able-bodied welfare recipients, especially women who are single parents, now becomes mandatory after a given period within countries where neoliberal policies have been adopted, in what some see as a shift from a welfare state to a Schumpetarian workfare state.

The rigidity of the distinction between the private and the public has broken down: commercial and private enterprises exist within or in partnership with many 'public' education institutions. Human capital theory is rejuvenated in a privatized rather than statist or public form. The neoliberal state has worked to make individual choice in the tertiary education market the overriding operative principle. Its aim has been to increase diversity—a prerequisite for choice—by abolishing the differences in the missions of the various institutions comprising the tertiary sector and to move to a fully consumer-driven system in which state funding is distributed to individual students by way of entitlements or vouchers rather than to the institutions or 'providers' themselves.

Under neoliberalism, questions of national economic survival and competition in the world economy have come increasingly to be seen as questions of cultural reconstruction. The task of reconstructing culture in terms of enterprise has involved remodeling public institutions along commercial lines as corporations and has encouraged the acquisition and use of so-called entrepreneurial qualities. Thus, and in accordance with this new discourse, both the welfare state and education systems have been criticized for leading to a 'culture of dependency.' It is against this general background that neoliberal states have abandoned the traditional goals of the universalist welfare state of equality and participation based on social rights in favor of a reduced conception of a 'modest safety net' based on targeting social assistance and institutionalizing user charges for social services. In addition, in some OECD countries there have been substantial cuts in welfare benefits, a tightening of eligibility criteria, the introduction of means testing, and a shift toward an increase in policing and surveillance by the state through the development of new information systems to reduce benefit fraud. This process has been referred to as the emergence of a 'shadow' state: the privatization of welfare through contestability of funding and the contracting out of welfare provision to the nongovernmental informal sector comprised of church-based groups, charity organizations, private foundations, and trusts which, increasingly, minister to the 'poor' and the 'disadvantaged' according to set criteria and performance targets.

Above all, the theme of 'responsibilizing the self,' a process at once economic and moral, is concomitant with a new tendency to 'invest' in the self at crucial points in the life cycle and symbolizes the shift in the regime and governance of education and welfare under neoliberalism. Risk and responsibility have been thematized in new ways. There has been a shift from a disciplinary technology of power, first, to welfarism—to programs of social security as governmentalized risk management and to new forms of actuarial or insurance-based rationalities—and, second, to new forms of prudentialism (a privatized actuarialism) where risk management is forced back onto individuals and satisfied through the market. O'Malley comments 'Within such prudential strategies, then calculative self-interest is articulated with actuarialism to generate risk management as an everyday practice of the self' (O'Malley, 1996, p. 200). The duty to the self—its simultaneous responsibilization as a moral agent and its construction as a calculative rational choice actor—becomes the basis for a series of investment decisions concerning one's health, education, security, employability, and retirement. The responsibilization of the self and its associated new prudential strategies go hand in hand with two related developments: a substitution of 'community' for 'society' and the invention of new strategies for government through information. The first development is significant because it implicitly recognizes a theoretical weakness in the strict neoliberal model of social policy based upon the market alone. Although they do not want to reinvent society (as government has been 'reinvented'), neoliberals want to substitute some notion of 'civil society' for the welfare state under the metaphor of community, where civil society means an association of free individuals based on self-rule. The second line of development issues from the new opportunities for state surveillance and control that accompany the growth of information and communications technologies. In one sense, this can be seen as 'government without enclosures' or 'government within an open system' (see Deleuze, 1995), which promotes more intensified visibility of both private and public spaces than ever before. Such unprecedented high levels of visibility are established through the new security and policing uses to which the video camera has been put in streets, malls, security systems within buildings, and the like and the advent of computerized citizen data, in the forms of 'information sharing' across separate government departments and the development of so-called smart card technology for specific purposes (for example, welfare recipients) or for more general 'governmental' purposes (for example, community cards). Information sharing and the application of new smart card technology have been applied to welfare 'problems' of benefit fraud and state calculation of welfare benefits and entitlements. This movement toward greater control under the theme of responsibilization of self is also seen in a new customized relation (a niche-market welfare) promoted between welfare officers who handle case loads and recipients. This involves risk-based targeting of services and the shift from an emphasis on a relationship based on professional authority (e.g., therapist, counselor, etc.), to an emphasis on self empowerment and self-help based on training, education, and the development of 'personal skills.' Increasingly, government strategies signal a shift in orientation from welfare to well-being through the promotion of self-reliance involving marketlike incentives in the redefinition of benefit regimes and governmentality associated with forms of 'investment' in at-risk children and families.

Neoliberalism represents a continuing critique of state reason; its governance of welfare and education consists in some strategic innovations in reconceptualizing the exercise of power, most notably the ideas of the responsibilization of the self effected through a series of marketlike arrangements. These new arrangements provide an increasingly accepted social recipe for individualizing the social by substituting notions of civil society, social capital or community for state. At the same time, however, they carry the combined dangers, on the one hand, of pathologizing and stigmatizing those who are structurally excluded from the labor market, and on the other, of weighing down with debt—of prematurely mortgaging the future lives of—the next generation. The full social consequences of instituting a neoliberal welfare system that individualizes and privatizes current welfare and education by deferring payment to the next generation via loans, user charges, forms of self-investment, and insurance schemes are yet to be investigated.

The theme of the 'responsibilization of the self' both in the governance of education and welfare and especially as a means for encouraging an enterprise society has been prominent in Third Way politics, even though neoliberal principles have been reworked within a different economic context. In the UK, New Labour's Third Way in an effort to hold on to the so-called radical centre places a great deal of emphasis on the economy and work as fundamental to the concept of citizenship. Indeed, through the concept of the 'knowledge economy' which served as the pivot for the Competitiveness Report, New Labour legitimizes the concepts of lifelong learning and entrepreneurship aimed at the production of flexible workers and the combined notions of 'education for work' and 'enterprise education' (see Peters, 2001). There is little doubt that New Labour remains committed to the principles of the neoliberal global economy based on protecting multinationals and extending free trade. In domestic economic policy the Blair government seems intent on privatizing public services such as railways and traffic control and introducing parallel forms of privatization in health and education through the contracting out of services or the creation of quasimarkets. Bryan Turner (2001) in his discussion of the erosion of citizenship and especially the impact of forces of globalization on the weakened nation-state, clearly indicates that high levels of economic participation mask a real change in the nature of the economy and obscures a transition from old to new welfare regimes. The new economic regime is based upon monetary stability, fiscal control and a relation in government regulation of the economy. In this new economic environment, one version of the Third Way strategy involves, not protecting individuals from the uncertainties of the market that had dominated welfare strategies between 1930 and 1970, but helping people to participate successfully in the market through education (lifelong learning schemes), flexible employment (family-friendly employment strategies) and tax incentives.

It seems clear that New Labour will seek to extend the neoliberal emphasis on enterprise culture in education as in other areas of society. Fairclough notes: 'The equivalence between country, nation, and business goes with a positive construction of business' (Fairclough, 2000, p. 33). Some commentators suggest that New Labour is fascinated with the glamour of business. The 'enterprise culture' was a central theme of the Thatcher Government in the 1980s. It seems that New Labour is taking over Thatcherite discourse in this as in other respects. In his speech to the South African parliament in January 1999, Tony Blair said that 'we need [a] culture of enterprise,' and the White Paper on competition calls for an 'enterprise culture' and an 'entrepreneurial culture.' The general idea that governments should seek social change through shifting 'culture' (implying an engineering of people's culture from above) has been taken over from the Tories, as too has the glorification of 'enterprise' . . . Tory initiatives to develop 'entrepreneurial skills' in school children are also being extended. To understand this emphasis on 'enterprise culture' we must go back to study its development through the Thatcher years.

THE RISE OF ENTERPRISE CULTURE AND ENTERPRISE EDUCATION

A notable feature of the early 1990s was the way in which the emphasis on the introduction of the new technologies has given way to a more general discourse that represents issues of economic and institutional reform in cultural terms (Keat and Abercrombie, 1991). In the case of Britain, questions of national economic survival and competition in the world economy came increasingly to be seen under the Conservative governments of Margaret Thatcher and John Major as questions of cultural reconstruction. According to Keat and Abercrombie, the idea of an enterprise culture 'emerged as a central motif in the political thought and practice of the . . . government' (Keat and Abercrombie, 1991, p.1). The task of constructing such a culture has involved remodeling institutions along commercial lines and encouraging the acquisition and use of enterprising qualities. Keat and Abercrombie see the ideological function of the political rhetoric of enterprise as a particular interpretation for making sense of the kind of economic and cultural changes that have been described under the banners of postindustrialism, the information society, postmodernism, and post-Fordism.

Morris (1991) traces the genesis and development of the concept of enterprise from its beginnings in the thinking of the Centre for Policy Studies in the link between Christianity and the 'new Conservatism' and in the work of Lord Young. He distinguishes three phases, the latest of which he christens 'partnership in cultural engineering.' This phase, which represents a massive cultural reconstruction, has concerned policies involving 'unprecedented government intervention in education (at all levels)' (Morris 1991, pp. 34–35). By contrast Schwengel provides a snapshot of a more liberal German concept than the British emphasis on enterprise. *Kulturgesellschaft* has a softer focus, containing a utopian element that also attempts to provide 'a framework for cultural change beyond corporatist state regulation' (Schwengel, 1991, p. 42). The emphasis on cultural solutions to the problems of the

1990s is worth mentioning here. *Kulturgesellschaft* is based on 'promoting direct and early interaction between economy and culture' (Schwengel, 1991, p. 42). Unlike enterprise culture it relies on public sector leadership.

> Kulturgesellschaft seems to mark a middle way between the 'soft' debate on aesthetic modernism and postmodernism, and the 'hard' debate on internationalist post-Fordist competition in the world market, ecological crisis and the dramatic risks of a class war between the north and the south (Schwengel , 1991, p. 139).

Hence, the emerging German solution also focuses on a cultural answer to the issues of rapid technological change and the structural dominance of the service sector. It is, however, less directly ideological and gives more space to the public sector. In an illuminating passage, Schwengel writes:

> We may have a post-Fordist theory of production, technology and consumption; we may understand the change from organized capitalism to disorganized institutions of regulation; we may understand the transformation of modernist texture into post-modernist figuration. But we have no alternative, political symbolic center as a necessary fiction. A new theory of modernization, which will be one of the most decisive intellectual battlefields between the right and the left in the 1990s, has explicitly to conceptualize the difference between social modernization and political modernity. The discourses of enterprise culture and Kulturgesellschaft are already providing arguments for both sides (Schwengel, 1991, p. 148).

These debates also became important in New Zealand during the 1990s. The Porter Project (Crocombe et al. 1991), for instance, focused very clearly on the notion of enterprise culture and the way in which the remolding of the education system is necessary to this end. The Minister of Education (Lockwood Smith) also picked up on this theme, commenting on the way 'imperatives of the modern world require a new culture of enterprise and competition in our curriculum' (Smith, 1991, p. 8). In the New Zealand context this kind of rhetoric had, to a large extent, both grown out of and been supplemented by a Treasury-driven emphasis on notions of consumer sovereignty and contestability. The concept of consumer sovereignty provides a particular interpretation of the link between subjectivist theories of values and the market that does not respect the integrity of cultural practices in the public domain. Keat makes the following apposite remark:

> The judgements made by democratic citizens are not regarded, at least in theory, as mere expression of personal preferences, but as resulting from a certain kind of critical engagement with the issues involved in the political sphere. But this is something that requires the acquisition and exercise of a number of skills and capacities, and hence also the availability of a wide range of cultural resources that provide, as it were, the necessary basis for relevant forms of 'educative experience.' There is thus a crucial role for certain cultural practices in contributing to this process, whose significance is itself at odds with any purely subjective theory of values (Keat, 1991, pp. 228–29).

Clearly, education has emerged as one of the newest starships in the policy fleet of governments around the world. The choice of metaphor is not entirely frivolous. Education has come to symbolize an optimistic future based on the increasing importance of science and technology as the engine of economic growth and the means by which countries can successfully compete in the global economy in years to come. The metaphor also captures and updates the past popular discourse and iconography that surrounded an ideology which motivated US educational reformers in the 1960s during the Sputnik catch-up-with-the-Russians debate, the Reagan era 'Star Wars' scenario of the 1980s, and the more recent Japanese threat to American enterprise. In the era of the 'new world order,' of structural adjustment policies, of international and regional free trade agreements, the focus has shifted away from exploiting fears of imminent destruction in superpower rivalry to the role that education, in conjunction with the new information, computer and communicational technologies, can play in the game of increasing national competitive advantage. The emphasis on possible economic decline in face of international competition and the need to 'catch up' with other nations now occupies center ground. Such a discourse, perhaps, is less naive, optimistic, and forthright than it once was, given the uncertainty of the prospect for continuous economic growth, of its ecological sustainability, and of its democratic potential for redistributing wealth. Yet it is also both more strategic and effective. Alongside economic globalization, there has been massive state asset sales programs, wholesale restructuring of the core public sector, a creeping privatization of health and commercialization of education. In conjunction with these policies enacted during the 1980s there has been, more broadly considered, a deliberate and sustained attempt at cultural reconstruction. At the heart of this attempt is the notion of enterprise culture and the importance of reconstructing education so that it will deliver the necessary research, skills and attitudes required to compete in an increasingly competitive international economy.

The notion of enterprise culture, designed for a postindustrial, information economy of the 1990s, can be seen in poststructuralist terms as the creation of a new metanarrative, a totalizing and unifying story about the prospect of economic growth and development based on the triumvirate of science, technology, and education. This master narrative, which projects a national ideological vision, differs from the social democratic narrative: it does not adopt the language of equality of opportunity, and it does not attempt to redress power imbalances or socioeconomic inequalities. The new neoliberal metanarrative is based on a vision of the future: one sustained by 'excellence,' by 'technological literacy,' by 'skills training,' by 'performance,' and by 'enterprise.'

The code words 'enterprise' and 'enterprise culture' are major signifiers in this new discourse, which emphasizes that there has been too much emphasis on social and cultural objectives and insufficient emphasis on economic goals in our education system. Henceforth, we must invest heavily in education as a basis for future economic growth by redesigning the system so that it meets the needs of business and industry. The curriculum must also be redesigned to reflect the new realities and the need for the highly skilled flexible worker who possesses requisite skills in management, information handling, communication, problem solving, and decision making. As the metanarrative has grown it has also been transformed to encompass a new emphasis on regional educational standards, portability and transferability of qualifications, performance management of teachers, systems of national testing, and so on.

THE ENTREPRENEURIAL SELF: THE SELF-CONSTITUTING AND SELF-CONSUMING 'CITIZEN-CONSUMER'

It is not a truism in social science to say that we have passed from a metaphysics of the self as producer, which characterised the era of Left politics and the Welfare State, to a metaphysics of self as consumer, which now characterizes politics on the Right, the neoliberal market economy and the provision of public services. In this shifting metaphysics it is possible to even talk of the symbolic economy of the self and the importance of understanding processes of self-capitalization, self-presentation, self-branding, and self-virtualisation as market processes that simultaneously involve political, ethical, and aesthetic elements.

Self-capitalization refers to decisions to invest in the self, especially where payment typically is undertaken over a period of years such as in advanced degrees often completed part-time. Self-presentation refers to the new emphasis on symbolic goods and the ways in which the ethos of self-presentation prevails in a symbolic economy and depends often on 'skills of self-presentation,' including personal grooming (e.g., hair, face, etc.), personal style, dress, body shape, body language, verbal presentation and increasingly the ability to change one's overall appearance regularly. This is very Goffmanesque although the creation of the self through the purchase of goods and services is given a much clearer market imperative that weighs on an 'aesthetics of self' and evidenced in examples of self-branding, (i.e., branding the self; 'I'm a ____ person'—substitute Levi, Coke, Gucci, Armani, etc.) self-virtualization (i.e., creation of personal web pages). We might follow Foucault's lead to talk in terms of processes of political, ethical and aesthetic self-constitution through choice-making involving the purchase of goods and services and, in some cases, longer-term investment decisions.

A genealogy of the entrepreneurial self reveals that it is the relationship, promoted by neoliberalism that *one establishes to oneself* through forms of personal investment (for example, user charges, top-up fees, student loans) and insurance that becomes the central ethical and political component of a new individualised, customised, and privatised consumer welfare economy. In this novel form of governance, responsibilized individuals are called upon to apply certain managerial, economic and actuarial techniques to themselves as new citizen-consumer subjects. Increasingly, under neoliberalism and the Third Way in the UK risk and security management is associated with the new consumer welfare regime where an entrepreneurial self invests in herself—a form of prudentialism—calculating the risks and returns on this investment in her education, health, employment and retirement. This process we describe as both self-constituting and self-consuming. It is self-constituting in the Foucauldian sense of choice-making shaping us as moral, economic and political agents. It is self-consuming in the sense that the entrepreneurial self creates and constructs herself through acts of consumption. Take for instance, the example of a self-investment in an advanced degree undertaken over a period of 4–5 years, where the entrepreneurial self is paying for the degree herself (let us assume £2,000 or $US 5,000 per year for 5 years). This is an investment in her future and it is made after a process of deliberation, of weighing up a range of factors including future security and employment prospects (a clear form of risk calculation and management). The investment is made in the self—in an activity that traditionally is held to be personally transformative—although it is made over a period of time and its success as an investment requires active participation ('work on the self') by the subject. Certainly, it differs from the normal acquisitive model of consumerism and one could argue that the purchase of (and investment in) services differs markedly from the purchase of commodities.

The neoliberal regime is, in part, supported by the rise of enterprise culture and what Peters calls 'enterprise education' which began under Thatcher's government (Peters, 2001a). Blair's Third Way is an attempt to go beyond neoliberalism and its conflation of autonomy with possessive, individualised consumerism and to subordinate the security of the producer to the freedom of the consumer. As Daniel Leighton notes 'The goal is to save the welfare state but to do so by privileging the efficiency of the private sector and the sovereignty of the consumer' (Leighton, 2003).

Tony Blair's speech on public service reform to public sector workers on October 16, 2001, defined the elements of a Third Way programme to remodel the government-citizen relationship along consumer lines:

> The key to reform is re-designing the system around the user—the patient, the pupil, the passenger, the victim of crime.

And later in the speech he defines its principles, thus:

First, high national standards and full accountability. Second, devolution to the front-line to encourage diversity and local creativity. Third, flexibility of employment so that staff are better able to deliver modern public services. Fourth, the promotion of alternative providers and greater choice.

All four principles have one goal—to put the consumer first. We are making the public services user-led, not producer or bureaucracy led, allowing far greater freedom and incentives for services to develop as users want. (For the full text of Blair's speech see The Guardian: http://society.guardian.co.uk/futureforpublicservices/story/0,8150,575220,00.html).[2]

The four reform principles—standards and accountability, devolution and diversity, flexibility of employment, and greater choice—define what Catherine Needham (2003) calls 'the consumerisation of citizenship' supported by an increasingly promotional and top-down form of communications, consultation focused on the 'self-regarding individual' without collective discussion, and a form of service delivery based on the combined objectives of maximising 'customer satisfaction and expanding individual choice and competition.' The four principles have a clear resonance with the principles articulated in *A Nation Still at Risk.*

Needham suggests that the government-citizen relationship is replicating patterns of choice and power found in the private economy where the 'consumer is primarily self-regarding, forms preferences without reference to others, and acts through a series of instrumental, temporary bilateral relationships.' She argues that there are limits to the relevance of consumerism to the public sector in that choice may have perverse effects and may be impossible to institutionalise. The most fundamental danger in her eyes is the erosion of democracy and, by contrast, she seeks alternatives in notions of active citizenship, community, coproduction and voluntarism (http://www.catalystforum.org.uk/pubs/pub10a.html).

The pressing question is whether Third Way New Labour can go beyond neoliberalism and loaded definitions of freedom in purely consumer terms to revitalise and perhaps, redefine, elements of traditional social democracy: participation and active engagement, access and equality, collective identity and mobilisation, and social justice. In this regard Chancellor Gordon Brown's foray into the discussion of the role and limits of the market in the context of globalisation has helped launch a new debate.

In the BBC4 series *The Commanding Heights: The Battle for the World Economy* (2003) based on the book by Daniel Yergin and Joseph Stanislaw, UK Chancellor Gordon Brown, who heads up the key policy-making IMF committee, told Yergin:

The problem for the Left in the past was that they equated the public interest with public ownership and public regulation, and therefore they assumed that markets were not in the public interest ... [Markets] provide opportunities for prosperity, but equally they're not automatically equated with the public interest.

He went on to say:

> The idea that markets must work in the public interest, the idea that governments have a responsibility for the level of employment and prosperity in the economy, the idea that governments must intervene on occasions—these are increasingly the ideas of our time.

The Chancellor accepts globalisation as a fact of life, but tells Yergin:

> The question is, can we manage it in the interests of a few or in the interests, as I want it to be, of all the people of the world.[3]

One of the most defining and controversial features of New Labour's second term is the way it has chosen to respond to the major constraint of underinvestment in public services through its public-private partnerships (PPP) and the private finance initiative (PFI). PPP refers to any private sector involvement in public services including 'contracting out' and transfers of ownership (as in the case of housing). PFI, the most well known form of PPP, refers to the contractualization of public services involving private companies in the provision of public services. Clearly, both forms represent the introduction of entrepreneurial values into public services. In the case of the later technically the risk is transferred from government to private consortia (although this does not discount the possibility of public 'bail outs'). There are also substantial risks to 'citizen-consumers' despite the emphasis on consumer public watch-dogs and provision of consumer information: effectively the process of contractualization and tendering does not involve 'the public' or the 'consumer' in any collective decision-making sense, and yet it mortgages the citizen-consumer to a form of hire-purchase the long-term financial and social costs of which are not often clear. In an age of consumerism, the fundamental question is to what extent, if at all, can the citizen-consumer shape privately funded public services in ways other than through their acts of consumption?

Postscript ON Subjectivity, Eros AND Pedagogy

In his so-called final ethical phase, Foucault moves 'back to the subject,' to the ethics of self-formation considered as an ascetic practice. Foucault argues that 'work' done on the self is not to be understood in terms of traditional left-wing models of liberation but rather as (Kantian) practices of freedom, for there is no essential, hidden, or true self, for Foucault, 'concealed, alienated, or imprisoned in and by mechanisms of repression' that is in need of liberation but only a *hermeneutics of the self,* a set of practices of self-interpretation. He emphasizes that freedom is the ontological condition for ethics and, in his works on the history of sexuality, he returns to the Stoics to entertain the notion of 'care for the self,' which has priority over and develops earlier than 'care for others.' Recently there has appeared a number of works focusing on the 'late' Foucault and his purported 'return to the subject' and to the ethical self-constitution of political subjects, yet this 'turn' can be seen as continuing a number of prescient themes in Foucault's thinking. To be sure Foucault is no longer concerned with 'the death of Man' so much as the ethical self-constitution of political subjects, and it seems that criticisms of his 'pessimism' to do with questions of agency no longer apply especially when the emphasis falls on self constitution under ethical liberalism and even with questions of freedom and human rights. Increasingly, it seems that Foucault's project revolves around the philosophy of the subject centering on the political technology of the body and the formation of the political subject. We will not pronounce here on whether there is an essential continuity in Foucault's thought or how to relate his 'late' ethics to his earlier work on normalizing power, except to say that we believe that there is a strong account of the self in relation to *practices* and thus to *culture* that emphasizes both active and passive elements of the shaping of subjectivity—both self-constitution and cultural/discursive shaping of individuals as two aspects of the making of subjects.

Sebastian Harrer (2005, p. 76) argues convincingly for such an interpretation against the view that holds

> that at some point in his oeuvre, Foucault turned away from analysing the power/knowledge mechanisms that fabricate subjects, and turned to analysing how subjects constitute themselves. This view sometimes implies the idea that these notions, 'constitution' and 'fabrication,' refer to two distinct phenomena.

Harrer, in his investigations of 'The Theme of Subjectivity in Foucault's Lecture Series *L'Herméneutique du Sujet*,' instead of a 'return of the subject' advocates a 'conceptual continuity traversing the whole of Foucault's oeuvre, rather than a rupture that separates the "early" from the "late" Foucault' (p. 76). Harrer assembles a range of internal evidence including Foucault's own recollections and interviews where he addresses his project as 'a history of the subject' (rather than a turn to ethics) and also develops a conceptual argument to support his interpretation, turning in particular to Foucault's *L'Herméneutique du Sujet*.

What is interesting for our purposes is the way in which Harrer makes central to his interpretation Foucault's account of subjectivity the notion of 'spiritual guidance' that is Foucault's concept for the ancient teacher-student relationship. 'Spiritual guidance,' Harrer claims, occupies the same position as 'surveillance' in Foucault's early work. Harrer finds a Nietzschean conception of power as the common denominator that links Foucault's earlier works on normalizing power and later works on ethical self-constitution. As he says:

> A subject arises through various modes of 'subjectivation,' some of them through normalizing power mechanisms, others through technologies or practices of the self ('*pratiques de soi*'). But the subject really is and remains only a 'hollow gap' in the field of power relations (p. 81).

He goes on to explain the significance of this position by suggesting

> The process of self-constitution is situated in a field of forces and starts out through a relationship to others, which in turn aims at producing a relation to self ('*rapport à soi*'). This is achieved by way of certain ascetic technologies of the self, which one practices first under supervision of a master. This relationship is then replicated inside the subject, who will eventually take a 'transcendental position' towards him- or herself (p.83).

He then focuses on 'dietetics' and 'spiritual guidance' as ascetic practices in Foucault's 'aesthetics of existence' used for the goal of ethical self-constitution.

Harrer reminds us that 'spiritual guidance' is the basis of Foucault's investigation of education in ancient schools of philosophy where the master did not teach a body of knowledge but rather participated in the development of a certain relation to self with his student, teaching his student to care for himself through engagement in ascetic practices of listening, reading, writing and speaking that establishes certain practices of self-discipline. Harrer's (2005) account is useful and informative although it does also miss something historically important in both Foucault and what we might call 'pederastic education' in the ancient schools of philosophy (briefly mentioned in chapter 3): the relationship of 'spiritual guidance' was between master and student was modelled on a form of pederasty, idealized by the Greeks in terms of a relationship and bond between an adolescent boy and an adult male. It became the basis for an aristocratic institution of education considered in moral terms—a form of homoeroticism closely connected with Greek ideals of athleticism and nudity. As part of philosophy, pederastic relationships often took a chaste form emphasizing the balance between desire and self-control. The *erastes-eromenos* relationship (Greek terms for 'lover' and 'beloved') constituted a complex moral system fundamental to ancient Greek society and to education, often forming a legal relationship of guardianship consecrated by a religious ceremony and requiring the consent of the boy's father. The relationship, mentioned uncritically by Plato in the *Symposium* and the *Phaedrus,* had strong educational purposes associated with introducing the youth into adult society by assuming certain citizen responsibilities and obligations. To this extent it was inseparable from the activities of the gymnasium, from pedagogy and from military training (see Percy, 1996).

We have to be careful to supplement our philosophical analyses with accurate historical accounts and to be wary of wanting to generalize investigations from one era to another to create universal necessities of human nature. This too is a message from Foucault.

The significance of Foucault's thought in relation to education is that he provides theoretical and methodological means to study the field of education part of the emergent human sciences, focusing the conditions under which subjects are constituted objects of knowledge and constitute themselves as subjects. Educationalists are only at the beginning of exploring the relevance and promise of Foucault's thought to their own field.

Notes

ONE. THE CULTURE OF SELF

1.   Colin Gordon comments: 'Foucault very seldom in these texts talks about the self. It is souci de soi, culture de soi, not souci, culture du soi. Arguably there is not such thing as 'the' self in classical thought. 'Culture of self', not 'culture of the self'. This is more natural in terms of modern thought and usage but it risks eliding a key historical and genealogical difference.' Personal communication, email 8/19/2007, Colin Gordon, reproduced with permission.

2.   For audio files of 'Michel Foucault: The Culture of the Self,' April 12, 1983: Berkeley Language Center—Speech Archive SA 1456 and 'Discussion,' April 19, 1983: Berkeley Language Center—Speech Archive SA 1462 at http://www.lib.berkeley.edu/MRC/audiofiles. html#foucault (accessed April 11, 2006).

3.   We are indebted to Colin Gordon, who at very short notice read a draft of Chapter 1 and offered a range of comments mainly focusing on our reference to Foucault's use of Hadot and Hadot's influence upon him. Rather than revise the text to reflect Colin Gordon's comments, especially at a very late stage in the production of the book, we decided to include as much of his commentary on this point as possible. It is, after all, a significant matter that requires correction. Gordon also questions the notion of a sharp break in Foucault's work in the mid 70s. He writes: 'While half of Foucault's lectures remain unpublished (including both first and last) it is maybe a bit hazardous to try partitioning them into clearly dis-

tinct periods. I do not see myself a key break between 75 and 76, and I see clear anticipations of the governmentality theme in the lectures of 74 and 75. Others have suggested a break between the 76 and 78 lectures—I don't find that convincing either.' Personal communication, email 8/19/2007, Colin Gordon, reproduced with permission.

Colin Gordon makes the following remark about the relationship between Foucault and Hadot: 'You refer in a couple of places to Foucault's well-known interest in the work of Hadot. You also refer to them at one point as friends. I think that may be an overstatement. Foucault was instrumental in Hadot's election to a chair at the College de France and on Hadot's account they had a certain number of conversations, but that was apparently about all. You refer to Hadot's criticisms of Foucault in his well-known paper (and which he develops in some later interviews, where signs of friendly sentiment on his part are hard to discern). However I am not sure that one is obliged to accept these criticisms as totally authoritative and final; in my opinion some are caricatures bordering on the homophobic, and others are little more than exercises in point-scoring. Hadot's account of Foucault's last books, and his reading of them as commending a form of dandyism, relies rather heavily on a tendentious interpretation of some remarks of Foucault's in an interview, rather than on what is said in the books themselves. One should also note that in the 1982 lectures Foucault himself takes issue with Hadot by suggesting there is a third conception of conversion in Seneca which differs from the two ancient conceptions, epistrophe and metanoia, identified by Hadot. Taking this volume as a whole one can perhaps see that Foucault is not quite as heavily reliant on Hadot as is sometimes supposed—or as lacking in scholarly equipment as Hadot and those who have endorsed Hadot's charges are inclined to suggest.' Personal communication, email 5/7/2007, Colin Gordon, reproduced with permission.

In a later email, Colin Gordon, writes: 'Hadot's essay was undoubtedly a significant stimulus to Foucault when his friend and research collaborator Pasquale Pasquino showed it to him some time in the late 70s. Foucault himself acknowledges this. But there is a great deal in Hadot's intellectual package that Foucault does not buy into—the idea of a perennial essence of philosophical practice, or the investment in a perennial Neo-Platonic model of philosophical spirituality centered on the oceanic experience of oneness with the cosmos. You say that 'Writing the self' 'clearly draws' on Hadot's work. Hadot himself criticizes this essay, remarking that he had written on some of the same sources. But can we not also consider the possibility that Foucault conducted his own independent research, very possibly stimulated and informed by Hadot's work, but addressing different issues and drawing different and independent conclusions? If we are interested in Foucault's relation to Hadot then why not discuss Foucault's own stated points of difference from Hadot? (Or indeed his use of other previous work: while Foucault respectfully cites Pierre Hadot, he also cites the important earlier work on the same subjects by Hadot's wife Ilsetraut.) One should also not exclude the possibility that Hadot's later work has discreetly taken on board certain themes which Foucault introduced and which were not previously much discussed by Hadot, including souci de soi.'

TWO. THE GENEALOGY OF THE CONFESSIONAL SELF

1.   Julian Young (2002, p. 44) argues that Lovitt's translation of das Gestell is unsatisfactory, because

it ignores 'das' and suggests human action rather than 'a mode of disclosure which determines the action.' He suggests that 'a better translation would be something like "the frame-up"' but opts to leave it untranslated.

2. The pronoun 'he' was used because these discussions about ancient Greek society only referred to free males, not slaves nor women as citizens.

THREE. THE BODY AND THE AESTHETICS OF EXISTENCE

1. The most developed contribution on Foucault in relation to counseling outside the narrative therapy approach of White and Epston (1989) is Besley (2000; 2001; 2002; 2003, 2006).
2. Only the date for English translations of Foucault's major works is provided in the Bibliography.
3. There are now many historians who disagree with Foucault on almost all aspects of his account but especially over the historical faithfulness of the 'great confinement.' For instance, Roy Porter (2002: 93) writes:

> Though there is a certain plausibility in Foucault's interpretation, it is simplistic and over-generalized. With the exception of France, the seventeenth century did not bring any spectacle surge in institutionalisation—it certainly did not become the automatic solution.

Porter suggests that state sequestration came late in England with the passing of an act in 1808 permitting the use of public funds for asylums. He argues that in Europe and North America 'the rise of the asylum is better seen not as an act of state but as a side effect of commercial and professional society' (p. 95).

4. In 'Of Other Spaces' Foucault contrasts the 19th century 'obsession with time' with the present epoch's preoccupation with space postulating three histories of space: a hierarchic ensemble of places in the Middle Ages—'sacred places and profane plates: protected places and open, exposed places: urban places and rural places'—which was opened up by Galileo when 'extension' (and infinite space) replaced 'emplacement' (or localization); and, today when 'site' and the relations between sites has been substituted for extension. As he says: 'Our epoch is one in which space takes for us the form of relations among sites,' which he explains as follows:

> The site is defined by relations of proximity between points or elements; formally, we can describe these relations as series, trees, or grids. Moreover, the importance of the site as a problem in contemporary technical work is well known: the storage of data or of the intermediate results of a calculation in the memory of a machine, the circulation of discrete elements with a random output (automobile traffic is a simple case, or indeed the sounds on a telephone line); the identification of marked or coded elements inside a set that may be randomly distributed, or may be arranged according to single or to multiple classifications.

The aesthetics of the body is, in part, an aesthetics of space and, therefore, in the Foucauldian sense as aesthetics of the movement or mobility of bodies.

5. These elements are based on on Schatzki and Natter's (1996) summary of the literature and discussion, although we have removed some features that they took from John O'Neill (see p. 4). We have also emphasized the importance of a rejuvenated concept of labour and notion of practice

to an analysis of the schooled body.

6. See Simons' essay 'Is *The Second Sex* Beauvoir's Application of Sartrean Existentialism?' at http://www.bu.edu/wcp/Papers/Gend/GendSimo.htm (accessed 18/5/05).

7. See the bibliography at http://www.cddc.vt.edu/feminism/bod.html (accessed 18/5/05).

8. For a bibliography of 'Feminist Aesthetics' see http://www.cddc.vt.edu/feminism/aes.html (accessed 18/5/05).

FOUR. SPACE AND THE BODY POLITIC

1. For a useful site on the politics of space see the website of the same title (http://www.urbitopia. com/Principal.htm), especially the link to Groupe de Recherche sur l'Architecture au Levant and the text by Michael F. Davie. For a variety of approaches to the study of social space see Lefebvre (1991), Ligget & Perry (1995), Doel (1999) and Casey (1997). In critical pedagogy: see Henry Giroux's (2001) *Public Spaces, Private Lives: beyond the Culture of Cynicism* as an argument for revitalised public spaces that provide 'the forum for debating norms, critical engaging ideas, making private issue public, and evaluating judgements' and thereby support the values of citizen participation and the public good (p. xi); see also Edwards & Usher (2000); Lankshear et al. (1996); Lankshear et al. (2000); Peters (1996); Peters (2001a).

SIX. RISK AND THE ETHICS OF SUBJECTIVITY: *PARRHESIA* IN ACTION

Websites

http://www.strath.ac.uk/government/awp/demo.html, accessed July 2003

http://www.messengers.org.uk, accessed April 2003

http://www.stopwar.org.uk/release, press release 20 March 2003, accessed April 2003

http://education.guardian.co.uk/Print/0,3858,4632153,00.html, accessed April 2003

http://www.eis.org.uk/latest.htm, accessed April 2003

http://www.nut.org.uk/, accessed April 2003

http://news.bbc.co.uk/nol/shared/spl/hi/programmes/panorama/transcripts/racetobaghdad.txt, accessed April 2003

http://www.ltscotland.com/citizenship/, accessed April 2003

http://www.qca.org.uk/ca/inclusion/respect_for_all/guidelines.asp, accessed April 2003

http://www.dea.org.uk, accessed April 2003

http://socrates.berkeley.edu/~hdreyfus/html/paper_heidandfoucault.html, accessed October 2002

http://education.guardian.co.uk/Print/0,3858,4631332,00.html, Geraldine Bedell, "Voices of tomorrow don't wait to protest," *The Observer*, 23 March 2003, accessed April 2003

http://education.guardian.co.uk/Print/0,3858,4632153,00.html, Dea Birkett, "It's their war too," *The Guardian*, 25 March 2003, accessed April 2003

http://argument.independent.co.uk/low_res/story.jsp?story=389745&host=6&dir=140, Zoe Pilger, "Generation Apathy has Woken Up," *The Independent*, 23 March 2003, accessed April 2003

Appendix 1. Respect for All: Valuing Diversity and Challenging Racism through the Curriculum—General Guidance for Teachers: Some Web Resources for UK Schools

www.dea.org.uk
http://www.citfou.org.uk/teaching_support/iraq_intro.php4
http://www.childrens-express.org/
http://www.espresso.co.uk/visitors/efs/staffroom/
http://www.dep.org.uk/globalexpress/index.htm
http://www.learn.co.uk/glearning/secondary/topical/default.htm
http://news.bbc.co.uk/cbbcnews
education@oxfam.org.uk
http://www.oxfam.org.uk/coolplanet
http://www.parentsonline.gov.uk/articles/2003/3/21–1048257578.html
http://www.runnymedetrust.org/meb/islamophobia/talking_teaching.html
http://www.teachingforchange.org/body_index.html

QCA
Guarding standards

Printed from the Qualifications Curriculum Authority website
Sunday 06th of April 2003 03:09 GMT Standard Time
http://www.qca.org.uk/ca/inclusion/respect_for_all/guidelines.asp

SEVEN. UNDERSTANDING THE NEOLIBERAL PARADIGM OF EDUCATION POLICY

1. This formulation comes from Alan Hunt, drawing on his characterization of liberalism and neoliberalism that was advanced in a series of three seminars given at the University of Auckland in May 1996. Besides the editors themselves, the collection edited by Barry, Osborne, and Rose (1996), includes the following contributors: Barry Hindess, Vikki Bell, Ian Hunter, Alan Hunt, Pat O'Malley, Mitchell Dean, and Barbara Cruikshank. (See also Dean, 1991, 1999; Hindess, 1996; Hunter, 1994; Hunt and Wickham, 1994; Rose, 1996). The Anglophone neo-Foucauldians might be distinguished from the French (e.g., Donzelot, 1979; Donzelot, 1991), and the U.S. neo-Foucauldians. They may also be distinguished from various feminist appropriations of Foucault, which are both too diverse and complex for us to outline here. In terms of education philosophy and policy see: Ball (1990), especially the essays by Marshall, Hoskin and Ball; Ball (1994); Besley (2000); Marshall (1996); Middleton (1998); Olssen (1999); Peters (1994, 1996, 2001); Peters & Marshall (1996); Popkewitz (1999).

2. In his Résumé du cours for 1979 (in Foucault, 2004b: 323) Foucault indicates that the method he will adopt is based on Paul Veyne's nominalist history and in this respect he writes:

    > Et reprenant un certain nombre de choix de méthode déjà faits, j'ai essayé d'analyser le <<libéralisme>>, non pas une théorie ni comme une idéologie, encore moins, bein entendu, comme une mannière pour la <<société>> de <<se\ représenter>>; mais

comme une pratique, c'est-à-dire comme une <<manière de faire>> orientée vers objec-
tifs et se régulant par une réflexion continue. Le libéralisme est à analyser alors comme
principe et méthode de rationalisation de l'exercice de gouvernement—rationalisation
qui obéit, et c'est là sa spécificité, à la règle interne de l'économie maximale.

Foucault (in 2001) explains in 'Questions of method' his emphasis on *practice* with an accent on
'eventalization' and 'the problem of rationalities.' He says, 'Eventalizing singular ensembles of practices, so as to make them graspable as different regimes of 'jurisdiction' and 'verification'' (p. 230)
and he ascribes the method to Veyne with the following remark 'it's a matter of the effect on historical knowledge of a nominalist critique itself arrived at by way of historical analysis' (p. 238).
The concept of practice here is crucial to understanding Foucault. Stern (2000: fn 33, p. 358) indicates in a footnote a reference to Dreyfus' course at the NEH Summer Institute on Practices on
24 July 1997, under the title 'Conclusion: How background practices and skills work to ground
norms and intelligibility: the ethico-political implications' and summarises Dreyfus' account of
five 'theories' (Wittgenstein and Bourdieu; Hegel and Merleau-Ponty; Heidegger; Derrida; and
Foucault). He summarises Foucault's notion as follows: 'Problematization. (Foucault) Practices
develop in such a way that contradictory actions are felt to be appropriate. Attempts to fix these
problems lead to further resistance. This leads to a hyperactive pessimism: showing the contin-
gency of what appears to be necessary and engaging in resistance to established order.' See also
Schatzki et al. (2001).

3.   Rousseau begins his famous 1755 text 'Discourse on Political Economy' with the following
     remark: 'The word Economy, or OEconomy, is derived from *oikos, a house,* and *vomos, law,* and
     meant originally only the wise and legitimate government of the house for the common good of
     the whole family. The meaning of the term was then extended to the government of that great
     family, the State.' Rousseau, as you know, goes on to distinguish between the government of the
     family and the State, and to deny there is anything in common except the obligations that the head
     or sovereign owe to their subjects. They are, he argues, based on different rules and that 'the first
     rule of public *economy* is that the administration of justice should be conformable to the laws' and
     to the general will. For the full text see: http://www.constitution.org/jjr/polecon.htm

4.   The Foucault archives have been recently relocated from the IMEC (Institut Mémoires de l'Édi-
     tion Contemporaine) Paris address (9, rue Bleue, F-75009 Paris) to Abbaye d'Ardenne (14280
     Saint Germaine la Blanche-Herbe), e-mail: bibliotheque@imec-archives.com. <<Il faut défend-
     er la société>>, a course Foucault delivered in 1975–1976, translated by David Macey as *Society
     Must Be Defended,* was published in 2003 by Penguin (Foucault, 2003). While courses for
     1977–78, 1978–79, as previously mentioned, and 1981–82 (<<L'Herméneutique de sujet>>) have
     been recently published (in the Gallimand/Seuill series), courses for the years 1979–80, 1980–81,
     1982–83, 1983–84 are still only available from the IMEC Foucault archive as recorded tapes.

5.   The governmentality literature has grown up around the journal *Economy and Society,* and includes
     the work of Cruickshank, Hindess, Hunter, Larner, Minson, O'Malley, Owen, and others, as well
     as those referred to above, most of whom have published in *Economy and Society* (for aims and
     scope, and table of contents, see http://www.tandf.co.uk/journals/titles/03085147.asp).

6.   See 'Why Foucault?' (Peters & Besley, 2007), which discusses Foucault studies in the English-
     speaking world by reference to the work of Marshall, Olssen, Ball, Popkewitz & Brennan, Besley,
     Baker, Middleton and Peters. Peters' work on Foucault's governmentality dates from Peters
     (1994), with additional work in 1996 (with Marshall), Peters (1996), Peters (1997a, 1997b), and
     Peters (2001d, e, f). For additional work on Foucault see Peters (2003a & b), Peters (2005a & b).
     Educational Philosophy and Theory published a special issue in 2006 entitled 'The Learning Society

and Governmentality' edited by Masschelein, Bröckling, Simons and Pongratz.

7. See the essay 'Foucault' by Maurice Florence written for a new edition of the Dictionnaire des philosophes (Foucault, 1998). The entry was written by Foucault and signed under a pseudonym. See also Rabinow's (1997) introduction to the history of systems of thought.

8. See the essay by Arnold Davidson where he reports upon and translates a fragment from a lecture Foucault gives in Japan in 1978 (roughly the point in which he was working up the notion of 'govenrmentality'). Foucault makes the following comment on Anglo-American philosophy in 'La philosophie analytique de la politique' (cited in Davidson, 1997, p. 3):

> For Anglo-Saxon analytic philosophy is a question of making a critical analysis of thought on the basis of the way in which one says things. I think one could imagine, in the same way, a philosophy that would have as its task to analyze what happens every day in relations of power, a philosophy that would try to show what they are about, what are the forms, the stakes, the objectives of these relations of power. A philosophy, accordingly, that would bear rather on relations of power than on language games, a philosophy that would bear on all these relations that traverse the social body rather than the effects of language that traverse and underlie thought. One could imagine, one should imagine something like an analytico-political philosophy.

9. Michael Peters does not describe himself as an Anglo- or neo-Foucauldian. He states: While acknowledging that the problematic developed out of his governmentality paper and related interviews holds theoretical promise, I think it is a mistake to want to base a problematic on such slender pickings. I would rather: (i) take Foucault's corpus as a whole and work on the relations between governmentality and his wider 'project'; (ii) view Foucault as part of a movement of contemporary French thought that have become homogenized as 'poststructuralism,' with historical relations to a range of thinkers (Kant, Nietzsche, Weber) and connections to his 'teachers' and contemporaries (Bataille, Blanchot, Althusser, Deleuze).

10. 'La Volonté de savoir' (1970–71), 'Théories et Institutions pénales' (1971–72), 'La Société punitive' (1972–73), 'Le Pouvoir psychiatrique' (1973–74), 'Les Anormaux' (1974–75).

11. 'Il faut défendre la société' (1975–76), 'Securité, Territoire, Population' (1977–78), 'Naissance de la biopolitique' (1978–79), 'Du gouvernement des vivants' (1979–80), 'Subjectivité et Vérité' (1980–81), 'L'Herméneutique du subjet' (1981–82), 'Le Gouvernement de soi et des autres' (1982–83), 'Le Gouvernement de soi et des autres: le courage de la verite' (1983–84).

12. As he writes in his Résumé du cours (in Foucault, 2004b: 323):

> Le thème retenu était doc la <<biopolitique>>: j'entendais par là la manière don't on a essayé, depuis le XVIII siècle, de rationaliser les problèmes posés à la pratique gouvenrement par les phénomènes propres à une ensemble de vivants constitutes en population: santé, hygiene, natalitié, longévité, races . . .

13. Foucault investigates the notion of civil society—a twin notion to *homo economicus* and indissociable elements of the technology of liberal government—by reference to Adam Ferguson (1996), a philosopher of the Scottish Enlightenment, whose *An Essay on the History of Civil Society,* first published in 1767, as an inquiry into the 'natural history of man,' seeks to elucidate the general characteristics of human nature (including principles of self-preservation, union, war, etc.), provide a 'history of rude nations,' policy and arts, and comments on the advancement of civil and commercial arts, as well as 'the decline of nations' and 'corruption and political slavery.'

14. Foucault refers to the work of F. Bilger (1964) *La Pensée économique libérale de l'Allemagne contemporaine*. For a brief chronological biography of Erhard see http://www.dhm.de/lemo/html/biografien/ErhardLudwig/

15. See also Broyer (1996) and Witt (2002). For the continued relevance of ordoliberalism and the social market model see Joerges & Rödl (2004).

16. This brief account is based on information provided by the New School University's (New York) History of Economic Thought website (http://cepa.newschool.edu/het/index.htm). The New School was founded in 1919 by a group of pacifist intellectuals, including John Dewey and Thorstein Veblen—some of whom resigned from Columbia—to set up an institution, modeled after the *Volkshochschulen* in Germany, where ideas could be exchanged freely. The School was designed to maintain close ties with Europe and during the 1920s, the then president, Alvin Johnson, aware of Hitler's threat to democracy set up a 'University in Exile' for scholars threatened by National Socialism. Any acknowledged quotations are from the History of Economic Thought website.

17. Despite, or perhaps as a result of, its mischievous but always unique perspective, the University of Chicago has taken in a lion's share of Nobel prizes in economics: Milton Friedman, T.W. Schultz, G.J. Stigler, R.H. Coarse G.S. Becker, M.H. Miller, R.W. Fogel and R.E. Lucas were all on the Chicago faculty when they received their awards. If we were to add Chicago-trained economists, the list of Nobelists would expand to include Hebet Simon, James Buchanan, Harry Markowitz and Myron Scoles.

EIGHT: ENTERPRISE CULTURE AND THE RISE OF THE ENTREPRENEURIAL SELF

1. These examples come from an anonymous reviewer of the paper from which this was drawn.

2. Blair makes the following comments about education in relation to the four principles:

Standards and accountability
In education, there are national tests in the basics for all 7-, 11- and 14-year-olds, regular inspection of schools; and national strategies including, literacy and numeracy hours to ensure basic minimum standards of teaching and learning school by school. . . .

Devolution and diversity
Specialist schools—schools that build a real center of excellence in one area while continuing to teach the whole curriculum—also represent significant change. Schools achieving highly in one respect tend to perform better across the board—GCSE results in specialist schools are nearly 10 percentage points higher than in non-specialist comprehensives with a single intake. Our program of diversity in secondary education is therefore vital to the future, which is why we have set a target of at least 1,500 specialist schools by 2005 as a staging post to specialist status for all secondary schools ready for it. . . .

Flexibility of employment

There are new training salaries for new post-graduate teacher trainees, a performance bonus of £2,000.00 to nearly 200,00 teachers. . . . In education, we have established the new National College for School Leadership. . . .

Greater choice

The fourth of our reform principles is the provision of far great choice to the consumer—not just formal choice, but the ability to make that choice effective. In education that means not only a wider variety of schools, but also expansion of successful schools and encouragement of the very successful to take over schools or set up new schools, so that more parents are able to secure their first preference school for their child.

3. His reported desire is not only to eliminate poverty at home but also to double aid to the Third World. In his capacity as chairman of the IMF committee he aims to improve mechanisms of international financial institutions for 'crisis prevention' and early warning systems.

Bibliography

Armstrong, A. (2003). Foucault and Feminism. <http://www.iep.utm.edu/f/foucfem.htm> (accessed 18/5/05).

Augustine, St. (1992 [original AD 397–401]). *Confessions.* Text and commentary, James J. O'Donnell. Oxford: Oxford University Press.

Bagley, C., and K. King. (1990). *Child Sexual Abuse: the Search for Healing.* London and New York: Tavistock/Routledge.

Baker, B. (2001). *In Perpetual Motion: Theories of Power, Educational History, and the Child.* New York: Peter Lang.

Ball, S. (1994). Education Reform: a Critical and Post-structural Approach. Buckingham and Philadelphia: Open University Press.

Ball, S. J., ed. (1990). *Foucault and Education: Disciplines and Knowledge.* London: Routledge.

Barry, A., T. Osborne, and N. Rose, eds. (1996). *Foucault and Political Reason: Liberalism, Neo-liberalism and Rationalities of Government.* London: UCL Press.

Bass, E., and L. Davis. (1988). *The Courage to Heal: A Guide for Women Survivors of Child Sexual Abuse.* London: Vermillion.

Baudrillard, J. (1998 [original 1970]). *The Consumer Society: Myths and Structures.* London: Sage.

Beck, U. (1992). Risk Society: Towards a New Modernity. In B. Adam, U. Beck, and J. von Loon, eds. (2000). *The Risk Society and Beyond: Critical Issues for Social Theory.* London: Sage.

Becker, G. (1964). *Human Capital: a Theoretical and Empirical Analysis with Special Reference to Education.* New York: National Bureau of Economic Research. (Columbia University Press, distributor).

Besley, A. C. (Tina). (2000). *Self, Identity, Adolescence and the Professionalisation of School Counselling in New Zealand: Some Foucauldian Perspectives.* PhD thesis, University of Auckland.

———. (2002a). *Counseling Youth: Foucault, Power and the Ethics of Subjectivity.* Westport, CT: Praeger.

———. (2002b). Foucault and the Turn to Narrative Therapy. *British Journal of Guidance and Counselling,* 30, (2), 125–43.

———. (2002c). Psychologised Adolescents and Sociologised Youth: Rethinking Young People in Education in the 21st Century. In B. Cope and M. Kalantzis, eds. *Learning for the Future: Proceedings of the Learning Conference 2001.* <www.theLearner.com>

———. (2002d). The Professionalisation of School Counselling in New Zealand in the 20th Century. Special issue ACCESS, 21, (2): 1–94.

———. (2003a). Hybridized and Globalized: Youth Cultures in the Postmodern Era. *Review of Education, Pedagogy and Cultural Studies,* 25, 2: 153–77.

———. (2003b). The Ethical Constitution of Educational Researchers. Paper presented at BERA Conference. Heriot-Watt University, Edinburgh. 12 September 2003.

———. (2003c). A Risky Business: a Teenager's Dilemma in Disclosing Sexual Abuse. *New Zealand Journal of Counselling,* 24, 2: 11–24.

———. (2003d). Truth-telling (*parrhesia*)—a Risky Practice in Education. Paper presented at Philosophy of Education Society of Australasia Conference. Auckland, 28–29 November 2003.

———. (2003e). The Body and the Self in the New Zealand Health and Physical Education Curriculum. *New Zealand Journal of Educational Studies,* 38 (1): 59–72.

———. (2006). *Counseling Youth: Foucault, Power and the Ethics of Subjectivity* (2nd Edition). Rotterdam: Sense Publishers.

Best, S., and D. Kellner. (2003). Contemporary Youth and the Postmodern Adventure. *The Review of Education, Pedagogy and Cultural Studies,* 25, 2: 75–94.

Blagg, H., J. A. Hughes, and C. Wattam. (1989). *Child Sexual Abuse: Listening, Hearing and Validating the Experiences of Children.* London: Longman.

Bordo, S. (1993). *Unbearable Weight: Feminism, Western Culture, and the Body.* Berkeley: University of California Press.

Bourdieu, P. (1985a). The Genesis of the Concepts of Habitus and Field. C. Newman, trans. *Sociocriticism, 2, Theories and Perspectives* 2. Pittsburgh: International Institute for Sociocriticism.

———. (1985b). The Social Space and the Genesis of Groups. *Theory and Society* 1, 4.

———. (1989). Social Space and Symbolic Power. *Sociological Theory* 7, 1: 14–25.

Brownmiller, S. (1976). *Against Our Will: Men, Women and Rape.* Harmondsworth: Penguin.

Broyer, S. (1996). The Social Market Economy: Birth of an Economic Style. Discussion paper FS I 96–318. Social Science Research Center, Berlin.

Buchanan, J. (1991). *Constitutional Economics.* Oxford and Cambridge, MA: Blackwell, 1991.

Burchell, D. (1997). Liberalism and Government: Political Philosophy and the Liberal Art of Rule. In C. O'Farrell, ed. *Foucault, the Legacy.* Brisbane: Queensland University of Technology.

Burchell, G. (1993). Liberal Government and Techniques of the Self. *Economy and Society,* 22 (3): 267–82. Also in A. Barry, T. Osborne, and N. Rose, eds. *Foucault and Political Reason,* London: UCL Press.

Burchell, G., C. Gordon, and P. Miller, eds. (1991). *The Foucault Effect: Studies in Governmentality.* Chicago: University of Chicago Press and Harvester.

Butler, J. (1990). *Gender Trouble: Feminism and the Subversion of Identity.* New York and London: Routledge, Chapman, and Hall.

———. (1993). *Bodies That Matter: On the Discursive Limits of "Sex."* New York and London: Routledge.

Casey, E. S. (1993). *Getting Back into Place.* Indianapolis: Indiana University Press.

Cavell, S. (1995). *Philosophical Passages: Wittgenstein, Emerson, Austin, Derrida.* Oxford and Cambridge,

MA: Blackwell.

——. (1996). Epilogue: the Investigations' Everyday Aesthetics of Itself. In S. Mulhall, ed. *The Cavell Reader.* Oxford and Cambridge, MA: Blackwell.

Chodorow, N. (1978). *The Reproduction of Mothering: Psychoanalysis and the Sociology of Gender.* Berkeley: University of California Press.

Conant, J. (2001). Philosophy and Biography. In J. C. Klagge, ed. *Wittgenstein: Biography and Philosophy.* Cambridge: Cambridge University Press.

Corby, B. (2000). *Child Sexual Abuse: Towards a Knowledge Base* (2nd edition). Buckingham and Philadelphia: Open University Press.

Corrigan, P. (1997). *The Sociology of Consumption.* London: Sage.

Crossley, N. (2001). *The Social Body: Habit, Identity and Desire.* London and Thousand Oaks, CA: Sage.

Curtis, B. (2002). Foucault on Governmentality and Population: the Impossible Discovery. *Canadian Journal of Sociology,* 27, 4: 505–35.

David, M., R. Edwards, and P. Alldred. (2001). Children and School-based Research: 'Informed Consent' or 'Educated Consent?' *British Educational Research Journal,* 27, (3): 347–66.

Davidson, A. I., ed. (1997a). *Foucault and His Interlocutors.* Chicago: University of Chicago Press.

——. (1997b). Structures and Strategies of Discourse: Remarks Towards a History of Foucault's Philosophy of Language. In A. Davidson, ed. *Foucault and His Interlocutors.* Chicago: University of Chicago Press.

——. (1997c). Introductory Remarks to Pierre Hadot. In A. I. Davidson, ed. *Foucault and His Interlocutors.* Chicago and London: University of Chicago Press.

Davis, M. (1996). Some Paradoxes of Whistle-blowing. *Business and Professional Ethics Journal,* 15, 1: 3–21.

Day, R. B. (2002). History, Reason and Hope: a Comparative Study of Kant, Hayek and Habermas. *Humanitas,* XV, 2, 4–24.

De Alba, A., E. González-Gaudiano, C. Lankshear, and M. A. Peters. (2000). *Curriculum in the Postmodern Condition.* New York: Peter Lang.

Dean, M. (1991). *The Constitution of Poverty: Toward a Genealogy of Liberal Governance.* London: Routledge.

——. (1999). *Governmentality: Power and Rule in Modern Society.* London: Thousand Oaks.

Dean, M., and B. Hindess, eds. (1998). *Governing Australia: Studies in Contemporary Rationalities of Government.* Cambridge: Cambridge University Press.

De Beauvoir, S. (1972). *The Second Sex.* H.M. Parshley, trans. and ed. Harmondsworth: Penguin.

Defert, D. (1991). 'Popular Life' and Insurance Technology. In G. Burchell, C. Gordon, and P. Miller, eds. *The Foucault Effect: Studies in Governmentality.* Hemel Hempstead: Harvester Wheatsheaf.

De Francis, V. (1969). *Protecting the Child Victim of Sex Crimes Committed by Adults.* Denver: American Humane Society.

Deleuze, G. (1995). Postscript on Control Societies. M. Joughin, trans. *Negotiations 1972–1990.* New York: Columbia University Press.

De Young, M. (1982). *The Sexual Victimisation of Children.* Jefferson, NC: McFarland.

Doel, M. (1997). *Poststructuralist Geographies.* Edinburgh: Edinburgh Press.

Donzelot, J. (1979). *The Policing of Families.* R. Hurley, trans. Foreword by G. Deleuze. New York: Pantheon Books.

——. (1991). The Mobilization of Society. In G. Burchell, C. Gordon, and P. Mille, eds. *The Foucault Effect: Studies in Governmentality.* Hemel Hempstead: Harvester Wheatsheaf.

Doody, T. (1980). *Confession and Community in the Novel.* Baton Rouge and London: Louisiana State

University Press.

Doyle, C. (1990). *Working with Abused Children.* Houndmills and London: Macmillan.

Dreyfus, H. (1972). *What Computers Can't Do: A Critique of Artificial Reason.* New York: Harper and Row.

———, ed. (1982). *Husserl, Intentionality, and Cognitive Science,* in collaboration with Harrison Hall. Cambridge, MA: MIT Press.

———. (1991). *Being-In-The-World: A Commentary on Heidegger's Being and Time, Division I.* Cambridge, MA: MIT Press.

———. (1992). *What Computers Still Can't Do: A Critique of Artificial Reason.* Cambridge, MA: MIT Press.

———. (1998). Being and Power: Heidegger and Foucault. Originally published as On the Ordering of Things: Being and Power. In Heidegger and Foucault, *Michel Foucault, Philosophe,* Le Seuil, Paris, (1989). Reprinted in *International Journal of Philosophical Studies, Vol. 4.* Also available at: <http://socrates.berkeley.edu/~hdreyfus/html/paper_being.html>

———. (2001). *On the Internet.* London and New York: Routledge.

———. (2002). *Heidegger and Foucault on the Subject, Agency and Practices.* Regents of University of California, Berkeley. < http://socrates.berkeley.edu/~hdreyfus/html/paper_heidandfoucault.html> (accessed October 2002).

Dreyfus, H., and S. Dreyfus, with T. Athanasiou. (1986). *Mind over Machine: The Power of Human Intuition and Expertise in the Era of the Computer.* New York: Free Press.

Dreyfus, H. L., and P. Rabinow. (1983). *Michel Foucault: Beyond Structuralism and Hermeneutics* (2nd edition). Chicago: University of Chicago Press.

Edwards, R., and R. Usher. (2000). *Globalisation and Pedagogy: Space, Place and Identity.* London and New York: Routledge.

Elden, S. (2001). *Mapping the Present: Heidegger, Foucault and the Project of a Spatial History.* London and New York: Continuum.

Ericson, R.V. (1997). *Policing the Risk Society.* Oxford: Oxford University Press.

Evans, K., H. Behrens, and J. Kaluza. (2000). *Learning and Work in the Risk Society: Lessons from the Labour Markets of Europe and Eastern Germany.* New York: St. Martin's Press.

Ferguson, A. (1996). *An Essay on the History of Civil Society (1767).* Introduction by Duncan Forbes, ed. Edinburgh: Edinburgh University Press.

Finkelhor, D. (1984). *Child Sexual Abuse: New Theory and Research.* New York: Free Press.

Foucault, M. (1954). Dream, Imagination and Existence. In M. Foucault and L. Binswanger, *Dream and Existence.* K. Hoeller, ed. Atlantic Highlands, NJ: Humanities Press, 1993. Studies in Existential Psychology and Psychiatry.

———. (1961). *Folie et deraison: Histoire de la folie a l'age classique.* Paris: Libraire Plon; *Madness and Civilization: A History of Insanity in the Age Reason.* London: Routledge, 2006.

———. (1963). *Birth of the Clinic.* New York: Pantheon. (Naissance de la clinique (Paris, PUF, 1963).

———. (1965). *Madness and Civilization: a History of Insanity in the Age of Reason.* Richard Howard, trans. New York: Pantheon Books.

———. (1966). *Les Mots et les Choses.* Paris: Gallimard. (*The Order of Things.* New York: Pantheon, 1970).

———. (1966). *Maladie mentale et psychologie.* Paris: PUF.

———. (1972). *The Archaeology of Knowledge.* New York:Pantheon Books. Translation from the French. *L'Archeologie du Savoir.* (Paris:Gallimard, 1969).

———. (1973). *The Birth of the Clinic: An Archaeology of Medical Perception.* A. M. Sheridan, trans.

London: Tavistock.

———. (1973). *The Order of Things: an Archaeology of the Human Sciences*. London: Tavistock.

———. (1977a). Nietzsche, Genalogy, History. In D. F. Bouchard, ed. *Language, Counter-Memory, Practice: Selected Essays and Interviews*. Ithaca, New York: Cornell University Press.

———. (1977b). *Language, Counter-Memory, Practice: Selected Essays and Interviews*. D. Bouchard, ed. Oxford: Blackwell.

———. (1977c). *Discipline and Punish: the Birth of the Prison*. London: Penguin.

———. (1978). La Philosophie analytique de la politique. In *Dits et écrits, 1954–1988. Vols.1–4*. D. Defert and F. Ewart, with J. Lagrange, eds. Paris, 3.

———. (1979). On Governmentality. *Ideology and Consciousness*, 6: 5–21.

———. (1980a). *The History of Sexuality, Vol. I*. New York: Vintage.

———. (1980b). The Confession of the Flesh. In C. Gordon, ed. *Power/Knowledge: Selected Interviews and Other Writings 1972–1977 by Michel Foucault*. Hemel Hempstead: Harvester Wheatsheaf.

———. (1980c). Two lectures. In C. Gordon, ed. *Power/Knowledge: Selected Interviews and Other Writings 1972–1977 by Michel Foucault*. Hemel Hempstead: Harvester Wheatsheaf.

———. (1982). The Subject and Power. In M*ichel Foucault: Beyond Structuralism and Hermeneutics*. H. L. Dreyfus and P. Rabinow. Chicago: University of Chicago Press.

———. (1983). The Subject and Power. In *Michel Foucault: Beyond Structuralism and Hermeneutics*. H. L. Dreyfus and P. Rabinow. Chicago: University of Chicago Press (2nd edition).

———. (1984a). Space, Knowledge and Power. In P. Rabinow, ed. *The Foucault Reader*. New York: Pantheon Books.

———. (1984b). Nietzsche, Genealogy, History. In P. Rabinow, ed. *The Foucault Reader*. New York: Pantheon Books.

———. (1984c). What Is Enlightenment? In P. Rabinow, ed. *The Foucault Reader*. New York: Pantheon Books.

———. (1984d). Polemics, Politics and Problematisation. In P. Rabinow, ed. *The Foucault Reader*. New York: Pantheon Books.

———. (1985). *The Use of Pleasure: The History of Sexuality, Vol. II*. New York: Vintage.

———. (1986a). *Kant on Enlightenment and Revolution*. Colin Gordon, trans. Economy and Society 15.1: 88–96.

———. (1986b). Of Other Spaces. Jay Miskowiec, trans. *diacritics*, 16, 1, Spring.

———. (1988a). Truth, Power, Self: an Interview with Michel Foucault. In L. H. Martin, H. Gutman, and P. H. Hutton, eds. *Technologies of the Self: a Seminar with Michel Foucault*. Amherst: University of Massachusetts Press.

———. (1988b). Technologies of the Self, in L. H. Martin, H. Gutman, and P. H. Hutton, eds. *Technologies of the Self: A seminar with Michel Foucault*. Amherst: University of Massachusetts Press.

———. (1988c). The Political Technology of Individuals. In L. H. Martin, H. Gutman, and P. H. Hutton, eds. *Technologies of the Self: a Seminar with Michel Foucault*. Amherst: University of Massachusetts Press.

———. (1989) *Resume des cours 1980–1982*. Paris: conferencs, essais et lecons du Collège de France, Paris, Julliard.

———. (1990). *The Care of the Self: the History of Sexuality, Vol. III*. London: Penguin.

———. (1991). Governmentality. In G. Burchell, C. Gordon, and P. Miller, eds. *The Foucault Effect: Studies in Governmentality—with Two Lectures by and an Interview with Michel Foucault*. Chicago: University of Chicago Press and Harvester Wheatsheaf.

———. (1997a). The Ethics of the Concern for Self as a Practice of Freedom. In P. Rabinow, ed. *Michel*

Foucault: Ethics, Subjectivity and Truth, The Essential Works of Michel Foucault 1954–1984, Vol 1. London: Allen Lane and Penguin Press.

———. (1997b). Writing the Self. In *Foucault and His Interlocutors.* Introduction by Arnold Davidson, ed. Chicago: University of Chicago Press.

———. (1997c). *Michel Foucault: Ethics, Subjectivity and Truth, The Essential Works of Michel Foucault 1954–1984, Vol. 1.* P. Rabinow, ed. London: Allen Lane and Penguin Press.

———. (1998a). *Aesthetics, Method, and Epistemology: Essential Works of Foucault, 1954–1984 Vol. 2.* J. Faubion, ed.; P. Rabinow, series ed. R. Hurley et al., trans. London: Allen Lane and Penguin Press.

———. (1998b). What Is an author? In *Aesthetics, Method, and Epistemology: Essential Works of Foucault, 1954–1984 Vol. 2.* J. Faubion, ed.; P. Rabinnow, series ed.; R. Hurley et al., trans. London: Allen Lane and Penguin Press.

———. (1998c). Structuralism or Poststructuralism. In *Aesthetics, Method, and Epistemology: Essential Works of Foucault, 1954–1984 Vol. 2.* J. Faubion, ed.; P. Rabinow, series ed.; R. Hurley et al., trans. London: Allen Lane and Penguin Press.

———. (1998d). A Critical History of Thought. In *Aesthetics, Method, and Epistemology: Essential Works of Foucault, 1954–1984 Vol. 2.* J. D. Faubion, ed.; P. Rabinow, series ed.; R. Hurley et al., trans. London: Allen Lane and Penguin Press.

———. (2000). The Subject and Power. In *Power: Essential Works of Foucault, 1954–1984 Vol. 3.* J. D.Faubion, ed.; P. Rabinow, series ed.; R. Hurley et al., trans. London: Allen Lane and Penguin Press.

———. (2001a). *Fearless Speech.* J. Pearson, ed. Los Angeles: Semiotext(e).

———. (2001b). The Political Technology of Individuals. In *Power: Essential Works of Michel Foucault 1954–1984, Vol 3.* J. D. Faubion, ed.; P. Rabinow, series ed.; R. Hurley et al., trans. London: Allen Lane and Penguin Press. (The Subject and Power, in Dreyfus and Rabinow [1982 and 1983]).

———. (2004a). *Sécurité, Territoire, Population: Cours au collège de France (1977–1978).* Édition établie sous la direction de Francois Ewald et Alessandro Fontana, par Michel Senellart, Paris, Éditions Gallimand et des Éditions du Seuill.

———. (2004b). *Naissance de la biopolitique: Cours au collège de France (1978–1979),* Édition établie sous la direction de Francois Ewald et Alessandro Fontana, par Michel Senellart, Paris, Éditions Gallimand et des Éditions du Seuill.

———. (2005). *The Hermeneutics of the Subject: Lectures at the College de France 1981–1982.* Graham Burchell, trans. New York: Palgrave Macmillan.

Giddens, A. (1984). *The Constitution of Society: The Outline of the Theory of Structuration.* Berkeley: University of California Press.

———. (1985). *The Nation-State and Violence.* Cambridge: Polity.

———. (1990). *The Consequences of Modernity.* Cambridge: Polity.

———. (1991). *Modernity and Self Identity.* Cambridge: Polity.

Gilligan, C. (1982). *In a Different Voice.* Cambridge: Harvard University Press.

Giroux, H. (1990). *Curriculum Discourse as Postmodern Critical Practice.* Geelong: Deakin University Press.

———. (1996). *Fugitive Cultures: Race, Violence and Youth.* New York: Routledge.

———. (1998). Teenage Sexuality, Body Politics, and the Pedagogy of Display. In J. Epstein, ed. *Youth Culture: Identity in a Postmodern World.* Oxford: Blackwell: 24–55.

———. (2001). *Public Spaces, Private Lives: Beyond the Culture of Cynicism.* Lanham, CO: Rowman and Littlefield.

Gordon, C. (1991). Governmental Rationality: an Introduction. In G. Burchell, C. Gordon, P. Miller, eds. *The Foucault Effect: Studies in Governmentality.* Hemel Hempstead: Harvester Wheatsheaf.

———. (1996). Foucault in Britain. In A. Barry, T. Osborne, and N. Rose, eds. *Foucault and Political Reason,* 253–70. London: UCL Press.

———. (2001). Introduction. In J. D. Faubion, ed. and R. Hurley et al., trans. *Power: Michel Foucault: Essential Works 1954–1984, Vol. 3.* London: Allen Lane and Penguin Press, xi–xli.

Gray, J. N. (1982). *F. A. Hayek and the Rebirth of Classical Liberalism, Literature of Liberty,* 4; 4. Winter. <http://www.econlib.org/library/Essays/LtrLbrty/gryHRC1.html> (accessed 20/7/07)

Gruber, K., and Jones, R. (1983). Identifying Determinants of Risk of Sexual Victimization of Youth. *Child and Abuse,* 7: 17–24.

Gutman, H. (1988). Rousseau's *Confessions:* a Technology of the Self. In L. H. Martin, H. Gutman, and P. H. Hutton, eds. *Technologies of the Self: a Seminar with Michel Foucault.* Amherst: University of Massachusetts Press.

Hadot, P. (1995). Spiritual Exercises and Reflections on the Idea of the 'Cultivation of the Self.' M. Chase, trans. Introduction by A. Davidson, ed. *Philosophy as a Way of Life.* Oxford: Blackwell.

———. (1995). *Philosophy as a Way of Life.* M. Chase, trans. and A. Davidson, ed. Oxford: University of Oxford Press.

———. (1997). Forms of Life and Forms of Discourse in Ancient Philosophy. In A. Davidson, ed. *Foucault and His Interlocutors.* Chicago: University of Chicago Press.

Hammersley, M. (1990). *Reading Ethnographic Research.* London: Longman.

Harrer, A. (2005). The Theme of Subjectivity in Foucault's Lecture Series, L'Herméneutique du Sujet, *Foucault Studies,* No 2, May: 75–96.

Hayek, F. A. (1960). The Constitution of Liberty. Chicago: University of Chicago Press.

Heidegger, M. (1962). Being and Time. J. Macquarrie and E. Robinson, trans. London: SCM Press.

———. (1971a). Building Dwelling Thinking. In *Poetry, Language, Thought.* A. Hofstadter, trans. and ed. New York: Harper Row.

———. (1971b). *Poetry, Language, Thought.* A. Hofstadter, trans. and ed. New York and London: Harper and Row.

———. (1977). *The Question Concerning Technology and Other Essays.* New York: Harper and Row.

Herman, J., and L. Hirschman. (1977). Father-daughter Incest. *Signs,* 2: 1–22.

Hindess, B. (1996). *Discourses of Power: From Hobbes to Foucault.* Oxford: Blackwell.

———. (1997). Politics and Governmentality. *Economy and Society,* 26 (2).

Høeg, P. (1993, GB) (1992 Denmark). *Miss Smilla's Feeling for Snow.* F. David, ed. London: Flamingo.

Hudson, B. (2003). *Justice in the Risk Society: Challenging and Re-affirming 'Justice' in Late Modernity.* London: Sage.

Huisman, D. (1984). *Dictionnaire des Philosophes.* Denis Huisman, ed. Paris: PUF.

Jacobs, J. L. (1994). *Victimised Daughters: Incest and Development of the Female Self.* London: Routledge.

Jameson, F. (1983). Postmodernism and Consumer Society. In H. Foster, ed. *Postmodern Culture.* London and Sydney: Pluto Press.

Joerges, C., and F. Rödl. (2004). 'Social Market Economy' as Europe's Social Model? European University Institute (Florence) Working paper LAW No. 2004/8. <ww.iut.it> (accessed 20/5/07)

Khuri, F. I. (2001). *The Body in Islamic Culture.* London: Saqi Books.

Korsmeyer, C. (2004). Feminist Aesthetics. In E. N. Zalta, ed. Stanford Encyclopedia of Philosophy (Summer 2004 Edition). <http://plato.stanford.edu/archives/sum2004/entries/feminism-aesthetics/> (accessed 20/5/05).

Lankshear, C., and Knobel, M. (2003). *New Literacies: Changing Knowledge and Classroom Learning.* Buckingham: Open University Press.

Lankshear, C., Peters, M. A., and Knoebel, M. (1996). Critical Pedagogy in Cyberspace. In C. Lankshear, H. Giroux, P. McLaren, and M. A. Peters. *Counternarratives, Cultural Studies and Critical Pedagogies in Postmodern Spaces*. London: Routledge.

———. (2000). Information, Knowledge, and Learning: Some Issues Facing Epistemology and Education in a Digital Age. In Nigel Blake and Paul Standish, eds. *Enquiries at the Interface: Philosophical Problems of On-line Education*. Special issue *Journal of Philosophy of Education*, 34 (1): 17–39.

Lasch, C. (1979). *The Culture of Narcissism: American Life in an Age of Diminishing Expectations*. New York, W.W. Norton.

———. *The Minimal Self: Psychic Survival in Troubled Times*. New York: W.W. Norton.

Lefebvre, H. (1991). *The Production of Space*. Oxford: Blackwell.

Leiber, Justin. (1997). On What Sort of Speech Act Wittgenstein's *Investigations* Is and Why It Matters. *The Philosophical Forum*, XXVIII, 3, Winter–Spring: 232–67.

Leighton, D. (2003). Happy Days? Freedom and Security in a Consumer Society. Archive, 11 (2) <http://www.renewal.org.uk/issues/2003_Volume_11>

Liggett, H., and D. C Perry, eds. (1995). *Spatial Practices*. London: Sage.

Lloyd, G. (1984). *The Man of Reason: 'Male' and 'Female' in Western Philosophy*. Minneapolis: University of Minnesota Press.

Luke, A. (2000). The Jig Is Up: an Alternative History of Psychology or Why Current Concepts of Identity and Development Are Part of the Problem Rather Than Part of the Solution. *NZAC Newsletter*, 20:3: 12–26.

Luke, A., and C. Luke. (2000). A Situated Perspective on Cultural Globalisation. In N. Burbules and C. Torres, eds. *Globalisation and Educational Policy*. New York: Routledge.

Macey, D. (1993). *The Lives of Michel Foucault*. London: Hutchinson.

Malcolm, N. (1994*). Wittgenstein: A Religious Point of View*. Response by P. Winch, ed. Ithaca, New York: Cornell University Press.

Malpas, J. (1999). *Place and Experience: a Philosophical Topography*. Cambridge: Cambridge University Press.

———. (2000). Uncovering the Space of Disclosedness: Heidegger, Technology, and the Problem of Spatiality in Being and Time. In M. Wrathall and J. Malpass, eds. *Heidegger, Authenticity, and Modernity: Essays in Honor of Hubert L. Dreyfus, Vol. 1*. Cambridge, MA: MIT Press.

Marshall, J. D. (1996). *Michel Foucault: Personal Autonomy and Education*. Dordrecht and Boston: Kluwer Academic Publishers.

———. (1997). Michel Foucault: Problematising the Individual and Constituting 'the Self.' Special issue: M. Peters, J. Marshall, and P. Fitzsimons, eds. Education and the Constitution of Self. *Educational Philosophy and Theory*, 29, 1: 20–31.

Masson, J. (1989). *Against Therapy*. London: HarperCollins.

McGuiness, B. (1990). *Wittgenstein, a Life: Young Ludwig 1889–1921*. Harmondsworth, Middlesex: Penguin Books.

McKerrow, R. (2001). Foucault and Surrealism of the Truth. Access at <http://oak.cats.ohiou.edu/~mck-errow/foucault.htm> (accessed 21/07/07)

McNamee, M. (2001). The Guilt of Whistle-blowing: Conflicts in Action Research and Educational Ethnography. In M. McNamee and D. Bridges, eds. Special issue: The Ethics of Educational Research, *Journal of Philosophy of Education*, 35, 3: 423–42.

McNay, L. (1992). *Foucault and Feminism: Power, Gender and Self*. Boston: Northeastern University Press.

Merleau-Ponty, M. (1962). *Phenomenology of Perception*. C. Smith, trans. London: Routledge and

Kegan Paul.

——. (1968). *The Visible and the Invisible.* A. Lingus, trans. Evanston: Northwestern University Press.

Meyers, D. (1999, 2000). Feminist Perspectives on the Self. In *Stanford Encyclopedia of Philosophy.* <http://plato.stanford.edu/entries/feminism-self/> (accessed 3/11/02).

Middleton, S. (1998). *Disciplining Sexuality: Foucault, Life Histories and Education.* New York, Peter Lang

Miller, P., and N. Rose. (1990). Governing Economic Life. *Economy and Society,* 19 (1): 1–31.

Morgan, J. (2000). Critical Pedagogy: the Spaces That Make the Difference. *Pedagogy, Culture and Society,* 8 (3): 27–89.

Needham, C. (2003). *Citizen-Consumers: Labour's New Marketplace Democracy.* London: Fabian Society.

Nelson, S. (1982). *Incest: Fact and Myth.* Edinburgh: Stramullion. New York and London: Teachers College Press.

New Zealand Association of Counsellors. (1995). *NZAC Handbook.* Hamilton: NZAC.

——. (2000). *NZAC Handbook.* Hamilton: NZAC.

New Zealand Children and Young Persons Service. (1995). *Breaking the Cycle: an Interagency Guide to Child Abuse.* Wellington.

——. (1996). *Breaking the Cycle: Interagency Protocols.* Wellington.

Nietzsche, F. (1956 [original 1887]). *The Genealogy of Morals.* New York: Doubleday.

——. (1989). *Beyond Good and Evil.* W. Kaufmann, trans. New York: Vintage Books.

Olssen, M. (1999). *Michel Foucault: Materialism and Education.* Westport, CT: Bergin and Garvey.

O'Malley, P. (1996). Risk and Responsibility. In A. Barry, T. Osborne, and N. Rose, eds. *Foucault and Political Reason: Liberalism, Neo-liberalism and Rationalities of Government.* London: UCL Press.

——. (1998). *Neo-liberalism, Advanced-liberalism and Neo-conservatism: Problems of Genealogy and Rationalisation in Governmentality.* Paper presented at the University of Auckland.

Paden, W. E. (1988). Theaters of Humility and Suspicion: Desert Saints and New England Puritans. In L. H. Martin, H. Gutman, and P.H. Hutton, eds. *Technologies of the Self: A Seminar with Michel Foucault.* Amherst: University of Massachusetts Press.

Parks, P. (1990). *Rescuing the 'Inner Child': Therapy for Adults Sexually Abused as Children.* London: Souvenir Press.

Peeples, S. E. (1999). *The Emperor Has a Body: Body-politics in the Between.* Tucson, AZ: Javelina Books.

Percy, W. A. (1996). *Pederasty and Pedagogy in Archaic Greece.* Urbana and Chicago: University of Illinois Press.

Peters, M. A. (1994). Governmentalidade Neoliberal e Educacao. In T. Tadeu da Silva, ed. *O Sujeito Educacao, Estudos Foucaulianos.* Rio de Janeiro: Editora Vozes.

——. (1996a). *Poststructuralism, Politics and Education.* Westport, CT and London: Bergin and Garvey.

——. (1996b). Architecture of Resistance: Educational Theory, Postmodernism and the 'Politics of Space.' In *Poststructuralism, Politics and Education.* Westport, CT and London: Bergin and Garvey.

——. (1997a). Neoliberalism, Welfare Dependency and the Moral Construction of Poverty in New Zealand. *New Zealand Journal of Sociology,* 12 (1): 1–34.

——. (1997b). What Is Poststructuralism? the French Reception of Nietzsche. *Political Theory Newsletter,* 8 (2), 39–55.

——. (1999a). Neo-Liberalism. In *Encyclopedia of Philosophy of Education.* M. A. Peters, and P. Ghiraldelli Jr., eds. < http://www.educacao.pro.br/>

——. (1999b). (Posts-) Modernism and Structuralism: Affinities and Theoretical Innovations, *Sociological Research Online,* 3 (4), September. Available at: <http://www.socresonline.org.uk/4/

3/peters.html>

———, ed. (1999c). *After the Disciplines? the Emergence of Cultural Studies.* Westport, CT and London: Bergin and Garvey.

———. (2000a). Wittgensteinian Pedagogics: Cavell on the Figure of the Child in the *Investigations. Studies in Philosophy and Education,* 20: 125–138

———. (2000b). Writing the Self: Wittgenstein, Confession and Pedagogy. *Journal of Philosophy of Education,* 34, 2: 353–68.

———. (2001a). Education, Enterprise Culture and the Entrepreneurial Self: a Foucauldian Perspective. *Journal of Educational Enquiry,* 2 (1), May. Available at <htp://www.education.unisa.edu.au/JEE/>

———. (2001b). Foucault and Governmentality: Understanding the Neoliberal Paradigm of Education Policy. *The School Field,* XII (5/6): 59–80.

———. (2001c). Foucault, Neoliberalism and the Governance of Welfare. In *Poststructuralism, Marxism, and Neoliberalism: Between Theory and Politics.* Lanham and Oxford: Rowman and Littlefield.

———. (2001d). National Education Policy Constructions of the 'Knowledge Economy': Towards a Critique. *Journal of Educational Enquiry,* 2 (1), May: 8–30.

———. (2001e). *Poststructuralism, Marxism, and Neoliberalism: Between Theory and Politics.* Lanham, MD: Rowman and Littlefield.

———. (2001f). Deleuze's 'Societies of Control': from Disciplinary Pedagogy to Perpetual Training in the Knowledge Economy. In *Poststructuralism, Marxism and Neoliberalism: Between Theory and Politics.* Lanham, MD: Rowman and Littlefield.

———. (2001g). Michel Foucault 1926–84. In J. A. Palmer, ed. *Fifty Modern Thinkers on Education: From Piaget to the Present.* London and New York, Routledge.

———. (2002a). Dreyfus on the Internet: Platonism, Body Talk and Nihilism. *Educational Philosophy and Theory,* 34 (4):

———. (2002b). Heidegger, Education and Modernity. In M. Peters, ed. *Heidegger, Education and Modernity.* Lanham, MD: Rowman and Littlefield.

———. (2003a). Truth-telling as an Educational Practice of the Self: Foucault, Parhessia and the Ethics of Subjectivity. *Oxford Review of Education,* 29. 2: 207–23.

———. (2003b). Educational Research, 'Games of Truth' and the Ethics of Subjectivity. Ethical Educational Research: Practices of the Self Symposium: M. A. Peters, T. Besley, and C. Caddell, BERA.

———. (2003c). Why Foucault? New Directions in Anglo-American Educational Research. Invited conference keynote, After Foucault: Perspectives of the Analysis of Discourse and Power in Education, 29–31 October, 2003. University of Dortmund. In L. Pongratz et al., eds. (2004). *Nach Foucault. Diskurs- und machtanalytische Perspectiven der Pädagogik,* Wiesbaden, VS Verlag Für Sozialwissenschaften.

———. (2004a) Education and the Philosophy of the Body: Bodies of Knowledge and Knowledges of the Body. In *Knowing Bodies, Moving Minds: Towards Embodied Teaching and Learning* L. Bresler (Ed.), Dordrecht, Kluwer, pp. 13–28.

———. (2004b). Citizen-Consumers, Social Markets and the Reform of Public Services. *Policy Futures in Education,* 2 (3–4): 621–32.

———. (2005a). Foucault, Counselling and the Aesthetics of Existence. In T. Besley and R. Edwards, eds. Poststructuralism and the Impact of the Work of Michel Foucault in Counselling and Guidance. Special issue symposium, *British Journal of Guidance and Counselling,* 33, 3: 383–96.

———. (2005b). The New Prudentialism in Education: Actuarial Rationality and the Entrepreneurial Self. In P. Hogan and P. Smeyers, eds. Special issue on education and risk *Educational Theory,* 55

(2): 123–37.

Peters, M. A., with A. C. Besley. (2005). *Building Knowledge Cultures: Education and Development in the Age of Knowledge Capitalism.* Lanham and Oxford: Rowman and Littlefield.

Peters, M. A. and A. C. Besley, eds. (2006). *Why Foucault? New Directions in Educational Research.* New York: Peter Lang.

Peters, M. A., and J. Marshall. (1996). *Individualism and Community: Education and Social Policy in the Postmodern Condition.* London: Falmer Press.

———. (1999). *Wittgenstein: Philosophy, Postmodernism, Pedagogy.* Westport, CT and London: Bergin and Garvey.

Pignatelli, F. (1993). Dangers, Possibilities: Ethico-Political Choices in the Work of Michel Foucault < http://www.ed.uiuc.edu/EPS/PES-Yearbook/93 _docs/PIGNATEL.HTM>

Plato. (1993). *The Last Days of Socrates. Euthyphro, Apology, Crito, Phaedo.* H. Tredenick and H. Tarrant, trans. Introduction and notes by H. Tarrant. London: Penguin Books.

Popkewitz, T., and L. Fendler, eds. (1999). *Critical Theories in Education: Changing Terrains of Knowledge and Politics.* New York and London: Routledge.

Popkewitz, T. S., and M. Brennan. (1998) *Foucault's Challenge: Discourse, Knowledge, and Power in Education.* New York: Teachers College Press.

Porter, Roy. (2003). *Flesh in the Age of Reason: The Modern Foundations of Body and Soul.* London: Allen Lane.

Proudfoot, M. (2003). *The Philosophy of the Body.* Oxford: Blackwell Publishing.

Rabinow, P. (1997). Preface and Afterword. In P. Rabinow, ed. *Michel Foucault: Ethics, Subjectivity and Truth, The Essential Works of Michel Foucault 1954–1984, Vol. 1.* London: Penguin Press.

Redman, D. (1997). *The Rise of Political Economy as a Science.* Cambridge, MA: MIT Press.

Ritzer, G. (1998). Introduction. In J. Baudrillard *The Consumer Society: Myths and Structures.* London: Sage.

Rose, N. S. (1989). *Governing the Soul: the Shaping of the Private Self.* London: Routledge.

———. (1993). Government, Authority and Expertise in Advanced Liberalism. *Economy and Society,* 22 (3).

———. (1996). Governing 'Advanced' Liberal Democracies. In A. Barry, T. Osborne, and N. Rose, eds. *Foucault and Political Reason: Liberalism, Neo-liberalism and Rationalities of Government.* London: UCL Press.

———. (1998). *Inventing Our Selves: Psychology, Power, and Personhood.* Cambridge: Cambridge University Press.

———. (1999). *Powers of Liberty.* Cambridge: Cambridge University Press.

———. (n.d.). Power in Therapy: Techne and Ethos. Academy for the Study of the Psychoanalytic Arts. Available at http://www.academyanalyticarts.org/rose2.htm

Rousseau, J-J. (1953). *The Confessions of Jean-Jacques Rousseau.* J. M. Cohen, trans. Harmondsworth: Penguin Books.

Rush, F. (1980). *The Best Kept Secret.* New York: Prentice-Hall.

Russell, D. (1983). Incidence and Prevalence of Intrafamilial and Extrafamilial Sexual Abuse of Female Children. *Child and Abuse,* 7: 133–46.

Sartre, J-P. (1948). *Existentialism and Humanism.* P. Mairet, trans. London: Methuen.

Schatzki, T., K. Knorr Cetiona, and E. Von Savigny, eds. (2001). *The Practice Turn in Contemporary Theory.* London and New York: Routledge.

Schatzki, T. R., and W. Natter. (1996). Sociocultural Bodies, Bodies Sociopolitical. In T. R. Schatzki and W. Natter, eds. *The Social and Political Body.* New York and London: Guilford Press.

Shields, P. (1997). *Logic and Sin in the Writings of Ludwig Wittgenstein.* Chicago: University of Chicago Press.

Shrift, A. (1995). *Nietzsche's French Legacy: A Genealogy of Poststructuralism.* New York and London: Routledge.

Silber, I. F. (1995). Space, Fields, Boundaries: the Rise of Spatial Metaphors in Contemporary Sociological Theory, *Social Research,* Summer, 62 (2): 323–33.

Smith, R. (1995). *Derrida and Autobiography.* Cambridge: Cambridge University Press.

Sontag, F. (1995). *Wittgenstein and the Mystical: Philosophy as an Ascetic Practice.* Atlanta: Scholars Press.

Strathern, A. J. (1996). *Body Thoughts.* Ann Arbor: University of Michigan Press.

Szabados, B. (1992). Autobiography after Wittgenstein. *The Journal of Aesthetics and Art Criticism,* 50 (1), Winter: 1–12.

Tolstoy, L. (1996). *Confession.* D. Patterson, trans. New York and London: W.W. Norton.

Trentmann, F. (2002). Beyond Consumerism: New Historical Perspectives on Consumption. Cultures of Consumption Working Paper Series. An ESRC-AHRB Research Programme. <www.consume.bbk.ac.uk>

Valverde, M. (1996). 'Despotism' and Ethical Legal Governance. *Economy and Society,* 25 (3), 357–72.

Vanberg, V. (2004). The Freiburg School: Walter Eucken and Ordoliberalism, Freiburg Discussion Papers on Constitutional Economics, at <http://opus.zbw-kiel.de/volltexte/2004/2324/pdf/04_11bw.pdf>

Van Gigch, J. P. (1998). The Epistemology of the Social Sciences According to Michel Foucault (1926–1984). (Design of the Modern Inquiring System, Part 14) *Systems Research and Behavioral Science,* March–April, 15, 2, 154–59.

Veyne, P. (1997). The Final Foucault and His Ethics. In *Foucault and His Interlocutors,* A. I. Davidson, ed. C. Porter and A. I. Davidson, trans. Chicago: University of Chicago Press.

Ward, E. (1984). *Father Daughter Rape.* London: Women's Press.

White, H. C. (1992). *Identity and Control: a Structural Theory of Social Action.* Princeton, NJ: Princeton University Press.

Witt, U. (2002). Germany's 'Social Market Economy': Between Social Ethos and Rent Seeking, *The Independent Review,* IV (3): 365–75.

Wittgenstein, L. (1953). *Philosophical Investigations.* Oxford: Blackwell.

Wittgenstein, Ludwig. (1975). Foreword. In *Philosophical Remarks,* Rush Rhees, ed., R. Hargrave and R. White, trans. Chicago: University of Chicago Press.

Wright, G. H. von. (1962) Memoir. In Norman Malcolm, *Ludwig Wittgenstein: A Memoir.* London: Oxford University Press.

Young, I. M. (1997). *Intersecting Voices: Dilemmas of Gender, Political Philosophy and Policy.* Princeton, NJ: Princeton University Press.

Young, J. (2000). What Is Dwelling? The Homelessness of Modernity and the Worlding of the World. In M. Wrathall and J. Malpass, eds. *Heidegger, Authenticity, and Modernity: Essays in Honor of Hubert L. Dreyfus, Vol. 1.,* Cambridge, MA: MIT Press.

———. (2002). *Heidegger's Later Philosophy.* Cambridge: Cambridge University Press.

Index

A

Abrahmaic religions, 65, 81
ACC (Accident Compensation Commission), 121
Accident Compensation Commission (ACC), 121
actuarial rationality and risk management, 159–163
Aesthetics, Method and Epistemology, 47–48
aesthetics of existence, 45–70
    arts of the self as, 14–15
    body's history in, 61–63
    body's relationship to, 58–61
    defined, 16, 54–57
    embodiment in, 63–65
    feminism and the female body in, 65–67
    Foucault on, 47–51
    globalisation and postmodern identity in, 110
    history of madness and, 51–54
    introduction to, 45–47, xvi
    masculinity and the male body in, 67–70

Alcibiades, 4
Alcibides Major, 94
aletheia, 22, 27, 43–44
Alfred Salter School, 114
Allen, Jeanne, 158
American neoliberalism
    education policy of, 131
    governmentality in, 136, 143–145
    human capital theory of, 150–154
analytic philosophy
    Anglo-Saxon, 184
    Foucault on, 51, 102
    regimes of truth vs. games of truth in, 91–92
analytics of truth tradition, 88
Anglo-Foucauldians, 138–139
Annales School, 58
antiquity. *see* Greco-Roman antiquity
Apology, 94, 97
The Archeology of Knowledge, 49
Archeology of Knowledge, 102
Aristotle, 3, 15
Armstrong, Aurelia, 67

Studies in the Postmodern Theory of Education

General Editors
Joe L. Kincheloe & Shirley R. Steinberg

Counterpoints publishes the most compelling and imaginative books being written in education today. Grounded on the theoretical advances in criticalism, feminism, and postmodernism in the last two decades of the twentieth century, Counterpoints engages the meaning of these innovations in various forms of educational expression. Committed to the proposition that theoretical literature should be accessible to a variety of audiences, the series insists that its authors avoid esoteric and jargonistic languages that transform educational scholarship into an elite discourse for the initiated. Scholarly work matters only to the degree it affects consciousness and practice at multiple sites. Counterpoints' editorial policy is based on these principles and the ability of scholars to break new ground, to open new conversations, to go where educators have never gone before.

For additional information about this series or for the submission of manuscripts, please contact:

> Joe L. Kincheloe & Shirley R. Steinberg
> c/o Peter Lang Publishing, Inc.
> 29 Broadway, 18th floor
> New York, New York 10006

To order other books in this series, please contact our Customer Service Department:

> (800) 770-LANG (within the U.S.)
> (212) 647-7706 (outside the U.S.)
> (212) 647-7707 FAX

Or browse online by series:
> www.peterlang.com